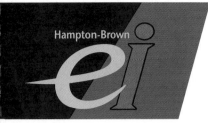

Edge Interactive
Practice Book

TEACHER'S ANNOTATED EDITION

Hampton-Brown

NATIONAL
GEOGRAPHIC

National Geographic School Publishing
Hampton-Brown
P.O. Box 223220
Carmel, California 93922
800-333-3510
www.NGSP.com

Printed in the United States of America

ISBN 13: 978-0-7362-3547-1
ISBN 10: 0-7362-3547-7

10 11 12 13 14 15 16 10 9

Unit 2

Unit 4

Unit 6

Prepare to Read

▶ **The Good Samaritan**
▶ **The World Is in Their Hands**

Key Vocabulary

A. How well do you know these words? Circle a rating for each word. Check your understanding of each word by circling *yes* or *no*. Then, complete the sentences. If you are unsure of a word's meaning, refer to the Vocabulary Glossary, page 852, in your student text.

Rating Scale	
1	I have never seen this word before.
2	I am not sure of the word's meaning.
3	I know this word and can teach the word's meaning to someone else.

Key Word	Check Your Understanding	Deepen Your Understanding
❶ affect (u-**fekt**) *verb* **Rating:** 1 2 3	What you choose to eat can **affect** your health. (**Yes**) No	One way I affect the environment positively is _____ *Possible response:* by recycling paper _____ _____ _____ .
❷ conflict (**kon**-flikt) *noun* **Rating:** 1 2 3	A **conflict** in a friendship is a good thing. Yes (**No**)	One conflict I recently had with another person was _____ *Possible response:* when my mom would not let me use the car _____ _____ .
❸ contribute (kun-**tri**-byūt) *verb* **Rating:** 1 2 3	You can **contribute** to a family meal by making a salad. (**Yes**) No	People can contribute to their community by _____ *Possible response:* volunteering their time _____ _____ _____ .
❹ disrespect (dis-ri-**spekt**) *noun* **Rating:** 1 2 3	When you give your seat on the bus to an elderly person, you are showing **disrespect**. Yes (**No**)	Teenagers in my school sometimes show disrespect by *Possible response:* being rude to teachers _____ _____ _____ .

Key Word	Check Your Understanding	Deepen Your Understanding
5 **generation** (je-nu-**rā**-shun) *noun* **Rating:** **1 2 3**	My grandparents and parents are part of my **generation**. Yes (No)	People in my parents' generation think _____ *Possible response:* teenagers spend too much time playing video games _____ _____ _____ .
6 **motivation** (mō-tu-**vā**-shun) *noun* **Rating:** **1 2 3**	One **motivation** for getting a job is to earn money. (Yes) No	A teenager's motivation for getting a part-time job might be *Possible response:* to earn gas money _____ _____ _____ _____ .
7 **privilege** (**pri**-vu-lij) *noun* **Rating:** **1 2 3**	Driving the family car is an example of a **privilege**. (Yes) No	Something I consider to be a privilege is _____ *Possible response:* being allowed to go on a trip with friends _____ _____ _____ .
8 **responsible** (ri-**spon**-su-bul) *adjective* **Rating:** **1 2 3**	If you check out a book from the library, you are **responsible** for returning it. (Yes) No	My parents say I am responsible for _____ *Possible response:* watching my younger brother after school _____ _____ _____ .

B. Use one of the Key Vocabulary words to write about a difficult choice you, or someone you know, recently had to make.

Answers will vary. _____

_____

Before Reading The Good Samaritan

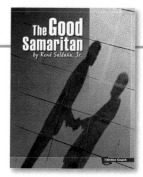

LITERARY ANALYSIS: Plot

The **plot** is the sequence of events in a story. A plot usually contains the following parts: exposition, conflict, complications, climax, and resolution.

A. Read the passage below. Write the complication, or the event that may contribute to a conflict, in the right column of the chart.

> **Look Into the Text**
>
> Mr. Sánchez told us, "If you help clean up the yard, you boys can use the pool any time you want so long as one of us is here." . . . After a hard day's work cleaning his yard, I so looked forward to taking a dip. I'd even worn my trunks under my work clothes. Then Mr. Sánchez said, "Come by tomorrow. I don't want you fellas to track all this dirt into the pool."

Characters	Setting	Complication
Narrator	modern day, somewhere warm	Mr. Sánchez promises that the boys can use the pool if they help him clean his yard. But then Mr. Sánchez says they cannot use the pool because they are dirty.
Mr. Sánchez		
The Boys		

B. What do you think the conflict of the story will be? Why do you think so?

1. The conflict of the story will probably be _Possible response: that the narrator and the other boys want to use the pool, but Mr. Sánchez does not keep his promise to let them use it. I think the conflict occurs because the characters made an agreement and Mr. Sánchez broke it right away_ .

2. What could happen that would bring about a resolution?
   Mr. Sánchez could honor his promise and apologize to the boys.

READING STRATEGY: Make and Confirm Predictions

How to Make and Confirm Predictions

1. **Read the Story's Title** You may find a clue about the plot.

2. **Look at Art and Quotations** They may give clues about story events.

3. **Make Predictions** Put the clues together to predict events.

4. **Confirm or Change Predictions** Notice story details; then change your prediction, or confirm that your prediction is correct.

A. Read the passage. Use the strategies above to make a prediction. Answer the questions below.

Look Into the Text

The **Good Samaritan**
by René Saldaña, Jr.

No way was I going to help him out again!

1. What do you predict the story is about?

   Possible response: This story is about a person who wants to do a good deed, but changes his mind.

2. Which of the four strategies did you use to answer question 1?

   Strategies 1, 2 and 3

B. As you read "The Good Samaritan," look for details that will help you confirm or change your prediction.

Selection Review The Good Samaritan

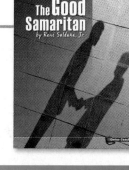

EQ **What Influences a Person's Choices?**
Explore the effect of family and friends on choices.

A. In "The Good Samaritan," you learn how Rey makes a choice despite the conflict he has with Mr. Sánchez. Briefly describe each part of the plot in the chart below.

Parts of the Plot	The Good Samaritan
Characters and Setting	main characters: Rey, Mr. Sánchez setting: somewhere warm, modern day, a Hispanic neighborhood
Conflict	Mr. Sánchez gets the boys to work for him with promises he does not keep.
Complications	Cleaning the yard, cleaning the neighbor's yard, building the basketball court and getting kicked off, and Mr. Sánchez's attitude all lead to Rey's decision to not have anything more to do with the Sánchez family.
Climax	Rey has another chance to help Mr. Sánchez. Rey struggles with the decision. Thoughts of his father help him to decide.
Resolution	Rey changes the tire and lets Mr. Sánchez know, in a respectful way, that he won't be coming over to his house.

B. Use the information in the chart to answer the questions.

1. Why is it difficult for Rey to make the choice to help Mr. Sánchez?

Mr. Sánchez asks Rey and other boys to help him do work with the promise that the boys will be

rewarded. Mr. Sánchez either doesn't keep his promises or rewards the boys with little.

2. What affects Rey's final choice to help Mr. Sánchez? Use **affects** in your answer.

Possible response: Rey thinks about his father. This affects his decision.

3. How might the resolution have been different if Mr. Sánchez had apologized for his behavior?

Possible response: Rey might have felt more respect for him and gone to the barbecue.

The World Is in Their Hands

by Eric Feil

Connect Across Texts

In "The Good Samaritan," Rey must decide whether to help a neighbor. What makes people choose to help others?

Changing the World

With sincere apologies to that old song, the children are not the future.

They are the present.

They are not going to lead the way one day.

They are leading it right now. (Youth) **activism levels** are at all-time highs. Nearly three-quarters of (young adults) say they have **donated** money, clothes, or food to a community or church organization over the past few years. They **get involved** at national and local levels, and their numbers are growing. Doing good, not **gaining recognition**, is their **motivation**.

"We've seen a huge demand from (young people) who want their voices

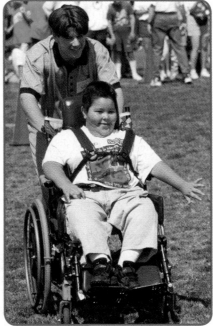

A volunteer helps out at an event for youth with special needs.

Key Vocabulary
● **motivation** *n.*, reason for doing something or thinking a certain way

In Other Words
Youth activism levels The numbers of young people who help others
donated given
get involved join, offer to help
gaining recognition getting attention

Interact with the Text

1. Preview
Underline the title, heading, and caption. What is this article about? List three possible topics.

Possible response:

The article is about

volunteering, youths,

and changing the world.

2. Set a Purpose
Who are the volunteers? Circle words that tell you who is volunteering. Then, think of a question you want answered, and write it below.

Possible response: The

volunteers are young

people who want to

make changes.

Why are so many young

people motivated to

volunteer?

3. Preview/Set a Purpose

Look at this page for visual clues about what the topic will be. What do you want to learn by reading this page?

Possible response:

More details about teen
volunteerism.

4. Text Features

Read the pie chart. Mark an *X* next to each of the largest portions. What do these reasons for volunteering have in common?

Each reason shows a
desire to help others
instead of volunteering
to fulfill a requirement or
to look good.

5. Interpret

According to the bar graph, more teens than adults do volunteer work. Why?

Possible response:

Students have more free
time; adults are focused
on work or raising
children.

heard and who feel they've got something to **contribute** to society," says **Youth Service America** president and CEO Steve Culbertson. "And they're not going to wait until they grow up to do it."

Clearly. Millions of youth volunteers will be out in force again this year, from five-year-olds visiting and decorating senior citizen homes to high school kids tutoring **peers**. Distributing HIV/AIDS educational materials, cleaning up the environment, **registering voters**—the list of projects is almost as limitless as the **enthusiasm** and energy of the people engaged in them. Young people are making a difference in their

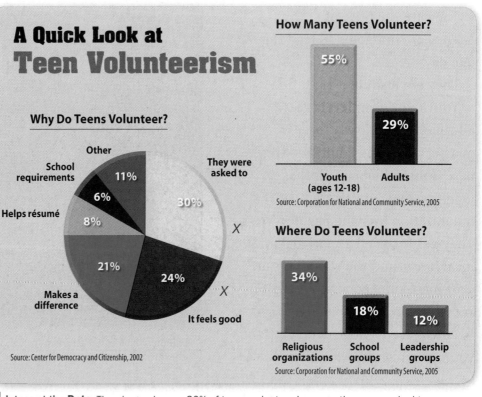

A Quick Look at Teen Volunteerism

Why Do Teens Volunteer?

- Other 11%
- School requirements 6%
- Helps résumé 8%
- Makes a difference 21%
- It feels good 24%
- They were asked to 30% X

Source: Center for Democracy and Citizenship, 2002

How Many Teens Volunteer?

- Youth (ages 12-18): 55%
- Adults: 29%

Source: Corporation for National and Community Service, 2005

Where Do Teens Volunteer?

- Religious organizations: 34%
- School groups: 18%
- Leadership groups: 12%

Source: Corporation for National and Community Service, 2005

▲ Interpret the **Data** The pie graph says 30% of teens volunteer because they were asked to. Who might have asked them?

Key Vocabulary
- **contribute** *v.*, to give with others

In Other Words
Youth Service America youth volunteer organization
peers people who are the same age
registering voters signing people up to vote
enthusiasm excitement, eagerness
Data Facts, Information

A volunteer paints a mural to celebrate Youth Service Day.

Interact with the Text

6. Preview/Set a Purpose
Think about the question you asked in question 2. Is your purpose for reading still the same? Why or why not? What questions do you have now?

Possible response:

No. Now I want to

know more. How can

I volunteer? When is

National Youth Service

Day?

communities. These volunteers also learn such life skills as planning events, raising funds, and holding leadership roles and responsibilities.

"Young people **have gotten sort of a negative rap**, when the majority of young people really are involved in their communities in very positive ways," says Carl Nelson. His company, State Farm, was the **Presenting Sponsor of** National Youth Service Day (NYSD) 2005, "a celebration of community service and service learning that goes on year-round."

Today's youth are building a unique background in **altruism**. <u>And they are not going to leave their service history behind them when they enter the workforce.</u> "We know that the one key predictor to lifetime service is whether you did it as a child," Culbertson states. "There's a whole **generation** of young people that have grown up giving back and

7. Interpret
Underline the author's main idea in the last paragraph. Write down one detail that supports the idea.

Possible response:

People who volunteered

when they were young

often keep volunteering

as they get older.

Key Vocabulary
- **generation** *n.*, people who are about the same age

In Other Words
have gotten sort of a negative rap are talked about in a bad way
Presenting Sponsor of company that paid for
altruism caring about the well-being of others

8. Interpret
Circle words that describe
this young generation
in the last paragraph.
What is so special about
this generation of young
people? Use one of the Key
Vocabulary words in your
explanation.

Possible response:

The author describes

this generation as

"passionate." They have

the motivation to help

others.

9. Text Features
Circle the sentence that
states information about
college freshmen. Why is
this information important?

Possible response:

This information

shows that many more

college freshmen are

volunteering now than

in 1989.

making that a **fundamental** part of their lives and it's not something
you give up."

Not when they are so (engaged) so (passionate.) Not where events like
NYSD show them that there is a (diverse) group of peers striving for a
common goal: a better world for everyone. "They're the most (tolerant)
generation we've ever seen in history," Culbertson says. "They can't
imagine that somebody should be left out of society simply because
they're black or they're gay or they have a disability or they come from
an ethnic background that's unusual. They just don't look at those
differences as anything more than just part of what it means to be a

Volunteer Work:
By the Numbers

Teenagers volunteer 2.4 billion hours
annually — worth $34.3 billion to the
U.S. economy.
Source: Independent Sector/Gallup, 1996, and 1999 hourly value

82.6% of incoming college freshmen
did volunteer work, compared to
66% in 1989.
Source: UCLA/Higher Education Research Institute Annual
Freshmen Survey, 2001

The number of high school students
involved in service learning increased
3,663% in the past decade from
81,000 to 2,967,000.
Source: U.S. Department of Education, 1999

A library volunteer keeps his audience's attention.

◤ **Interpret the Data** How do the numbers in this boxed feature support the main ideas of this article?

In Other Words
fundamental basic and important
engaged interested
diverse mixed
tolerant accepting, open-minded

human. They don't let those differences get in the way of progress. That's what makes this the greatest generation I think we've ever seen in this country, and nobody knows it."

They do now. ❖

Interact with the Text

10. Interpret

Reread the last sentence. What does this last sentence tell you about what the author's purpose for writing the article might be?

Possible response: The author wrote the article to inform others about how young people in this country are volunteering.

Selection Review   The World Is in Their Hands

A. The text features in this selection, graphs, photos, and captions provide useful information about teen volunteerism. Answer the questions below.

1. Reread the information in the graphics on pages 12 and 14. What do these facts suggest about the future of teen volunteerism?

   Possible response: The future of teen volunteerism looks good. The facts show many teens are volunteering, and they enjoy how it makes them feel.

2. Which text feature in the article gave you the most information? Why?

   Answers will vary.

Selection Review continued

B. Answer the questions.

1. How did using the text features in the article help you understand the rise of teen volunteerism in this country?

   Answers will vary.

   _____

   _____

   _____

   _____

2. The article suggests that the current generation of teens is more altruistic than previous generations. List the details that support this main idea in the diagram below.

   Main-Idea Diagram

Main Idea: Teens today are more altruistic than previous generations.

Detail: More teens are volunteering than ever before.
Detail: Teens are volunteering because thay want to, not because they have to.

   Do you agree with the main idea of this article? Why or why not?

   Answers will vary.

   _____

   _____

   _____

   _____

   _____

   _____

   _____

   _____

Reflect and Assess

WRITING: Write About Literature

A. Plan your writing. List examples from both texts of reasons that teens choose to help others. Then list your reasons. *Answers will vary.*

The Good Samaritan	The World Is in Their Hands	My Reasons
Rey wants to use Mr. Sánchez's pool.	Teens want their voices to be heard.	

Rank your reasons in order of importance.

1. Most Important: _____

2. Second: _____

3. Third: _____

4. Fourth: _____

B. Write a paragraph presenting your reasons in order of importance, ending with the reason you think is most important. Use examples from both selections to support your ideas.

Students should support their answers with examples from the selections.

_____

_____

_____

_____

_____

Integrate the Language Arts

LITERARY ANALYSIS: Analyze Theme

The **theme** of a selection is the central idea or message. It can be stated directly or implied. Clues about the theme can be found in the story events, characters, dialogue, and title.

A. List examples from "The Good Samaritan" of events, characters, and dialogue that can be used as clues to figure out the theme.

Answers will vary. Possible responses are shown.

Event:	**Character:**	**Dialogue:**
Rey changes Mr. Sánchez's tire.	Rey helps his neighbor, even though Mr. Sánchez had taken advantage of him many times. Rey is honest and respectful.	Rey says, "And I'm doing it for my dad really, not Mr. Sánchez."

Theme:
The theme is that people should help each other whether or not that person deserves help.

B. Answer the questions.   *Answers will vary. Possible responses are shown.*

1. What do you think is the theme of "The Good Samaritan"?

The theme is that people should help each other whether or not that person deserves help.

2. How does the title give a clue to the theme?

I knew the story would be about helping others because the phrase "good Samaritan" means a person who helps others in need.

C. Write about a time you or someone you know was a "Good Samaritan."

Answers will vary.

VOCABULARY STUDY: Prefixes

A **prefix** is a word part that comes at the beginning of a word and changes the meaning of that word.

A. *Mis-* is a common prefix that means "wrong" or "badly." Add *mis* to each word. Write what the new word means. Use a dictionary to confirm the meaning of the word.

Word	New Word	Meaning
behave	misbehave	to behave badly
count	miscount	to count wrong
fortune	misfortune	something bad or bad luck
inform	misinform	to give wrong information
understand	misunderstand	to understand something wrong

B. Use each word from the list below and make a new word by adding it to one of the prefixes in the chart. Then write the definition of the new word.

believable   build   cycle   order

Prefix	Meaning	New Word	Definition
bi-	two	bicycle	something with two wheels
dis-	reverse, opposite	disorder	the opposite of order
re-	again, repeatedly	rebuild	to build again
un-	not	unbelievable	not believable

C. Use the chart above to write a definition for each of these words. *Answers will vary.*

bilingual _____

disengage_____

react _____

unlock _____

Prepare to Read

▷ **Thank You, M'am**
▷ **Juvenile Justice from Both Sides of the Bench**

Key Vocabulary

A. How well do you know these words? Circle a rating for each word. Check your understanding of each word by circling *yes* or *no*. Then complete the sentences. If you are unsure of a word's meaning, refer to the Vocabulary Glossary, page 852, in your student text.

Rating Scale	
1	I have never seen this word before.
2	I am not sure of the word's meaning.
3	I know this word and can teach the word's meaning to someone else.

Key Word	Check Your Understanding	Deepen Your Understanding
1 circumstances (**sur**-kum-stans-uz) *noun* **Rating:** **1 2 3**	Choosing your friends and what you wear are **circumstances** within your control. (Yes)　　No	Some of the positive circumstances in my life are _____ *Possible response:* a loving family, supportive _____ teachers _____ _____ _____.
2 commit (ku-**mit**) *verb* **Rating:** **1 2 3**	It is irresponsible to **commit** yourself to a job you can't finish. (Yes)　　No	Many people commit acts of heroism, such as _____ *Possible response:* stopping to help someone who is ____ hurt _____ _____ _____.
3 consequence (**kon**-su-kwens) *noun* **Rating:** **1 2 3**	The **consequence** of failing a class is always positive. Yes　　(No)	The consequence of breaking rules at school is _____ *Possible response:* privileges are taken away, _____ detention, suspension, losing the respect of parents ____ and teachers _____ _____.
4 contact (**kon**-takt) *noun* **Rating:** **1 2 3**	Sending a letter through the mail is the fastest way to get in **contact** with a person. Yes　　(No)	When I want to get in contact with my friends, I use a ____ *Possible response:* telephone or a computer _____ _____ _____ _____.

Key Word	Check Your Understanding	Deepen Your Understanding
5 empathy (**em**-pu-thē) *noun* **Rating:** 1 2 3	Being sensitive to a person's feelings is an example of how a person shows **empathy**. (**Yes**) No	A friend of mine showed empathy by *Possible* *response:* understanding what it is like to be sick and offering to help me _____ .
6 juvenile (**joo**-vu-nīl) *adjective; noun* **Rating:** 1 2 3	**Juvenile** people are considered mature and responsible. Yes (**No**)	Teenagers are juvenile when they *Possible response:* decide to go to a party when there is work to be done _____ .
7 maturity (mu-**choor**-u-tē) *noun* **Rating:** 1 2 3	Expecting someone else to fix your mistakes is an example of **maturity**. Yes (**No**)	I showed maturity when I *Possible response:* offered to clean my grandmother's yard _____ .
8 salvage (**sal**-vuj) *verb* **Rating:** 1 2 3	Spreading rumors about a friend is a good way to **salvage** a bad friendship. Yes (**No**)	If I am doing poorly in class, I can salvage my grade by *Possible response:* studying harder or asking for a tutor _____ .

B. Write a sentence about yourself using one of the Key Vocabulary words.

Answers will vary.

_____

Before Reading Thank You, M'am

LITERARY ANALYSIS: Characterization

Authors use **characterization** to show what a character is like.

A. Read the passage below. Find the character clues that tell you what Mrs. Jones is like. Write the clues in the chart.

> **Look Into the Text**
>
> She was a large woman with a large purse that had everything in it but a hammer and nails. It had a long strap, and she carried it slung across her shoulder. It was about eleven o'clock at night, dark, and she was walking alone, when a boy ran up behind her and tried to snatch her purse. The strap broke with the sudden single tug the boy gave it from behind. But the boy's weight and the weight of the purse combined caused him to lose his balance. Instead of taking off full blast as he had hoped, the boy fell on his back on the sidewalk and his legs flew up. The large woman simply turned around and kicked him right square in his blue-jeaned sitter. Then she reached down, picked the boy up by his shirt front, and shook him until his teeth rattled.

Type of Clue	Mrs. Jones
Physical traits	large woman
Words or thoughts	was probably angry
Actions	kicked the boy and then picked him up and shook him
Reactions of others	the boy was probably startled or frightened by her

B. Complete the sentence about Mrs. Jones's character.

Mrs. Jones seems like a character who <u>is a strong woman. She is not afraid to stand up for herself</u>

_____

_____.

READING STRATEGY: Clarify Ideas

How to CLARIFY IDEAS

1. Reread Go back to see if you missed something important.

2. Read On Keep reading. The author may answer your question later.

A. Read the passage. Use the strategies above to clarify the ideas as you read. Answer the questions below.

Look Into the Text

> After that, the woman said, "Pick up my pocketbook, boy, and give it here."
> She still held him tightly. But she bent down enough to permit him to stoop and pick up her purse. Then she said, "Now ain't you ashamed of yourself?"
> Firmly gripped by his shirt front, the boy said, "Yes'm."
> The woman said, "What did you want to do it for?"
> The boy said, "I didn't aim to."
> She said, "You a lie!"
> By that time two or three people passed, stopped, turned to look, and some stood watching.
> "If I turn you loose, will you run?" asked the woman.
> "Yes'm," said the boy.
> "Then I won't turn you loose," said the woman. She did not release him.
> "Lady, I'm sorry," whispered the boy.

1. Why didn't the boy run?

Mrs. Jones would not let him go.

2. Which of the two strategies did you use to answer question 1?

Possible response: Reread

B. Return to the passage above and circle the words or sentences that gave you the answer to the first question.

 What Influences a Person's Choices?
Find out how circumstances affect choices.

A. In "Thank You, M'am," you found out how circumstances can affect the choices people make. Complete the charts below.

Mrs. Jones	
Her circumstances:	Her choices:
does not have much money	she understands the boy's struggle
used to steal, too	tries to teach him right from wrong
works in a hotel beauty shop	

Roger	
His circumstances:	His choices:
nobody at home to take care of him	steals to get money
does not have much money	

B. Use the information in the charts to answer the questions.

1. Why does Mrs. Jones make the choice to help Roger?

   Mrs. Jones makes the choice to help Roger because she understands his struggle and wants to help him.

2. How could Roger's circumstances change because of Mrs. Jones? Use **circumstances** in your answer.

   Possible response: Roger's circumstances have caused him to think that he has to steal to get money, but because of Mrs. Jones' example, Roger might realize that he can work hard in order to get the things that he needs.

3. How might Roger's choices be different in the future? Why?

   Possible response: Roger might not steal from people in the future because Mrs. Jones stood up to Roger and let him know that it is not acceptable to steal a woman's purse on the street.

Juvenile Justice
from Both Sides of the Bench
by Janet Tobias and Michael Martin

Connect Across Texts

In "Thank You, M'am," Mrs. Jones shows **empathy** *for Roger despite what he does. In these interviews, read how real-life judges and attorneys deal with teens who* **commit** *crimes.*

Interact with the Text

    Recent legislation in many U.S. states makes it easier to try, or judge, **juvenile** offenders in adult criminal court and not in juvenile court. As a result, more and more teen offenders are **doing time** alongside adults in prison.

    Teens who are tried as adults can also receive longer sentences, or periods of punishment. Many people believe such punishment is a better fit for more serious crimes. They see this as more important than how old the person is.

    Public opinion has changed over the last hundred years. In 1899, the first juvenile court was set up in Illinois. Then, most people believed juveniles were not as responsible for their actions as adults. Illinois wanted to protect each young person, even while it protected the public from crime. The goal of juvenile court was to help offenders make better choices about the future.

    Today, however, many people believe that harsh punishment is the better way to stop teens from committing crimes in the future. To explore this topic, the Public Broadcasting System's *Frontline* TV news team interviewed **people from both sides of "the bench."**

1. Clarify Ideas/Paraphrase

Circle a sentence that supports the idea that juvenile offenders should be tried in juvenile court. Write the sentence in your own words.

Possible response:

In the past, people

believed that teens

were too young to be

responsible for their

actions.

2. Clarify Ideas/Paraphrase

Underline a sentence that supports the idea that juvenile offenders should be tried in adult court. Write the sentence in your own words.

Possible response:

People believe that

if teens are given a

stronger punishment,

they will not commit

crimes in the future.

Key Vocabulary

empathy *n.*, the understanding of someone else's problems, feelings, or behavior
• **commit** *v.*, to perform, do, or carry out something, often a crime
juvenile *adj.*, young; *n.*, young person

In Other Words

Recent legislation New laws
doing time being punished
people from both sides of "the bench" judges, who sit on one side of the bench, or desk, and lawyers, who stand on the other side

3. Clarify Ideas/Paraphrase
Underline the main points in Judge Edwards's answer to the second question. Write a paraphrase of his answer.

Possible response:

There are not many, but

sometimes there are

kids who definitely need

to be tried in adult court.

4. Interpret
What is the Judge's strongest or most powerful idea? Use one of the Key Vocabulary words in your response.

Possible response:

Sometimes a child in

juvenile court belongs in

an adult court trial and

deserves to suffer the

consequences of his or

her actions.

Judge Thomas Edwards
Until recently he was the presiding judge of the Juvenile Court of Santa Clara County, a division of the California Superior Court. He heard between 300 and 350 cases a month.

Q. Why should we treat a 14-year-old offender differently than a 24-year-old offender?

A. It depends on many, many **circumstances**. But very generally, the 14-year-old does not have the level of **maturity**, thought process, decision-making, experience, or wisdom that a 24-year-old presumably has.

Secondly, a 14-year-old is still growing, may not appreciate the **consequences** of that type of behavior, and **is susceptible to** change, at least to a higher degree than a 24-year-old is. . . . I think we have a real shot at trying to straighten out the 14-year-old, and even the people who are a little bit hard-nosed in the system, such as your average **prosecutor**, will sometimes grudgingly admit that, with a 14-year-old, given the proper level of accountability and the proper types of programs to change their behavior, we have a chance at **salvaging** these kids.

Q. Are there kids who don't belong in juvenile court?

A. Oh, sure. Yes. I've had **sociopaths** in court here. I've had only a few of them, and I've been doing this for a long time. I can only really count maybe a half a dozen, and only two in particular that I would be very frightened to see on the street. But I see them from time to time.

Key Vocabulary
- **circumstances** *n.,* situation
  maturity *n.,* the time when a person has all the abilities of an adult
- **consequence** *n.,* result
  salvage *v.,* to save or rescue

In Other Words
is susceptible to probably will
prosecutor lawyer whose job is to get punishment for criminals
sociopaths people who do not know right from wrong

Judge LaDoris Cordell
A state court trial judge since 1982, until recently she served on the Superior Court of Santa Clara County, where she heard both juvenile and adult cases.

Q. Why should we treat a 14-year-old offender differently than a 24-year-old offender?

A. The problem is that we're taking 14-year-olds, 15-year-olds, 16-year-olds, and we're giving up on them. We're saying, "You've committed a crime, and we're just going to give up on you. You're out of here; society has no use for you." We're throwing away these kids. And I have found, in my own experience, that there are salvageable young people. They have committed some very horrible kinds of crimes, but they are able to get their lives together and **be productive members of society**. I think it is a mistake to just . . . give up on these young people. There is so much more that goes into why that person got there at that point in time so young in their lives.

Q. Do you think any kid ever belongs in adult court?

A. Yes. . . . I have come across some young people who are so **sophisticated** and who have committed such **heinous** crimes that the adult system is the place for them to be. I haven't come across a lot, but there have been some. . . . It can happen, and it does [happen].

In Other Words

be productive members of society work and be responsible like other people
sophisticated clever in a grown-up way
heinous horrible, evil

Interact with the Text

5. Text Features

Captions provide additional information. In this article, the writer states that judges "hear" cases. Reread the caption and describe what you think hearing a case means, in your own words.

Possible response:

Hearing a case means to

be the judge for a trial.

6. Text Features

Remember that brackets and ellipses are important text features. Circle the text features in Judge Cordell's answer. Write what each text feature means.

The first ellipses means

that the person being

interviewed paused

between words. The

second ellipses means

that some text is not

included. The bracketed

word means that it was

not spoken, but implied.

7. Clarify Ideas/Paraphrase
Underline the main points in Jones's answer. Paraphrase her answer.

Possible response: A
fourteen year old still
has a chance to make a
change in his or her life,
and we should support
him or her in making
that change. A severe
punishment will not help
the child later in life.

8. Interpret
Do you agree that a young person needs the support of his or her community? Why or why not?

Answers will vary.

Bridgett Jones
Former supervisor of the Juvenile Division of the Santa Clara County Public Defender's Office

Q. Why should we treat a 14-year-old offender differently than a 24-year-old offender?

A. I think the community understands, or should understand, that the younger a person is, <u>the more likely it is that they can change</u>. And the best way I've heard it put is from a **victim** in a very serious case.

This person had been **maimed** for life. He had **indicated to** the young person who shot him, or was **alleged** to have shot him, that <u>he would rather meet up with this person ten years down the road as a graduate from a college versus a graduate from [prison].</u>

He [understood] that this person was eventually going to get back out and be in our community. They don't go away. They come back. And <u>the younger they are, the more likely it is that they are going to come back into our community.</u> So I guess as a community we have to decide what is it we're willing to get back in the long run.

<u>Children are not little adults. They think differently. They respond and react to things differently than adults do.</u> . . . . So why should the consequences be the same as for an adult?

<u>The only thing that's going to work with kids like [these] is a willingness of the community to **redeem** them and saying, "Look, your life's not over, there's still hope for you."</u>

In Other Words
victim person hurt by a crime
maimed physically hurt, wounded
indicated to told or shown
alleged suspected
redeem help and forgive

Social Studies Background
A district attorney prosecutes, or seeks punishment for, someone charged with a crime. If the person cannot afford a lawyer, a public defender has the job of advising and representing the person.

Kurt Kumli

The supervising deputy district attorney for the Juvenile Division of the Santa Clara County District Attorney's Office, he has practiced exclusively in juvenile court.

Q. Why should we treat a 14-year-old offender differently than a 24-year-old offender?

A. If we could take every kid and surround the kid with full-time staffs of psychologists and drug and alcohol counselors, then perhaps no kid should be in adult court. But the fact is, there are only a limited number of **resources** in the juvenile justice system. . . . You have to make **the hard call**, sometimes, as to whether or not the high-end offenders really are the **just recipients of** the [limited] resources that the juvenile justice system has available to it.

Q. What does it take to rehabilitate young offenders?

A. What works is different for every kid, but the one rule that I think is applicable, after years of seeing this, is "the sooner, the better." We need to reach these kids with **alternatives**, with opportunities, before they start to feel [like nobody cares]. If we took half of the money that we spend on **incarceration** and put it in **front-end programs** to give these kids alternatives, then we wouldn't have as many **back-end kids** that we needed to incarcerate. And I think that is the immediate answer.

In Other Words

resources staff people and services
the hard call a difficult decision
just recipients of people who should receive
rehabilitate help, fix the problems of
alternatives other choices
incarceration keeping people in jail

front-end programs programs that help
  kids before they get into trouble
back-end kids kids who have already
  committed crimes

Interact with the Text

9. Text Features
Draw a circle around the information that is in italics. Write a sentence about why this background information is important.

Possible response: This information is important because Kumli has only worked in juvenile court, so his opinion is based on his experiences in juvenile court and not in the adult system.

10. Interpret

Which person's opinion in this article surprised you the most? Why?

Answers will vary.

Judge Nancy Hoffman

Judge Hoffman served on the Superior Court of Santa Clara County, where she handled both juvenile and adult cases. She is currently retired.

Q. What does it take to rehabilitate young offenders?

A. I would like to see groups . . . working with troubled families and youth, before they get to middle school and . . . high school. Something is causing the **minor** to do things like not go to school, stay out till three o'clock in the morning . . . We **intervene** with a minor, but there's very little done with the family, and we're sending the minor right back in that situation. ❖

In Other Words

minor person under the age of 18

intervene get involved to prevent or solve problems

Selection Review   Juvenile Justice from Both Sides of the Bench

A. Choose a topic and write three details from the interview that relate to it. Identify the speaker of each viewpoint.

| Topic 1: | **Differences between young and adult offenders** |
| Topic 2: | **Ideas about rehabilitating young offenders** |

Details for Topic ___1___ :

1. A fourteen year old does not have the maturity a twenty-four year old has. — Judge Thomas Edwards

2. Children are not little adults. They think differently. — Bridgett Jones

3. A fourteen year old has to see that there are alternatives to the life they are leading. — Kurt Kiumli

B. Answer the questions.

1. How did the text features help you to find the information?

Possible response: Words that are in brackets or italicized stand out from the rest of the text. It is easier to see what information is important.

2. Which speaker's views are closest to your own? Which speaker do you disagree with? Why?

Answers will vary.

Reflect and Assess

WRITING: Write About Literature

A. Plan your writing. Read the opposing opinions. Put an *X* next to the opinion you agree with. Then list examples from each text to support the opinion. *Answers will vary.*

☐ **Opinion 1:** Juvenile offenders should be treated differently than adult offenders.

☐ **Opinion 2:** Most juvenile offenders should be treated the same as adult offenders.

Thank You, M'am	Juvenile Justice

B. What is your opinion? Write an opinion statement. Remember to use the text evidence you listed in the chart to support your statement.

Students should support their answers with examples from both selections.

_____

_____

_____

_____

_____

_____

_____

_____

Integrate the Language Arts

LITERARY ANALYSIS: Analyze Dialogue

What a character says, or **dialogue**, is an important part of characterization. Writers use speaker words and quotation marks to show what characters say and how they say it.   *Answers will vary. Possible responses are shown.*

Example: "Lady, I'm sorry," <u>whispered</u> the boy.

A. Brainstorm words that show how characters speak. List them in the chart.   *Answers will vary. Possible responses are shown.*

Speaker Words	
1. shouted	**5.** proclaimed
2. mumbled	**6.** yelled
3. said	**7.** whimpered
4. asked	**8.** cheered

B. Rewrite these sentences as dialogue. Use quotation marks and the speaker words from the chart, above.   *Answers will vary. Possible responses are shown.*

1. Mrs. Jones told Roger to pick up her pocketbook.

   "Pick up my pocketbook, Roger," said Mrs. Jones.

2. Roger apologized to Mrs. Jones.

   Roger mumbled, "I'm sorry, Mrs. Jones."

3. Mrs. Jones asked Roger if he would run.

   "Roger, will you run?" asked Mrs. Jones.

4. Mrs. Jones told Roger she would not let him go.

   "I will not let you go!" shouted Mrs. Jones.

C. Write a conversation you have had with a friend recently using dialogue. The dialogue is started for you.   *Answers will vary.*

"_____," I shouted to my friend in the hallway._____

_____

_____

_____

_____

_____

VOCABULARY STUDY: Greek Roots

Greek roots are word parts in many English words. If you know the meaning of a word part, you can figure out the meaning of the word. *Answers will vary.*

A. *Tele* is a common Greek root that means "far off." Write what you think each word means. Confirm the definition for each word in the dictionary.

Word	What I Think It Means	Definition
telecom		
telecommute		
telegram		
telephoto		
telescope		

B. The chart below shows some common Greek roots and their meanings. Complete the chart by listing words you've heard that contain each root.

Greek Root	Meaning	Words I've Used
auto	self	automobile
bio	life	
graph	write, draw	
phone, phono	sound	
log	word, thought, speech	

C. Use the chart above to write a definition of each of these words.

autobiography _____

biology _____

telegraph _____

phonograph _____

logic _____

Prepare to Read

▶ **The Necklace**
▶ **The Fashion Show**

Key Vocabulary

A. How well do you know these words? Circle a rating for each word. Check your understanding of each word by circling the synonym. Then write a definition of the word in your own words. If you are unsure of a word's meaning, refer to the Vocabulary Glossary, page 852, in your student text.

Rating Scale

1	I have never seen this word before.
2	I am not sure of the word's meaning.
3	I know this word and can teach the word's meaning to someone else.

Key Word	Check Your Understanding	Deepen Your Understanding
❶ humiliating (hyū-**mi**-lē-ā-ting) *adjective* **Rating:** 1 2 3	A **humiliating** experience is _____. secretive (embarrassing)	My definition: *Answers will vary.*
❷ imitation (im-u-**tā**-shun) *noun* **Rating:** 1 2 3	An **imitation** of something is _____. an original (a copy)	My definition: *Answers will vary.*
❸ inspire (in-**spīr**) *verb* **Rating:** 1 2 3	To **inspire** people is to _____ them. (motivate) criticize	My definition: *Answers will vary.*
❹ luxury (**luk**-shu-rē) *noun* **Rating:** 1 2 3	If something is a **luxury**, it is _____. a necessity (an extravagance)	My definition: *Answers will vary.*

Key Word	Check Your Understanding	Deepen Your Understanding
5 perceive (per-**sēv**) *verb* **Rating:** 1 2 3	To **perceive** is to _____ something in a particular way. (see) ignore	My definition: *Answers will vary.* _____ _____ _____ _____
6 poverty (**pov**-er-tē) *noun* **Rating:** 1 2 3	To live in a state of **poverty** is to live in a state of _____. (need) rest	My definition: *Answers will vary.* _____ _____ _____ _____
7 symbol (**sim**-bul) *noun* **Rating:** 1 2 3	A **symbol** is a _____ of something else. (representation) recommendation	My definition: *Answers will vary.* _____ _____ _____ _____
8 value (**val**-ū) *verb* **Rating:** 1 2 3	To **value** something is to _____ it. summarize (appreciate)	My definition: *Answers will vary.* _____ _____ _____ _____

B. Use one of the Key Vocabulary words to write about a person who has had a positive influence on you.

Answers will vary.

Before Reading The Necklace

LITERARY ANALYSIS: Setting

The **setting** tells when and where a story takes place. It also includes details about the characters' circumstances.

A. Read the passage below. Pay attention to clues in the text that tell you about the setting. Write the clues in the chart.

> **Look Into the Text**
>
> Then one evening, her husband came home and proudly handed her a large envelope . . .
>
> She . . . threw the invitation onto the table and murmured, "What do you want me to do with that?"
>
> "But my dear, I thought you would be so pleased. This is a big event! I had a lot of trouble getting this invitation. All the clerks in the Ministry want to go, but there are only a few invitations reserved for workers. You will meet all the most important people there."
>
> She gave him an irritated look and said, impatiently, "I do not have anything I could wear. How could I go?"

Setting Chart
What is happening?   A couple disagrees about going to a fancy party for rich people.
Who are the characters?   The characters are a husband and a wife.
Where does this scene occur?   It takes place at the home of the characters.
When does this scene take place?   It takes place in the evening.
Why does the husband think his wife will be pleased?   The party will be in a fancy place with important people.

B. Complete this sentence about the setting.

The couple's social status and disagreement is an important part of the setting because they are not rich. The wife is upset because she does not have anything to wear to the party .

READING STRATEGY: Clarify Vocabulary

HOW TO CLARIFY VOCABULARY

1. **Look for Context Clues** When you read an unfamiliar word, other words or phrases near it can give you hints to its meaning.

2. **Figure Out Word Meaning** What *doesn't* the word mean? This will give you a clue about the word's meaning.

3. **Test Your Meaning** Does your meaning make sense in the sentence?

A. Read the passage below. Use the strategies above to clarify the vocabulary as you read. Then answer the questions.

Look Into the Text

He was stunned and said, "Mathilde, how much would it cost for a suitable dress that you could wear again?"

She thought for several seconds, wondering how much she could ask for without a (shocked refusal) from her thrifty husband.

Finally, she answered, "I am not sure exactly, but I think I could manage with four hundred francs."

(His face turned pale) because that was exactly the amount of (money he had saved) to buy a new rifle. He wanted to go hunting in Nanterre the next summer with some of his friends.

However, he said, "All right. I'll give you four hundred francs, but try to find a beautiful dress."

1. Read the sentences around the word *thrifty*. What does the word *thrifty* not mean? Explain.

Thrifty does not mean extravagant or wasteful. The husband became shocked and upset when his wife

asked for money.

2. What strategy did you use to find out what the word *thrifty* means?

Possible response: I used the first strategy, finding context clues. I also could have tested my own

definition.

B. Reread the passage above and circle the clues that told you what *thrifty* means.

Selection Review The Necklace

EQ **What Influences a Person's Choices?**
Discover how society influences choices.

A. In "The Necklace," you found out how circumstances can influence the choices people make. Complete the chart below with the consequences of the Loisels' circumstances.

Cause-and-Effect Chart

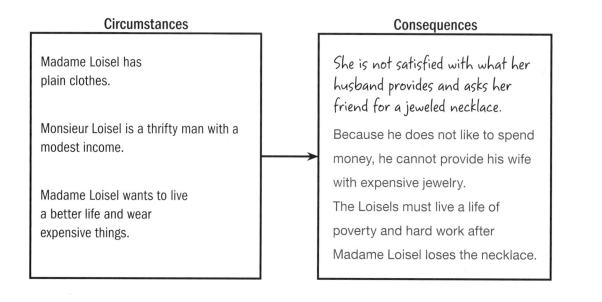

Circumstances	Consequences
Madame Loisel has plain clothes. Monsieur Loisel is a thrifty man with a modest income. Madame Loisel wants to live a better life and wear expensive things.	She is not satisfied with what her husband provides and asks her friend for a jeweled necklace. Because he does not like to spend money, he cannot provide his wife with expensive jewelry. The Loisels must live a life of poverty and hard work after Madame Loisel loses the necklace.

B. Use the information in the chart to answer the questions.

1. What circumstances cause Madame Loisel to want to live a different life?

She is embarrassed by her simple things and low social status. She thinks she deserves a better life.

2. Why does Madame Loisel choose to borrow a luxury item? Use the word **luxury** in your response.

Possible response: Madame Loisel thinks wearing a luxury item to the party will help get her noticed. She does not want to go to the party without all of the fancy things the people there will be wearing.

3. How might their final situation have been different if the Loisels had told the truth to Madame Forestier? Why?

Possible response: The Loisels would not have had to live a life of poverty and hard work. They may have been able to eventually buy the things they want.

Connect Across Texts

In "The Necklace," Madame Loisel makes a choice because she worries about what others think. Now read this memoir. How do the opinions of others affect Farah's decision?

THE FASHION SHOW

by Farah Ahmedi
with Tamim Ansari

At just 17, Farah Ahmedi entered an essay contest. Since then, her memoir, *The Other Side of the Sky*, has inspired people everywhere with her life story as a proud Afghan American.

▲ Farah Ahmedi was a junior in high school when she published *The Other Side of the Sky: A Memoir*.

Interact with the Text

1. Interpret
Circle the words and phrases that are clues to what this selection is about. What do you think the author's reason for writing might be?

Possible response: I think Ahmedi wrote this memoir to share her story and express her feelings about what it's like to be an Afghan American.

Farah Ahmedi didn't have much of a childhood. She was still recovering from losing her leg in **a land mine accident** when a rocket attack destroyed her home in Kabul, Afghanistan. Four years and many challenges later, Farah and her mother found their way to a **suburb of** Chicago. Farah learned English, started high school, and began to make choices that would change her life. Despite her disability, she wanted to fit in. She wanted to "wear high-heeled shoes." Here, Farah remembers one of those choices.

During our second summer in America, I switched schools. The **ESL department** at my new high school had an international club. Kids from other countries met every Wednesday after school to play games, talk, and have

From Kabul to Chicago

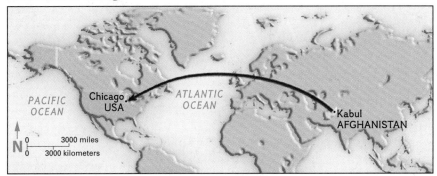

▲ Interpret the Map Use the scale to calculate how far Farah and her mother traveled to their new home.

fun. Ms. Ascadam, the teacher who sponsored this group, decided that the international kids should throw a party at the end of the year and present a show. She told us each to bring food from our country to the party, and she encouraged us to think about participating in the show as well.

The first part of the show would be a dance performance by the kids from Mexico. The next part would be a **fashion show**. Kids from any country could be in the fashion show, and they would model clothes from their own culture, but no one had to do it.

In Other Words

a land mine accident an explosion caused by a bomb buried in the ground
suburb of town outside of
ESL department English classes for students who spoke other languages
fashion show display of special clothes

Historical Background

Afghanistan has been at war for more than forty years. In 2001, the U.S. and other countries invaded the country to force the Taliban, the ruling group, to leave.

I felt (torn and confused) I could not take part in the dance, of course, but should I be in the fashion show? (I really wanted to do it.) I had two beautiful **Afghan outfits** I could model. But I was also thinking, *My leg is damaged.* (What if I fall down?)

Finally, I said to myself, *Okay, next Wednesday I'll sit in on the practice session and see what it's like, and then I'll decide.*

That day the girl who always picked on me came to the practice session, because she was planning to be in the fashion show. The moment she saw me sitting there, she could tell I was thinking of entering the show, too. She didn't tell me to my face that I could not

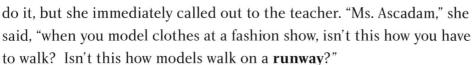

WHAT IF I FALL DOWN?

do it, but she immediately called out to the teacher. "Ms. Ascadam," she said, "when you model clothes at a fashion show, isn't this how you have to walk? Isn't this how models walk on a **runway**?"

Then she began to walk the way she thought a model should walk—with long strides, placing one foot in front of the other in a straight line that made her back end swing from side to side. "Is this the way you should walk?" she said. "If someone can't walk like this, should she be in the fashion show? She would just spoil the whole thing, wouldn't she?" And she kept walking back and forth, swinging from side to side.

It made me so angry, because I knew that she was really saying, *Farah can't do this. She has a problem with her legs. She shouldn't be in the fashion show.* She didn't say my name, but she was talking about me and only me, and everyone knew it.

That girl broke my heart. I felt as if somebody had punched me or slapped me. I felt as if someone had gotten into my throat and started pushing me and pressing me and choking me. I could not stay in that room. I turned and **fled**, my eyes stinging with tears. At home I

In Other Words
torn and confused mixed up, upset
Afghan outfits sets of clothes from Afghanistan
runway stage
fled ran away

Interact with the Text

2. Memoir
Circle the words and phrases in the first paragraph that tell you about Ahmedi feelings. Explain why she felt confused about participating in the fashion show.

Ahmedi wanted to participate, but she was afraid to walk on stage. She did not want to humiliate herself by falling down.

3. Interpret
Underline the action words and phrases that describe how Ahmedi was humiliated. Explain, using **humiliated** in your answer.

Possible response: Ahmedi felt humiliated by what the girl said to the teacher. The girl implied that Ahmedi could not walk like a model.

threw myself on my bed and just lay there, weeping and feeling sorry for myself—sorry about being only half a woman. I felt like everyone knew that I was not whole and that's what they thought about every time they looked at me. That girl had finally succeeded in getting through my defenses and poking me right where it hurt the most and where I would always hurt.

Farah Ahmedi shares her memoir with First Lady Laura Bush.

And what happened just then?

My friend Alyce called.

"Hey," she said. "How are you, sweetie? Are you well?"

I started to **bawl**.

She said, "What is it? What are you crying about?"

I spilled the whole story.

Alyce said, "Now don't **get all hung up on** what other people say. You just go ahead and do it. You tell your teacher you want to be in the fashion show."

But I just went on crying. "You don't understand. It's not *just* what 'other people say.' The terrible thing is, that girl is right! I *can't* be in a fashion show! It's true. How can someone like me be in a fashion show? With my limp? I can't walk like a model." That girl's cruelty **wounded** me, to be sure, but what really hurt was the truth she was telling. "Why are you trying to **inspire** me to do something I should never even try?" I **ranted** at Alyce.

It was one of those moments, you see. And Alyce just let me rage.

Key Vocabulary
• **inspire** v., to encourage someone to take action

In Other Words
bawl cry hard
I spilled the whole story. I told her everything.
get all hung up on worry about, feel upset about
wounded hurt
ranted yelled angrily

But then she said, "No, people aren't looking at you that way. Here, we **value** who you are as a person. You go right ahead and enter the fashion show fearlessly."

Well, I thought about it. I thought I should do it just to **spite** the girl who tried to keep me out of the show. I decided I had to do it, even if it meant falling down in the middle of the runway—because if I let that girl get away with talking about me as if I were half human, she would never stop. She would make me **her scapegoat**, and others would take up her view as well. I had to stand up for myself, because this was not just about a fashion show. It was about claiming my humanity. I had to do it.

I went to my teacher the next day and told her I wanted to enter the fashion show. She hugged me. "Farah," she said, "this makes me so, so happy!"

After that I started to practice walking. No, I started to practice *strutting* down a runway.

On the day of the fashion show, I hurried to the dressing room to get ready. I had two dresses to wear, an orange one and a purple

one. Backstage the makeup people put cosmetics on my face and curled my hair, so that I looked really different than usual. The teacher saw me and said, "Oh my gosh, you look so pretty!"

The fashion show began. Each model was supposed to go out and walk around the stage in a diamond-shaped pattern. At each point of the diamond we were supposed to pause, face the audience, and **strike a pose**.

When my turn came, I <u>went strutting out</u>. I <u>threw my shoulders back</u> and <u>held my head up high</u> so that my <u>neck stretched long</u>. I didn't fall, and I didn't shake. I <u>didn't even feel nervous</u>.

Interact with the Text

4. Interpret
Ahmedi decided to participate in the fashion show. What can you conclude about Ahmedi's values? Explain.

Ahmedi is a strong

person. She values

herself and does not

allow others to make her

feel bad about her injury.

_____

_____

_____

5. Memoir
Underline the words and phrases in the last paragraph that give you an idea about how the author felt when she walked down the runway. How are her feelings different from her earlier feelings? Why did they change?

Ahmedi felt confident

and strong, and she

enjoyed herself. This

is different from how

she felt at first about

participating in the

fashion show because

Ahmedi had decided to

"claim her humanity."

_____

_____

6. Clarify Vocabulary

Circle the words and phrases that tell you what *beamed* means. Explain how you found your answer.

Possible response: I read the sentences before and after the word, and I used the clues in the rest of the paragraph.

Alyce told me later that no one could tell about my legs. I moved in time to the music, showed the clothes off well, and smiled—I did just fine! My mother **beamed**. She didn't say much at the time, but later on, at home, she told me she (felt proud) of me. Imagine that! (Proud) that her daughter stood up before an audience of strangers and modeled our beautiful Afghan clothes: She, too, has come a long way since we arrived in America.

After the show the party began. We had all brought special foods from our various cultures. My mother had cooked a fancy Afghan rice dish. We ate and chatted and felt happy. That night, though it wasn't **literally** true, I felt that I was wearing high-heeled shoes at last. ❖

Key Vocabulary
• **perceive** *v.*, to see someone or something in a certain way

In Other Words
beamed smiled with joy
literally actually

Selection Review The Fashion Show

A. Answer the questions.

1. The author of "The Fashion Show" chose to write her story as a memoir. How did writing this way make the story more powerful?

Possible response: The story was told from Ahmedi's point of view. It included feelings and opinions. The story was more powerful because the account was from someone who had experienced a war firsthand.

2. Who do you think inspired Ahmedi? Why?

Ahmedi was inspired by the girl who picked on her. Ahmedi did not want someone making fun of her and wanted to show the girl that she could do it. She wanted to "claim her humanity."

B. List the words that were difficult for you to understand. Circle one of the words and explain how the reading strategy helped you.

1. Words that were difficult: *Answers will vary.*

2. Reading strategy I used: *Answers will vary.*

Reflect and Assess

WRITING: Write About Literature

A. Plan your writing. Think about how Madame Loisel in "The Necklace" and Farah Ahmedi in "The Fashion Show" make choices that have surprising consequences. List examples from both texts in the chart below. *Answers will vary.*

	Choice	Consequence
Madame Loisel	borrows a friend's necklace	loses the necklace
Farah Ahmedi		

B. Write a response log, describing a time when a choice you made had surprising consequences. Compare your experience to Madame Loisel's and Farah's. Use examples from the chart to support your writing.

Students should support their answers with examples from the selections.

_____

_____

_____

_____

_____

_____

Integrate the Language Arts

LITERARY ANALYSIS: Analyze Setting and Theme

Setting is the time and place in which a story unfolds. A story's setting affects the characters and the **theme**, or message, of the story.

A. Complete each chart below with details from each selection.

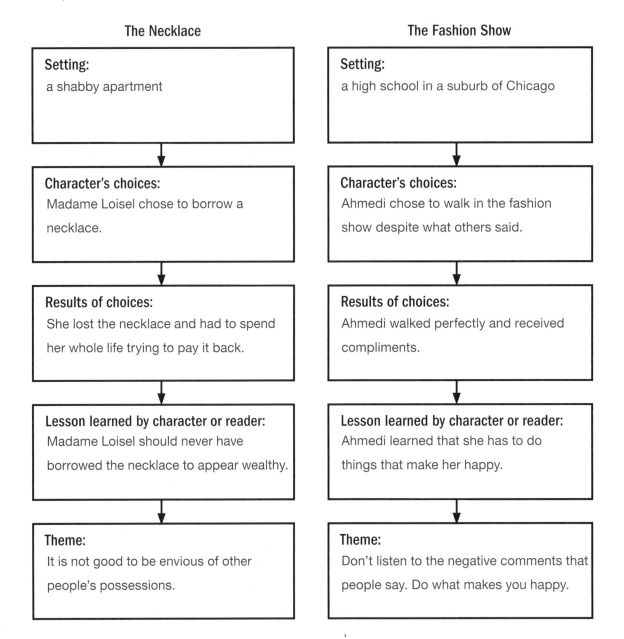

The Necklace

Setting:
a shabby apartment

↓

Character's choices:
Madame Loisel chose to borrow a necklace.

↓

Results of choices:
She lost the necklace and had to spend her whole life trying to pay it back.

↓

Lesson learned by character or reader:
Madame Loisel should never have borrowed the necklace to appear wealthy.

↓

Theme:
It is not good to be envious of other people's possessions.

The Fashion Show

Setting:
a high school in a suburb of Chicago

↓

Character's choices:
Ahmedi chose to walk in the fashion show despite what others said.

↓

Results of choices:
Ahmedi walked perfectly and received compliments.

↓

Lesson learned by character or reader:
Ahmedi learned that she has to do things that make her happy.

↓

Theme:
Don't listen to the negative comments that people say. Do what makes you happy.

B. How does setting affect the actions of Madame Loisel and Farah Ahmedi? Compare the themes.

Both Madame Loisel and Farah Ahmedi felt pressure from the people around them, but ultimately learn that it is important to ignore what others say. Do what makes you happy and be yourself.

VOCABULARY STUDY: Suffixes

A **suffix** is a word part added to the end of a word. Suffixes can change verbs or adjectives into nouns.

A. Change each verb or adjective in the chart into a noun by adding the suffix. Then write the meanings of each noun. Use a dictionary to check the meanings.

Verb or Adjective	Suffix	Noun	Meaning
work	-er	worker	one who works
enjoy	-ment	enjoyment	the act of enjoying
kind	-ness	kindness	the state of being kind
aggravate	-tion	aggravation	the act of annoying someone

B. List two more nouns for each suffix in the chart above.
Answers will vary. Possible responses are shown.

1. farmer, player

2. creation, sensation

3. establishment, detainment

4. fullness, happiness

C. Write sentences using one of the words you wrote containing each suffix. *Answers will vary.*

1. _____

    _____

2. _____

    _____

3. _____

    _____

4. _____

    _____

Key Vocabulary Review

A. Use the words to complete the paragraph.

affect	consequence	disrespect	salvage
conflict	contribute	juvenile	value

Shawn and Jacob argued about the direction of our project. Their continued ___conflict___
(1)

began to ___affect___ the group. They showed ___disrespect___ to each other, and
(2) (3)

they refused to ___contribute___ any new ideas. The ___consequences___ of their actions were
(4) (5)

getting serious, and we were afraid we wouldn't finish on time. The rest of us worked hard to

___salvage___ the project and create something we could ___value___. Their immature and
(6) (7)

___juvenile___ behavior almost cost us a good grade.
(8)

B. Use your own words to write what each Key Vocabulary word means.
Then write a synonym for each word. *Answers will vary. Possible responses are shown.*

Key Word	My Definition	Synonym
1. empathy	ability to understand how others feel	sympathy
2. generation	people born around the same time	peers
3. humiliating	shameful or foolish	embarrassing
4. imitation	something that is not the real thing	copy
5. inspire	to motivate a person's actions	encourage
6. luxury	something that is not necessary	treat
7. perceive	to see something in a certain way	see
8. poverty	a state of not having what is necessary	need

• affect	• consequence	empathy	• inspire	• motivation	responsible
• circumstances	contact	• generation	juvenile	• perceive	salvage
• commit	• contribute	humiliating	luxury	poverty	• symbol
• conflict	disrespect	imitation	maturity	privilege	value

• **Academic Vocabulary**

C. Answer the questions using complete sentences. *Answers will vary. Possible responses are shown.*

1. What **circumstances** might cause a person to make a bad decision?

   If someone is scared, he or she might make a bad decision.

2. Describe how you show **maturity**.

   I arrive at work on time, and I treat my family with respect.

3. Why might two people lose **contact** with each other?

   One person might move away, or they might lose each other's phone numbers.

4. What **privilege** do you enjoy the most?

   I enjoy the privilege of driving my parents' car.

5. What **symbol** do you see every day?

   I see the American flag.

6. What is your **motivation** to succeed?

   My dream of helping others is my motivation to succeed.

7. Why might someone **commit** a crime?

   He or she might be hungry or in danger.

8. Why are you **responsible**?

   I have a part-time job and do chores around the house.

Prepare to Read

▶ **Creativity at Work**
▶ **The Hidden Secrets of the Creative Mind**

Key Vocabulary

A. How well do you know these words? Circle a rating for each word. Check your understanding of each word by circling *yes* or *no*. Then complete the sentences. If you are unsure of a word's meaning, refer to the Vocabulary Glossary, page 852, in your student text.

	Rating Scale
1	I have never seen this word before.
2	I am not sure of the word's meaning.
3	I know this word and can teach the word's meaning to someone else.

Key Word	Check Your Understanding	Deepen Your Understanding
❶ career (ku-**rear**) *noun* **Rating:** 1 2 3	Doctors, artists, and teachers are examples of people who have a specific **career**. (**Yes**) No	A career I might be interested in pursuing some day is *Possible response:* engineering _____ _____ _____ _____ .
❷ collaborate (ku-**lab**-u-rāt) *verb* **Rating:** 1 2 3	World leaders sometimes **collaborate** to find peaceful solutions. (**Yes**) No	I collaborate with other people to ___ *Possible response:* finish a project _____ _____ _____ .
❸ commitment (ku-**mit**-mint) *noun* **Rating:** 1 2 3	Employees show their **commitment** to their jobs by doing as little work as possible. Yes (**No**)	I show commitment when I ___ *Possible response:* practice the piano every day _____ _____ _____ .
❹ evaluate (i-**val**-ū-āt) *verb* **Rating:** 1 2 3	Judges **evaluate** contestants in talent shows. (**Yes**) No	I can evaluate a video game by *Possible response:* playing it and comparing its graphics to other games _____ _____ _____ .

Key Word	Check Your Understanding	Deepen Your Understanding
5 **expectation** (ek-spek-**tā**-shun) *noun* **Rating:** 1 2 3	An **expectation** is something you do not think will happen. Yes (No)	One expectation I have for myself is *Possible* *response:* doing well at school _____ _____ _____ .
6 **insight** (**in**-sīt) *noun* **Rating:** 1 2 3	Reading several books about a subject can provide **insight** into the topic. (Yes) No	I have always wanted insight into *Possible response:* how to run a successful business _____ _____ _____ .
7 **talent** (**tal**-unt) *noun* **Rating:** 1 2 3	Someone who can sing, dance, and play many musical instruments has very little **talent**. Yes (No)	One talent I have is *Possible response:* dancing well _____ _____ _____ _____ .
8 **transform** (trans-**form**) *verb* **Rating:** 1 2 3	A painter can **transform** a blank canvas into a beautiful image. (Yes) No	Two things in my life that I wish I could transform are *Possible response:* my grades and my poor eating habits _____ _____ .

B. Use one of the Key Vocabulary words to explain how you think using your creativity helps you in your everyday life.

Answers will vary.

_____

_____

Before Reading Creativity at Work

LITERARY ANALYSIS: Author's Purpose

An **author's purpose** for writing a news article is to share factual information with readers in a clear and interesting way.

A. Read the passage below. Write the details in the passage in the Five-Ws Chart. Then answer the question about the article.

Look Into the Text

Pushing the Limits

The program began in 1991 as a collaboration between Susan Rodgerson—a white, middle-class artist—and five African American teen friends who started painting in her studio. The friends needed to sell their artwork in order to buy supplies and make more art. Sheer economics inspired an entrepreneurial zeal, and they approached Boston colleges, nonprofits, and corporations as potential customers. An audience was found and a program bloomed—with youth at the helm.

Five-Ws Chart

Who?	What?	Where?	When?	Why?
Susan Rodgerson and five African American teen friends	The friends started painting, then went to colleges, nonprofits, and corporations to sell their work.	Susan's studio in Boston	1991	They needed to sell their artwork to buy more art supplies.

B. Why do you think the author wrote the article?

Possible response: The author wanted to inform readers about the program. The author may have also wanted to describe the founders' purpose for starting the program.

READING STRATEGY: Identify Main Ideas and Details

HOW TO IDENTIFY MAIN IDEAS AND DETAILS

1. **Find the Important Details** Find information that tells *who, what, where, when,* and *why.*

2. **State the Main Idea** What is the overall message of the paragraph? Restate it in your own words.

A. Read the passage. Highlight the most important words, phrases, or sentences. Then answer the 5W questions.

> ### Look Into the Text
>
> Last year, a large Boston bank commissioned a large-scale painting of modern Boston. It was based on Paul Gauguin's signature masterpiece, *Where Do We Come From? What Are We? Where Are We Going?* After hanging alongside the colorful Gauguin original in the Museum of Fine Arts, this painting now greets travelers at Logan Airport, where it is on permanent display.

Write the main idea of the paragraph in your own words.

1. Who? _a large Boston bank_
2. What? _commissioned a painting_
3. Where? _Museum of Fine Arts and Logan Airport_
4. When? _last year_
5. Why? _to create a painting of modern Boston_

Main Idea: _Last year, a Boston bank asked for a large painting of modern Boston to be painted. It was on display at the Museum of Fine Arts. It is now in Logan Airport._

Selection Review Creativity at Work

 Does Creativity Matter?
Consider ways to express your creativity.

A. In "Creativity at Work," you learned how students express their creativity. Write four important benefits of Artists for Humanity, using the web below.

Details Web

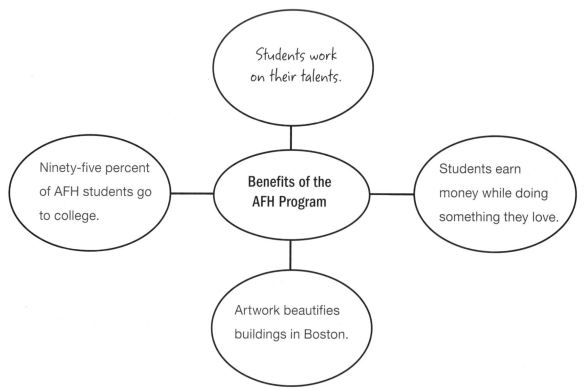

Students work on their talents.

Ninety-five percent of AFH students go to college.

Benefits of the AFH Program

Students earn money while doing something they love.

Artwork beautifies buildings in Boston.

B. Use the information in the web to answer the questions.

1. Why is AFH so important to people in Boston?

AFH is important to people because it is a way for students to express their creativity and for people in Boston to appreciate art.

2. How do the students in this program collaborate to enhance their creativity? Use **collaborate** in your answer.

Students collaborate as they work with their mentors to create their own projects. Their mentors help them learn new skills.

3. How might a program like this benefit your community?

Possible response: Young people would be able to use their time and energy to learn something new and to express themselves. They also would be able to earn money and contribute to the community.

The Hidden SECRETS of the Creative Mind

by Francine Russo

Connect Across Texts

"Creativity at Work" describes teens who use their creativity to begin careers in art. In this interview, a psychologist tells artists, inventors— and all of us—how to make the most of our creativity.

What is creativity? Where does it come from? The workings of the creative mind have been studied over the past twenty-five years by an army of researchers. But no one has a better **overview** of this mysterious mental process than Washington University psychologist R. Keith Sawyer. In an interview with journalist Francine Russo, <u>he suggests ways in which we can **enhance** our creativity, not just in art and science, but in everyday life.</u>

Q: Has new research changed any of our popular ideas about creativity?

A: Virtually all of them. Many people believe creativity comes in a sudden moment of **insight** and that this "magical" burst of an idea is different from our everyday thinking. But research has shown that when you're creative, your brain is using the same **mental building blocks** you use every day—like when you figure out a way around a traffic jam.

Q: Then how do you explain the "aha!" moment we've all had in the shower or the gym—or anywhere but at work?

A: In creativity research, we refer to the three Bs—for the bathtub, the bed, and the bus. They are places where ideas have famously and suddenly emerged. When we take time off from working on a problem, we change what we're doing and **our context**. That can

---

Key Vocabulary

- **insight** *n.*, understanding

In Other Words

overview understanding
enhance improve
Virtually Almost
mental building blocks ways of thinking
our context where and how we are doing it

Interact with the Text

1. Identify Main Ideas and Details

Underline the sentence that tells what this article will be mostly about. Write the main idea of the article in your own words.

Possible response: There are ways to be creative every day.

2. Interpret

Why do you think the writer chose Sawyer to interview? Does he seem credible?

Possible response: Yes, he seems very credible because he refers to the creativity research he has done and attempts to explain it.

3. Author's Purpose and Effectiveness

How does the author respond to Sawyer's explanation about the "aha" moment? Is this effective? Explain.

Possible response: She

asks for an example. It is

effective because it helps

the reader understand his

answers.

4. Identify Main Idea and Details

What idea does the author want the reader to learn from this graphic? Circle the sentence that answers this question. Then explain how you can apply this concept to your own life.

Possible response: I

should exercise all my

skills, especially my

imagination. Using all my

skills exercises my ability

to think creatively.

activate different areas of our brain. If the answer wasn't in the part of the brain we were using, it might be in another. If we're lucky, in the next context we may hear or see something that relates to the problem that we had temporarily put aside.

Q: Can you give us an example of that?

A: In 1990 a team of NASA scientists was trying to fix the lenses in the Hubble telescope, while it was already in orbit. An expert suggested that tiny mirrors could correct the images, but nobody could figure out how to fit them into the hard-to-reach space inside. Then

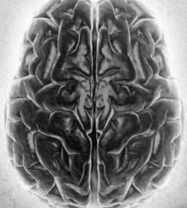

THE BRAIN: Use It or Lose It

There are two hemispheres, or sides, in the human brain. Both sides work together, although certain **mind functions** are only controlled by one hemisphere.

Take note: What we do during our teenage years may affect how our brains develop. If a skill is not used, the part of the brain needed for that skill dies.

Left Brain Functions

Language and Reading

Math and Science

Reasoning

Right-Hand Control

Right Brain Functions

Insight

Art and Music

Imagination

Left-Hand Control

▲ **Interpret the Diagram** How does the diagram help you understand how the brain functions?

In Other Words
activate turn on
mind functions jobs done by the brain

engineer Jim Crocker, taking a shower in a German hotel, noticed the European-style showerhead on **adjustable rods**. He realized the Hubble's little mirrors could be **mounted onto** similar folding arms. And this **flash** was the key to fixing the problem.

Q: How have researchers studied this creative flash?

A: Some psychologists set up video cameras to watch creative people work, asking them to describe their thought processes out loud or interrupting them frequently to ask how close they were to a solution. In other experiments, subjects worked on problems that, when solved, tend to result in the sensation of sudden insight. In one experiment, they were asked to look at words that came up one at a time on a computer screen and to think of the one word that was associated with all of them. After each word they had to give their best guess. Although many swore they had no idea until a sudden burst of insight at about the twelfth word, their guesses got closer to the solution. Even when an idea seems sudden, our minds have actually been working on it all along.

Q: Are there other generalizations you can make about creative people?

A: Yes. They have tons of ideas, many of them bad. The trick is to **evaluate** them and **purge** the bad ones. But even bad ideas can be useful. Sometimes you don't know which sparks are important until later. But the more ideas you have, the better.

Q: So how can the average person get more ideas?

A: Ideas don't magically appear from nowhere. They always build on what came before. And collaboration is key. Look at what others are doing. Brainstorm with different people. Research and evidence suggest that this leads to new ideas.

Key Vocabulary
- **evaluate** *v.*, to decide how good or valuable something is

In Other Words
adjustable rods metal bars that can move back and forth
mounted onto placed on
flash idea, understanding
purge get rid of

Interact with the Text

5. Identify Main Idea and Details

Highlight the most important idea in the answer to the first question. Underline the detail that supports it. In your own words, write a sentence that tells how scientists explain the creative flash.

Possible response:

Experiments show that even though the creative flash feels sudden, the mind has been working on solving the problem for a while.

6. Author's Purpose and Effectiveness

Why does the interviewer ask how the average person could get more ideas? Circle Sawyer's advice. Is her question effective?

Possible response: Yes. Most people need help to be creative. She wants the reader to learn something from her interview.

7. Identify Main Idea and Details

Summarize Sawyer's advice about how to encourage your own creativity. Do you agree? Why or why not?

Possible response:

Creativity develops over

time, and inspiration

does not always happen

overnight, so it is

important to work hard.

Q: What advice can you give us nongeniuses to help us be more creative?

A: Take risks, and expect to make lots of mistakes. Work hard, and take frequent breaks, but stay with it over time. Do what you love, because creative breakthroughs take years of hard work. Develop a **network of colleagues**, and schedule time for free, unstructured discussions. Most of all, forget those romantic myths that creativity is all about being artsy and gifted and not about hard work. They **discourage** us because we're waiting for that one full-blown moment of inspiration. And while we're waiting, we may never start working on what we might someday create. ❖

In Other Words
network of colleagues group of people who are interested in working on the same things
discourage take hope away from

Selection Review   The Hidden Secrets of the Creative Mind

A. Write three details from the article that best support how people develop creative thinking skills.

Detail 1: _*Possible response:* People describe thought processes out loud._

Detail 2: _*Possible response:* People change the context and task at hand._

Detail 3: _*Possible response:* People collaborate and brainstorm with others._

B. Answer the questions.

1. How did the author help you understand the interview?

The author asked informative questions, then followed up by asking for examples or asked new questions. This helped me understand Sawyer's research better.

2. Which main idea from the article did you find difficult to understand? Which detail made it clearer for you?

Possible response: Main idea: I am not sure I understand how researchers studied the creative flash. *Detail:* Ideas build on what came before.

Reflect and Assess

▶ **Creativity at Work**
▶ **The Hidden Secrets of the Creative Mind**

WRITING: Write About Literature

A. Plan your writing. Read what you wrote in the Anticipation Guide on page 112 of your student text. Choose one of the statements. List ideas from each text that confirm or change the opinions you made in the chart below. *Answers will vary.*

Creativity at Work	Hidden Secrets

B. What are your thoughts and feelings about creativity now that you have read both selections? Write an opinion paragraph responding to one of the statements from the chart. Support your opinion with information from both texts and your own experiences.

Students should support their answers with their own experiences and examples from both selections.

LITERARY ANALYSIS: Analyze Description

Description is the way writers use words to help readers create pictures in their minds. Description is used in both fiction and nonfiction. *Answers will vary.*

A. Choose descriptions from "Creativity at Work" and write them below. Then write what the description helped you picture.

Description	What You Picture
"high-contrast, hyper-realistic paintings"	the colors and types of paintings

B. Rewrite these sentences using words that appeal to the five senses.

1. The spaghetti was good.

The spaghetti had a delicious sauce made out of sweet, ripe tomatoes and spicy basil.

2. The flower was pretty.

_____

3. The house is small.

_____

4. The boy was tired.

_____

C. Write a paragraph describing how cats and dogs are different. Be sure to use words that appeal to the reader's five senses.

Students should support their answers with words that appeal to the five senses.

_____

_____

_____

_____

_____

VOCABULARY STUDY: Context Clues

Context clues are words and phrases in a sentence that can help you figure out the meaning of an unfamiliar word. Context clues include definitions or examples.

A. Read the sentences below, and underline the context clues that you can use to figure out the meaning of the underlined word.

1. Half of the profit, or money made on the project, is given back to the organization.

2. The student's dedication, or commitment, is very strong.

3. Many people believe creativity comes in a sudden moment of insight and that this "magical" burst of an idea is different from our everyday thinking.

4. We ask market value. We don't give it away or devalue the work. We charge a fair dollar.

B. Write what each word means by using the context clues you underlined above.

Word	What It Means
dedication	loyalty
insight	a sudden idea
market value	a fair price
profit	money made

C. Write a sentence for each of the words from the chart above. *Answers will vary.*

1. _____

_____

2. _____

_____

3. _____

_____

4. _____

_____

Prepare to Read

▶ Hip-Hop as Culture
▶ I Am Somebody

Key Vocabulary

A. How well do you know these words? Circle a rating for each word. Check your understanding of each word by circling *yes* or *no*. Then, write a definition in your own words. If you are unsure of a word's meaning, refer to the Vocabulary Glossary, page 852, in your student text.

	Rating Scale
1	I have never seen this word before.
2	I am not sure of the word's meaning.
3	I know this word and can teach the word's meaning to someone else.

Key Word	Check Your Understanding	Deepen Your Understanding
❶ **achieve** (u-**chēv**) *verb* **Rating:** 1 2 3	Athletes train to **achieve** physical excellence. (Yes) No	My definition: *Answers will vary.* .
❷ **assert** (u-**surt**) *verb* **Rating:** 1 2 3	Many people who call in to radio talk shows do so to **assert** their opinions. (Yes) No	My definition: *Answers will vary.* .
❸ **culture** (**kul**-chur) *noun* **Rating:** 1 2 3	People can share their **culture** with others by explaining their customs and beliefs. (Yes) No	My definition: *Answers will vary.* .
❹ **evolve** (ē-**volv**) *verb* **Rating:** 1 2 3	Clothing styles and trends rarely **evolve** over time. Yes (No)	My definition: *Answers will vary.* .

Key Word	Check Your Understanding	Deepen Your Understanding
5 heritage (**her**-u-tij) *noun* **Rating:** 1 2 3	Your **heritage** never affects how others treat you. Yes (No)	My definition: *Answers will vary.* .
6 innovator (in-nu-**vā**-tur) *noun* **Rating:** 1 2 3	A clothing designer strives to be an **innovator** of fashion. (Yes) No	My definition: *Answers will vary.* .
7 perspective (pur-**spek**-tiv) *noun* **Rating:** 1 2 3	A writer can use charts and graphs to help explain his or her **perspective** on an issue. (Yes) No	My definition: *Answers will vary.* .
8 self-esteem (**self** es-**tēm**) *noun* **Rating:** 1 2 3	Failure increases people's **self-esteem**. Yes (No)	My definition: *Answers will vary.* .

B. Use one of the Key Vocabulary words to write about how music affects your life.

Answers will vary.

Before Reading Hip-Hop as Culture

LITERARY ANALYSIS: Author's Purpose

In an essay, the **author's purpose** is to entertain, inform, or share opinions and ideas about a subject.

A. Read the passage below. Find details that show the author's purpose. Write the details in the chart.

> **Look Into the Text**
>
> Hip-hop has taken over the music industry in the same way the Williams sisters have taken over tennis. Look at the way the National Basketball Association uses hip-hop players like Shaquille O'Neal and Allen Iverson—and hip-hop culture in general—to sell soda, candy, and clothes to young people. To see hip-hop as simply rap is to not understand the impact and influence of a greater movement.
>
> Rap music is just one element of hip-hop. In fact, true hip-hop heads understand that hip-hop isn't just about music. It's a culture, a way of life, a language, a fashion, a set of values, and a unique perspective.

To Entertain	To Inform	To Share Opinions and Ideas
The author mentions celebrities like Shaquille O'Neal, Allen Iverson, and the Williams sisters.	The NBA uses hip-hop to sell products, including soda, candy, and clothes.	If you think hip-hop is only about rap, you are missing the point. Hip-hop is a culture with a specific language, style, and point of view.

B. Complete the sentence about the author's purpose.

I think the author chose to write about hip-hop because _Possible response: the author wanted to_ inform readers that hip-hop is about more than music. He wanted to share his opinion that hip-hop is a special culture in an entertaining way.

READING STRATEGY: Summarize Nonfiction

HOW TO SUMMARIZE NONFICTION

1. Identify the Topic Repeated words and ideas often point to the main topic.

2. Read Carefully Picture what the author is describing.

3. Summarize Each Section Pause when you finish each section. List important details and main ideas.

4. Think Beyond the Text After reading, ask what you have learned and how your thinking has changed.

A. Read the passage. Use the strategies above to summarize the section. List three important details. Then, write the main idea.

Look Into the Text

> Hip-hop tells the stories of the multiethnic urban youth and the communities they live in. Hip-hop is about inner-city and lower-class life. It's about trying to live out the American dream from the bottom up. It's about trying to make something out of nothing. Hip-hop is about the youth culture of New York City taking over the world. <u>Hip-hop is about dance, art, expression, pain, love, racism, sexism, broken families, hard times, overcoming adversity, and even the search for God.</u>

Detail 1: <u>Hip-hop tells the stories of diverse young people living in poorer sections of the inner city.</u>

Detail 2: <u>Hip-hop reflects young people's hopes of finding success and making a difference.</u>

Detail 3: <u>Hip-hop addresses both creative expression and serious issues affecting communities, such as racism, sexism, and broken families.</u>

Main Idea: <u>Hip-hop is about youth culture and gives inner-city youth a way to express many different experiences.</u>

B. Return to the passage above. Underline which details changed your thinking or taught you something new about hip-hop.

Selection Review Hip-Hop as Culture

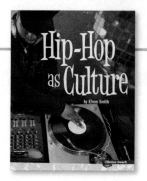

EQ **Does Creativity Matter?**
Explore the effect of music on our lives.

A. In "Hip-Hop as Culture," you found out that hip-hop is a way of life that influences many people in many ways. Complete the T Chart below.

T Chart

What Hip-Hop Is	What Hip-Hop Influences
a way for young people to express frustration	fashion
an inner-city movement	television and movies
a method of communication	language
a set of values	social issues
	dance

B. Use the information in the chart to answer the questions.

1. Why is hip-hop important to youth culture?

Hip-hop gives urban youth a voice and a way to express their ideas and frustrations.

2. How has hip-hop influenced American culture? Use **culture** in your answer.

Possible response: American culture has changed because hip-hop is hugely popular with young people.

It influences the way people dress, the movies they watch, and the way they talk.

3. What other types of "cultures" have led to changes in our society? Explain.

Possible response: The skateboard culture has influenced people's tastes in clothing, art, and music.

I AM SOMEBODY

BY GRANDMASTER FLASH

Connect Across Texts

In "Hip-Hop as Culture," Efrem Smith says that hip-hop tells the stories of "youth and the communities they live in." The following song lyrics describe how a legendary hip-hop artist feels about his own community.

Hey people
We got a little something that we wanna tell you all,
   so listen, understand
Yo, God made one no better than the other
Every girl becomes a woman, every boy a man

5 While you're livin' in your **mansion**, drivin' big cars
There's another on the street, cold sleepin' on the ground
And when you walk by, yo, don't act **cold-blooded**
'Cause it just ain't fair to **kick a man when he's down**

'Cause he is somebody (Say it loud)
10 Like I am somebody
You are somebody
Like I am someone (Say it loud)

In Other Words

mansion big, expensive house
cold-blooded in a rude, heartless way
kick a man when he's down treat a man badly
   when he is already hurting

Interact with the Text

1. Song Lyrics
Describe how the lyrics are like a poem.

The words at the end of

the lines rhyme just like

poems do. The writer

also uses imagery to

help the reader picture

the writer's ideas.

2. Summarize Lyrics
Circle the words and phrases that are repeated in the chorus. What is the main idea these words suggest?

The main idea is that

we are all human

beings who should

be respected, and we

should celebrate that

fact.

3. Summarize Lyrics

Write the main idea of lines 17–20 in your own words. Circle the words and phrases that helped you determine the main idea.

Possible response:

People shouldn't wait

for something good to

happen. People need to

make things happen and

focus on their positive

qualities.

Whether you're here or you're gone, you're right or you're wrong
You were meant to be somebody from the second you were born
15 Don't **criticize** and knock one another
It ain't really that hard to just be a brother

So be good, (speak up,)(don't wait for it to happen)
Life is passing you by, and homeboy, you're **cold nappin'**
Don't be gettin' hung up on what you're not
20 (Be proud of what you are) and whatever you got

'Cause it's a cold, cruel world causing kids to cry
If you're hangin' your head, cold kiss it goodbye
Stand up for your **heritage**, **rejoice in** the fact
Whether you're red, white, tan, yellow, brown, or black

25 **'Cause you are somebody (Say it loud)**
Like I am somebody
He is somebody
Like I am someone (Say it loud)

There are firemen, bankers, messengers, preachers
30 **Brokers**, policemen, executives, teachers,
Journalists, janitors, architects, doctors,
Restaurant workers, nurses, chief rockers

Key Vocabulary
heritage *n.*, background, race, or
ethnic group you belong to

In Other Words
criticize talk badly about
cold nappin' wasting your time
Don't be gettin' hung up on Don't worry about
rejoice in be happy about
Brokers People who trade stocks
Journalists News writers and reporters

If you feel you're (somebody,) be proud, and show it

'Cause everybody's (somebody,) (ugh) and ya know it

35 It doesn't matter if you're black, white, or Chinese

Livin' in the States or **reside overseas**

'Cause you and I are special, same as everyone else

If you don't believe me, you're only cheating yourself

We all got a purpose in life to **achieve**

40 That's a fact, and here's another that you better believe

That I am somebody (Say it loud)

Like you are somebody

He is somebody

Like I am someone (Say it loud)

45 You got wealth, good health, and you're **stuck on yourself**

Well let me tell you that you're better than nobody else

'Cause you got no **self-esteem**, so I'm richer

And when you leave this earth, you can't take money witcha

So play your dumb game, **call me out my name**,

50 But nothing you can do could make me feel shame

We're all created equal, we live and we die

So when you try to bring me down, I keep my head up high

Interact with the Text

4. Summarize Lyrics

Circle the words in lines 33–36 that also appear in the chorus. What does this repetition suggest?

The repetition suggests

that the word is important

to the main idea of the

song.

5. Song Lyrics

Underline the rhyming words in lines 49–52. Write a 5th line for this verse that rhymes with the last line.

Possible response: And no

matter what you try to do

to me, I won't ever cry.

6. Summarize Lyrics

Write the main idea of lines 49–52 in your own words.

Possible response: If you

have self-esteem, other

people will not be able to

hurt you.

7. Interpret

Highlight the advice the songwriter gives in the first verse on this page. Write in your own words what these song lyrics mean to you.

Possible response:

These lyrics mean that

we should never make

assumptions about

people based on the way

they look.

Don't judge a book by its cover
'Cause it's never what it seems

55 Now I know what I'm sayin',
And I feel I gotta scream

That I am somebody (Say it loud)
Like you are somebody
He is somebody
60 Like I am someone

So be yourself, HUH! ❖

Selection Review I Am Somebody

A. Return to the text, and reread the main ideas you wrote in your answers to questions 2, 3, and 6. Based on these three main ideas, how would you summarize the message of this song?

> *Possible response:* You are somebody if you respect others, are proud of who you are, and have self-esteem.

B. Answer the questions.

1. How did knowing that song lyrics are like poems help you as you read?

> *Possible response:* The descriptive imagery helped me see the pictures in my mind as I read. I also knew that the words at the ends of the lines or phrases rhymed.

2. Imagine you are the songwriter and want to write an additional verse. Who would you write it to? What message would it have?

> *Answers will vary.*

Reflect and Assess

WRITING: Write About Literature

A. Plan your writing. In the Venn Diagram, list the important ideas from
each selection. Then write one important idea that fits both selections
in the center. *Answers will vary.*

Venn Diagram

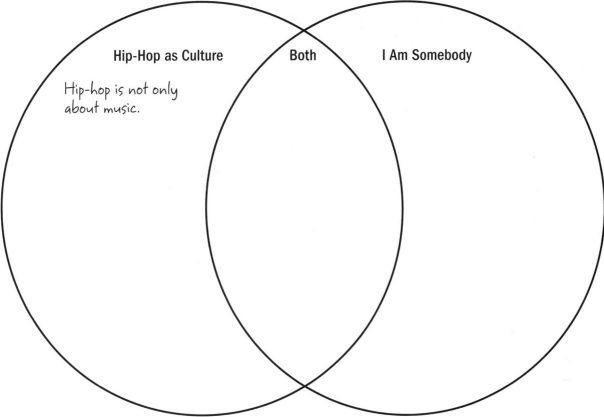

Hip-Hop as Culture

Hip-hop is not only
about music.

Both

I Am Somebody

B. Write your own song lyrics. Create a four-line verse that expresses the
main idea found in both selections. *Answers will vary.*

_____

_____

_____

_____

_____

_____

_____

_____

_____

Integrate the Language Arts

LITERARY ANALYSIS: Analyze Style and Word Choice

Word choice is the kind of language a writer uses. It is an important part of a writer's **style**, or particular way of writing. Word choice often changes based on a writer's audience. *Answers will vary.*

A. List examples of word choice and style from each selection

Hip-Hop as Culture	I Am Somebody

B. Explain why the author of each selection may have chosen the style that was used.

1. "Hip-Hop as Culture"

_____

_____

_____

2. "I Am Somebody"

_____

_____

_____

C. The author of "Hip-Hop as Culture" uses a formal style with informal quotes from students. How effective was his style in getting his message across?

_____

_____

_____

VOCABULARY STUDY: Context Clues for Idioms

Idioms are expressions that mean something different from the literal, or exact, meaning of their words. **Context clues** can help you figure out the meaning of an idiom.

A. Read the song lyric below. Underline the common idioms in the passage. (Hint: There are five.)

> So be good, <u>speak up</u>, don't wait for it to happen
> <u>Life is passing you by</u>, and <u>homeboy</u>, you're <u>cold nappin'</u>
> Don't be gettin' <u>hung up</u> on what you're not
> Be proud of what you are and whatever you got

B. Write the meaning of each idiom below. Use a resource to help you figure out the meaning, if needed. *Answers will vary. Possible responses are shown.*

1. *speak up:* make your voice heard
2. *life is passing you by:* you are wasting the time you have
3. *hung up:* depressed

C. Read the sentences that contain common idioms. Use the context of each sentence to figure out the meaning. Rewrite the sentence to show the idiom's real meaning. *Answers will vary. Possible responses are shown.*

1. The man's son is a <u>chip off the old block</u>.

   The man's son looks just like him.

2. I'm very tired, so I think I will <u>hit the hay</u>.

   I'm very tired, so I think I will go to bed.

3. I'm undecided about going out tonight, so let's <u>play it by ear</u>.

   I'm undecided about going out tonight, so let's be spontaneous.

4. I wanted to throw a surprise party for my friend, but my sister <u>let the cat out of the bag</u>.

   I wanted to throw a surprise party for my best friend, but my sister told everyone and ruined the surprise.

5. The teacher wanted the children to sit down, so she told them to <u>take their seats</u>.

   The teacher wanted the children to sit down, so she told them to sit in their chairs.

Prepare to Read

▶ **Slam: Performance Poetry Lives On**
▶ **Euphoria**

Key Vocabulary

A. How well do you know these words? Circle a rating for each word. Check your understanding of each word by marking an *X* next to the correct definition. Then, complete the sentences. If you are unsure of a word's meaning, refer to the Vocabulary Glossary, page 852, in your student text.

Rating Scale

1	I have never seen this word before.
2	I am not sure of the word's meaning.
3	I know this word and can teach the word's meaning to someone else.

Key Word	Check Your Understanding	Deepen Your Understanding
❶ **compose** (kum-**pōz**) *verb* **Rating:** 1 2 3	[X] to create something [ ] to read something thoroughly	I like to compose *Possible response:* short stories and poems _____ _____ _____ _____ .
❷ **euphoria** (ū-**for**-ē-u) *noun* **Rating:** 1 2 3	[X] extreme happiness [ ] a very loud noise	I was filled with euphoria when I *Possible response:* was voted student council president _____ _____ _____ .
❸ **expression** (eks-**pre**-shun) *noun* **Rating:** 1 2 3	[ ] the act of compromising [X] the act of communicating	One type of creative expression that is important to me is *Possible response:* painting pictures _____ _____ _____ .
❹ **improvisation** (im-prah-vi-**zā**-shun) *noun* **Rating:** 1 2 3	[X] acting without a plan [ ] speaking with notes	I used improvisation when I *Possible response:* had to speak at a school assembly _____ _____ _____ .

Key Word	Check Your Understanding	Deepen Your Understanding
5 **phenomenon** (fi-**nahm**-i-nahn) *noun* **Rating:** **1 2 3**	[X] a unique situation or occurrence [ ] an ordinary situation or occurrence	A current phenomenon in technology is _____ *Possible response:* a cell phone that plays movies _____ _____ _____ .
6 **recitation** (re-si-**tā**-shun) *noun* **Rating:** **1 2 3**	[ ] a private thought [X] a public reading	I would like to hear a recitation of _____ *Possible response:* a poem I have never heard before _____ _____ _____ .
7 **structure** (**struk**-chur) *noun* **Rating:** **1 2 3**	[X] the way something is organized [ ] the way something looks	I like structure when I *Possible response:* am learning something new or difficult _____ _____ _____ .
8 **transcend** (tran-**send**) *verb* **Rating:** **1 2 3**	[X] to rise above something [ ] to sink below something	In my dreams, I transcend my limits when I _____ *Possible response:* dream that I can fly _____ _____ _____ .

B. Use one of the Key Vocabulary words to write about a time when you were proud of something you created.

Answers will vary. _____

_____

Before Reading Slam: Performance Poetry Lives On

LITERARY ANALYSIS: Author's Purpose

An **essay** is a short nonfiction piece on a single topic that informs, persuades, or entertains. When you read an essay, think about the author's purpose for writing.

A. Read the passage below. Look for clues in the passage that tell you what the author thinks about poetry and poetry slams. Then list the clues in the Idea Web.

Look Into the Text

Poetry doesn't have to be the twelve lines on a page in a book that is sitting in the dustiest corner of the library. Poetry doesn't have to be something you don't understand. Poetry is moving, breathing, ever changing.

Want proof? Take a trip to the Urban Word Annual Teen Poetry Slam at the Nuyorican Poets Cafe in New York City.

Gathered in this tight space are hundreds of teens from every corner of the city. They've come together to compete for one of five top spots in Brave New Voices, the Eighth Annual National Youth Poetry Slam Festival.

Idea Web

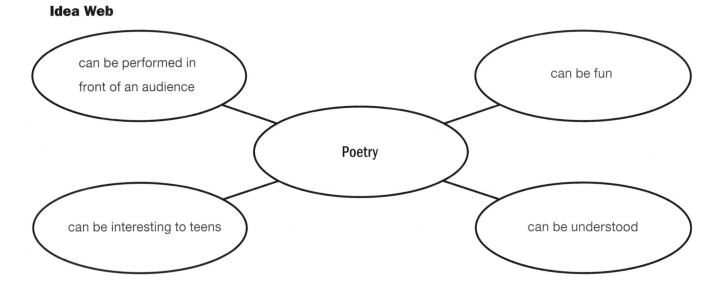

B. Use the information in the web to complete the sentence about the author's purpose.

The author wrote this essay about poetry slams because <u>the author wanted to show that poetry can</u>

<u>be fun and that the popularity of slam poetry is growing among teenagers</u> .

READING STRATEGY: Determine What's Important to You

HOW TO DETERMINE WHAT'S IMPORTANT TO YOU

1. **Read Carefully** Ask yourself how the text relates to your life.

2. **Record Your Ideas** In a Response Journal, write ideas and details that affect you.

3. **Make the Text Your Own** Explain what is important to you and why your reaction is positive or negative.

A. Read the passage. Record your reactions to the details in the chart below. Use the strategies above to determine what's important to you.

Look Into the Text

"A poetry slam is like a lyrical boxing match that pits poets against other poets in a bout," according to journalist Shilanda L. Woolridge. In simpler words, a slam is a competition in which poets perform original works alone or in teams. They recite their poems for an audience that boos and cheers as it votes on the best performers. Each poet's work is judged as much on the manner of its performance as on its content or style.

Details	My Reaction
A slam is like a lyrical boxing match.	The energy and passion in a slam sounds so exciting.
Possible response: Poets recite and perform.	*Possible response:* Performing takes courage.
Possible response: The audience boos and cheers.	*Possible response:* I would be embarrassed if the audience booed me.
Possible response: The poet is judged on performance and content.	*Possible response:* It must be difficult to choose the best performer.

B. Which detail do you find most noteworthy or important to you? Explain your reaction to it.

Possible response: I don't like the idea of being booed. When I write a poem, I want the audience to like it.

Selection Review Slam: Performance Poetry Lives On

 Does Creativity Matter?
Discover one way to find your voice.

A. In "Slam: Performance Poetry Lives On," you found out how slam poetry encourages creativity and self-expression. Complete the Main-Idea Diagram.

Main-Idea Diagram

> **Main Idea:**
>
> Slam poetry helps teens and young adults express their creativity.
>
> > **Detail:** Poets speak about how they feel and what they experience.
> >
> > **Detail:** Poets perform their own poems.
> >
> > **Detail:** Poets compete, and the audience judges them.

B. Use the information in the Main-Idea Diagram to answer the questions.

1. How does slam poetry encourage people to be creative?

Poets can express themselves in a supportive environment and share their ideas with others.

2. Why is slam poetry such a popular form of expression with teens and young adults? Use **expression** in your answer.

Slam poetry allows young people to have free expression of their feelings and ideas in front of an audience.

3. Why is it important for teens to have a way to express their creativity?

Possible response: An outlet for creative expression can help them deal with feelings that they may not be able to show in other ways.

Connect Across Texts

The article "Slam: Performance Poetry Lives On" describes how storytelling has become a modern creative art. How does the author of the following slam poem show the ways that creativity matters to her?

Euphoria
by Lauren Brown

today I'm filled with such a feeling of greatness and immortality
I must sit on my hands to control them from dancing
I find blinking a hazard
it takes too much time and leaves me in the darkness
5   when I could be seeing and living the manic colors
everything in me is magnified and exposed
but no one seems to notice
the air caresses my flesh
and my heart beats faster
10   and my pulse pulses with the concrete rhythm of the song
permanently playing

in my mind
I want to write everything I have ever felt before in my whole existence and

15   paste them on
the walls
I want to dance with such balance and magnificence
that the whole world will want to dance too

Key Vocabulary
euphoria *n.*, great joy and happiness
• **structure** *n.*, the way something is set up, organization

In Other Words
immortality the ability to live forever
hazard danger
manic wild, excited
magnified and exposed made bigger and visible for everyone to see
caresses softly touches

Interact with the Text

1. Poetry
Free verse poems have a loose structure. Give three examples of the loose structure in this poem.

Possible responses:

The lines do not rhyme;

the lines have different

rhythms; there is no

punctuation.

2. Determine What's Important to You
Reread lines 15–18. Underline a phrase that shows the poet's feelings. Write how you feel when you read these words.

Possible response:

These words make me

feel happy and free.

3. Interpret

A simile uses the words *like* or *as* to compare two things. Identify the simile in the last stanza. What is the simile comparing? What do you think the poet means?

Possible response: By comparing feeling other people's emotions to sandpaper on her tongue, the poet is saying how she wants to experience the intensity of other people's emotions.

I want to sing like the angels
20 to part my lips and have the loveliness of my song drip out of the corners of

my mouth
and to echo into everyone's ears and have a piece of my song glued into their minds
25 I want to be able to use my hands in ways I never have before
and to feel other people's emotions like sandpaper on my tongue . . .
. . . maybe I will

Key Vocabulary
expression *n.*, creative communication

In Other Words
sandpaper rough paper used to make wood smooth

Selection Review Euphoria

A. Reread the poem, and choose one or two lines that are especially meaningful to you. Complete the sentences.

The poet says *Answers will vary.*

These words make me feel   *Answers will vary.*

B. Answer the questions.

1. How does the free form of this poem help you understand the poet's feelings?

Possible response: The long and short lines show the poet's excitement and remind me of movement.

2. How does the poet want to express her feelings and ideas? List one example from the poem.

Possible response: She says she wants to "write everything I have ever felt before in my whole existence."

Reflect and Assess

WRITING: Write About Literature

A. Plan your writing. List words and phrases from each text that would make students interested in attending or participating in a poetry slam. *Answers will vary.*

Slam: Performance Poetry Lives On	Euphoria

B. Imagine you are holding a poetry slam at your school. Create a flyer to advertise the event. Use phrases from both texts for ideas.

Students should use phrases and ideas from the selections in their flyers.

Integrate the Language Arts

LITERARY ANALYSIS: Literary Movements (Poetry Across Cultures)

Poetry, like many other forms of literature, changes across different times and cultures. A category of poetry, such as slam poetry, has many different roots.

A. There are many roots of slam poetry. Reread "Slam: Performance Poetry Lives On" to find the roots and list them in the Details Web.

Details Web

B. Which forms of poetry that you listed above seem similar? Write a description of how you think slam came to be.

Answers will vary.

_____

_____

_____

C. What form of poetry do you find the most interesting? Write a short paragraph explaining why.

Answers will vary.

_____

_____

_____

_____

_____

VOCABULARY STUDY: Context Clues for Idioms

The context in which an **idiomatic expression**, or idiom, appears can help you figure out what it means. *Answers will vary. Possible responses are shown.*

A. Read the idiomatic expressions. Find the context, then write what you think each idiom means.

Idiomatic Expression	What I Think It Means
His eyes are bigger than his stomach when he is hungry.	He took more to eat than he could consume.
I can read the writing on the wall, it's so obvious.	I know the truth.
Cut it out, or I will make you stop.	Stop what you are doing now.

B. Read the sentences that include idiomatic expressions. Underline each idiom, then circle the context clues that gives you the idiom's meaning.

1. My mom wanted us to (stop,) so she told us to hold our horses.

2. I wanted to wish the actor (good luck,) so I told him he should break a leg.

3. My identical twin (looks so much like me) that he's a dead ringer.

C. Write a paragraph describing a recent event you have attended. Use at least two idiomatic expressions in your writing.

Answers will vary.

_____

_____

_____

_____

_____

_____

_____

_____

Key Vocabulary Review

A. Use these words to complete the paragraph.

achieve	compose	innovator	talent
career	expression	recitation	transform

What is your special skill or _____talent_____ (1)? Maybe you might _____compose_____ (2) songs or can perform a _____recitation_____ (3) of a famous poem. You might even be an _____innovator_____ (4) of your style and begin new clothing trends. The possibilities are endless. Creative _____expression_____ (5) has the power to _____transform_____ (6) your life. Who knows, you may even _____achieve_____ (7) success and make a _____career_____ (8) out of it!

B. Use your own words to write what each Key Vocabulary word means. Then write a synonym for each word. *Answers will vary. Possible responses are shown.*

Key Word	My Definition	Synonym
1. **collaborate**	to work with others toward a goal	cooperate
2. **commitment**	a promise	dedication
3. **euphoria**	great happiness	joy
4. **evaluate**	to decide the importance or worth of something	judge
5. **evolve**	to develop or change slowly	grow
6. **improvisation**	something that is done without planning	something unrehearsed
7. **insight**	unique understanding	awareness
8. **phenomenon**	something that is impressive and extraordinary	marvel, miracle

• achieve	• commitment	• evaluate	heritage	• perspective	• structure
assert	compose	evolve	improvisation	• phenomenon	talent
career	• culture	expectation	innovator	recitation	transcend
collaborate	euphoria	expression	• insight	self-esteem	• transform

• **Academic Vocabulary**

C. Complete the sentences. *Answers will vary. Possible responses are shown.*

1. My **perspective** on books and movies might change when __I go to college or grow up__ _____.

2. Some holidays my **culture** celebrates are __Cinco de Mayo and Christmas__ _____.

3. One way I **assert** my beliefs is __writing poetry__ _____.

4. I admire people who **transcend** __people's expectations by overcoming obstacles__ _____.

5. I learn about my **heritage** from __my family members__ _____.

6. My **expectation** for the future is __I will get married and have children__ _____.

7. One way I can improve my **self-esteem** is to __not care what other people think about me__ _____.

8. **Structure** is important when you write because __it helps the reader understand my ideas__ _____.

Prepare to Read

▶ **The Sword in the Stone**
▶ **Was There a Real King Arthur?**

Key Vocabulary

A. How well do you know these words? Circle a rating for each word. Check your understanding of each word by circling the correct synonym. Then write a definition. If you are unsure of a word's meaning, refer to the Vocabulary Glossary, page 852, in your student text.

Rating Scale

1 I have never seen this word before.

2 I am not sure of the word's meaning.

3 I know this word and can teach the word's meaning to someone else.

Key Word	Check Your Understanding	Deepen Your Understanding
❶ conscientiously (kon-shē-**en**-shus-lē) *adverb* **Rating:** 1 2 3	If you do something **conscientiously,** you do it _____. carelessly (**carefully**)	My definition: *Answers will vary.*
❷ endure (in-**dyur**) *verb* **Rating:** 1 2 3	To **endure** is to _____. (**continue**) end	My definition: *Answers will vary.*
❸ evidence (**e**-vu-duns) *noun* **Rating:** 1 2 3	**Evidence** is _____. theory (**proof**)	My definition: *Answers will vary.*
❹ genuine (**jen**-yū-win) *adjective* **Rating:** 1 2 3	If something is **genuine**, it is _____. (**real**) false	My definition: *Answers will vary.*

Key Word	Check Your Understanding	Deepen Your Understanding
5 **historian** (hi-**stor**-ē-un) *noun* **Rating:** 1 2 3	A **historian** is an _____. amateur (expert)	My definition: *Answers will vary.*
6 **investigation** (in-ves-ti-**gā**-shun) *noun* **Rating:** 1 2 3	An **investigation** is a _____. (search) class	My definition: *Answers will vary.*
7 **just** (**just**) *adjective* **Rating:** 1 2 3	A **just** person is _____. unfair (fair)	My definition: *Answers will vary.*
8 **skeptic** (**skep**-tik) *noun* **Rating:** 1 2 3	A **skeptic** is a _____. believer (doubter)	My definition: *Answers will vary.*

B. Use one of the Key Vocabulary words to write about one of your heroes.

Answers will vary.

_____

Before Reading The Sword in the Stone

LITERARY ANALYSIS: Point of View

A narrator is the character who tells the story. A narrator with a **third-person omniscient** point of view is an outsider who knows what every character thinks, feels, says, and does using third-person pronouns such as *he*, *she*, and *they*. The narrator can also comment on other story elements, such as setting.

A. Read the passage below. As you read, look for text clues that tell you that this is third-person omniscient point of view. Then, write the clues in the chart.

> **Look Into the Text**
>
> The dragon loomed large in front of Arthur's eyes, then . . . the smoke faded away.
>
> Arthur sat up in his own bed and rubbed his eyes. He had been having the most wonderful dream. He started to tell his brother Kay about his strange adventures but just then someone knocked loudly at the door. Everyone in the household had to get up early that morning because they were starting the hay-making.
>
> This was Arthur's favorite time of year. Lessons were suspended so that he and Kay could join the men out in the fields. It was all hands to the wheel to get the harvest in before the autumn rains.

Elements of Third-Person Omniscient Point of View	Text Clues
Narrator uses third-person pronouns	*he, they, his*
Narrator comments about people, events, and setting	Everyone in the household had to get up early that morning because they were starting the hay-making.
Narrator reveals characters' thoughts	This was Arthur's favorite time of year.

B. Use the information in the chart to answer the question about the narrator's point of view.

What does the narrator know about Arthur? The narrator knows that Arthur is dreaming about a dragon in his bed in his household. The narrator also knows that harvest time is Arthur's favorite time of year.

READING STRATEGY: Make Inferences

HOW TO MAKE INFERENCES

1. **Read and Record** Write the author's important ideas.

2. **Think About What You Know** Add your knowledge about the topic.

3. **Consider All the Information** Infer new ideas about the topic from the information you have.

4. **Read On** Find out if the text proves or changes your inferences.

A. Read the passage. Think about the author's important ideas as you read. Then use your knowledge about the ideas to make inferences.

Look Into the Text

Tossing the hay onto the wagon was men's work. Arthur was not yet strong enough to lift a sheaf, but Kay had grown several inches in the last few months and was almost a man. In a few weeks' time he would leave the schoolroom for good to take up his duties as a squire. Kay could toss the heavy sheaves as well as any of the farmhands. At the end of the day he would climb up on top, pulling Arthur after him, and together they would ride back to the hay barn for supper—a splendid feast of rabbit stew and apple pies which the women had been preparing for most of the day, washed down with jugs of frothing cider.

Author's Ideas	My Knowledge	My Inference
"Tossing the hay onto the wagon was men's work."	In the past, there were separate jobs for men and women.	Arthur might be envious of his brother Kay.
"Kay would leave the schoolroom for good and take up his duties as a squire."	Squires take their work very seriously.	Boys prepare at a young age to become squires.

B. Highlight key words and phrases in the passage that helped you make inferences.

Selection Review The Sword in the Stone

EQ **What Makes a Hero?**
Discover how legends begin.

A. In "The Sword in the Stone," you learn how an ordinary boy becomes a king. Complete the Cluster with examples of Arthur's heroism and the qualities that a hero possesses.

Cluster

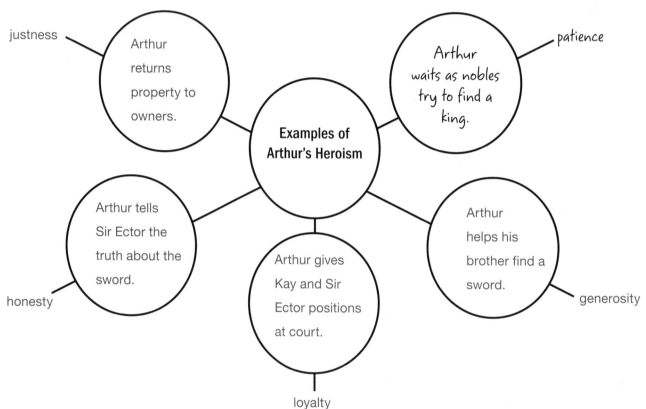

justness

Arthur returns property to owners.

Examples of Arthur's Heroism

Arthur waits as nobles try to find a king.

patience

Arthur tells Sir Ector the truth about the sword.

honesty

Arthur gives Kay and Sir Ector positions at court.

loyalty

Arthur helps his brother find a sword.

generosity

B. Use the information in the Cluster to answer the questions.

1. How might Arthur have been different had he known he would eventually be king?

Possible response: Arthur might not have wanted to work hard in the fields or help his brother if he had known he had noble blood. He might have been impatient and wanted to become king immediately.

2. What events in the story show that Arthur will be a just king? Use **just** in your answer.

Possible response: Arthur shows he is just by telling the truth about where the sword came from, and by returning land to the people who owned it.

3. Does Arthur have the qualities of a hero? Why or why not?

Possible response: Yes, I think these qualities make Arthur a hero, because he is looked up to by many and is a very good leader.

Was There a Real King Arthur?

Interactive

by Robert Stewart

Connect Across Texts

The short story "The Sword in the Stone" retells a heroic legend that has been told for centuries. The following article examines its lasting appeal. What makes this hero's legend **endure**?

King Arthur is a mysterious figure, and his tale has a long and complex history. Writers from every age have constructed their own version of Arthur, tailored to suit the spirit of their times. But was there a real King Arthur? If so, exactly who was the **historical figure** behind the folk tale? How did the world-famous legend **emerge**? It is one of history's greatest unsolved riddles.

Almost everyone has heard of King Arthur. He was the ancient British king who pulled the sword from the stone. He consulted the magician Merlin, led the knights of the Round Table, married the beautiful Guinevere, and set an example of bravery and chivalry. According to British legend, though he is long dead, he lies somewhere in the hills, waiting for the moment when his countrymen need him most. Then he will awake and save them.

Is this history? Much of it certainly is not. The magical Merlin sounds **suspect**, and how could a sword possibly be embedded in a stone in the first place? That all sounds like **folklore**. But just because the story is folklore now does not necessarily mean that it did not have a historical seed. It is for that seed that **historians** and **archaeologists** have long been looking.

Key Vocabulary
endure v., to continue or go on
historian n., person who studies the past and interprets it

In Other Words
historical figure real person from the past
emerge come about
suspect hard to believe
folklore tales or beliefs shared by many people
archaeologists scientists who study past cultures

Interact with the Text

1. Text Structures
Remember that nonfiction authors often organize their ideas into text structures. Circle a word that signals sequence in the second column. How does this phrase help you follow the author's thinking?

The author uses *then* to signal that Arthur will rise from the dead at the time his countrymen need him.

2. Interpret
Look at visuals in the time line on pages 92–93. How do the maps help you understand the events?

The first map shows where the invading tribes came from. The second map shows how England is split and when it happened.

British and World History Before 1100

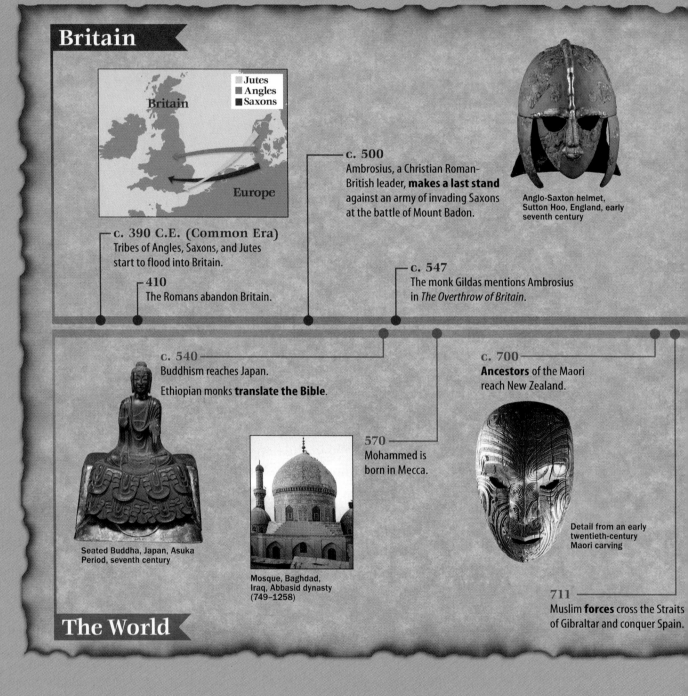

Britain

Jutes
Angles
Saxons

Britain

Europe

c. 390 C.E. (Common Era)
Tribes of Angles, Saxons, and Jutes start to flood into Britain.

410
The Romans abandon Britain.

c. 500
Ambrosius, a Christian Roman-British leader, **makes a last stand** against an army of invading Saxons at the battle of Mount Badon.

Anglo-Saxton helmet, Sutton Hoo, England, early seventh century

c. 547
The monk Gildas mentions Ambrosius in *The Overthrow of Britain*.

The World

c. 540
Buddhism reaches Japan.

Ethiopian monks **translate the Bible**.

Seated Buddha, Japan, Asuka Period, seventh century

Mosque, Baghdad, Iraq, Abbasid dynasty (749–1258)

570
Mohammed is born in Mecca.

c. 700
Ancestors of the Maori reach New Zealand.

Detail from an early twentieth-century Maori carving

711
Muslim **forces** cross the Straits of Gibraltar and conquer Spain.

In Other Words

c. about (abbreviation used for estimated dates)
makes a last stand fights to defend his land
translate the Bible change the Bible from one language to another

Ancestors Family members from past generations
forces armies, soldiers

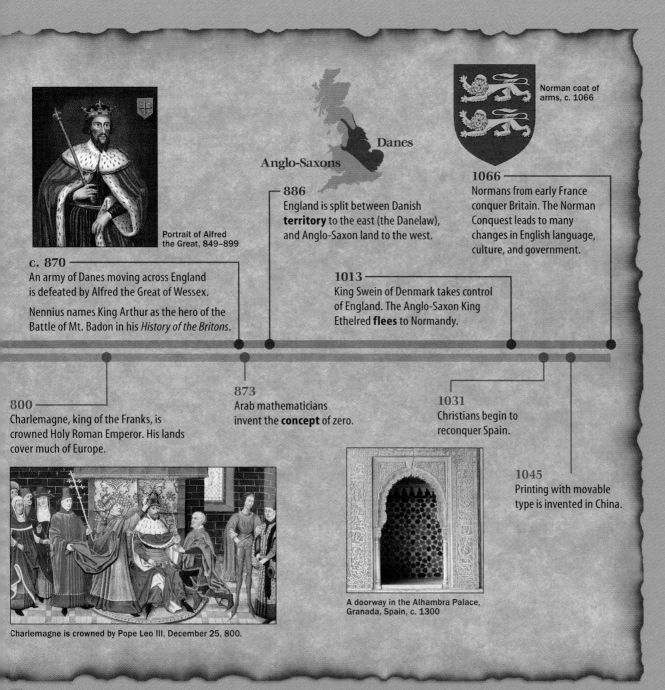

Norman coat of arms, c. 1066

Danes

Anglo-Saxons

886
England is split between Danish **territory** to the east (the Danelaw), and Anglo-Saxon land to the west.

1066
Normans from early France conquer Britain. The Norman Conquest leads to many changes in English language, culture, and government.

Portrait of Alfred the Great, 849–899

c. 870
An army of Danes moving across England is defeated by Alfred the Great of Wessex.

Nennius names King Arthur as the hero of the Battle of Mt. Badon in his *History of the Britons*.

1013
King Swein of Denmark takes control of England. The Anglo-Saxon King Ethelred **flees** to Normandy.

800
Charlemagne, king of the Franks, is crowned Holy Roman Emperor. His lands cover much of Europe.

873
Arab mathematicians invent the **concept** of zero.

1031
Christians begin to reconquer Spain.

1045
Printing with movable type is invented in China.

A doorway in the Alhambra Palace, Granada, Spain, c. 1300

Charlemagne is crowned by Pope Leo III, December 25, 800.

▲ **Interpret the Time Line** This time line shows major world events that occurred at the same time. What does this show about the legend of Arthur?

In Other Words
concept idea or notion
territory land
flees escapes

3. Text Structures

Circle a signal word that compares one piece of information with another. What is the author trying to indicate?

The author is showing

the contrast between

the text evidence and

what some historians

believe about Arthur.

4. Make Inferences

Mark an *X* at each place on the map where stories were heard about someone like Arthur. Summarize the information about these places.

Possible response: Tales

of Arthur were found in

many locations. I can

infer that Arthur was

famous and travelers

spread the stories about

him across land and sea.

Where Is Arthur?

A historian usually starts by looking for written **evidence**. The first mention of someone who might be Arthur is in a book called *The Overthrow of Britain* **compiled** by the British monk Saint Gildas (c. 516–570 C.E.). In this book, a British leader named Ambrosius slows the **advance** of the invading Angles and Saxons, who are later defeated at the Battle of Mount Badon in about 500 C.E. Gildas does not mention Arthur, nor say that Ambrosius fought at Badon. However, some historians have wondered if Ambrosius and Arthur are **one and the same**. This is historical evidence, but was it Arthur?

At the same time, **bards** in Wales and Brittany, in France, were entertaining their hosts with stories of a hero named Arthur. This one had a personality much like that of

Europe in the Early Middle Ages (c. 500–800 C.E.)

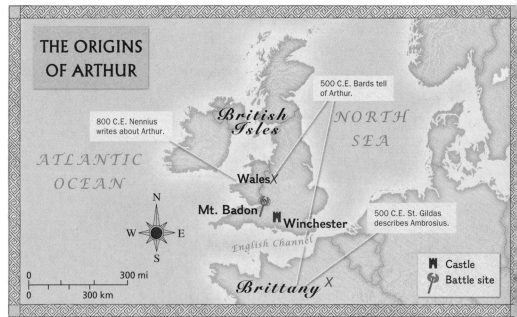

THE ORIGINS OF ARTHUR

800 C.E. Nennius writes about Arthur.

500 C.E. Bards tell of Arthur.

500 C.E. St. Gildas describes Ambrosius.

British Isles

NORTH SEA

ATLANTIC OCEAN

Wales X

Mt. Badon

Winchester

English Channel

Brittany X

N W E S

0   300 mi
0   300 km

◪ Castle
⚲ Battle site

▲ Interpret the Map What do the captions on the map show?

Key Vocabulary
• **evidence** *n.*, information that helps prove something

In Other Words
compiled put together from different sources
advance forward movement
one and the same the same person
bards storytellers from ancient times

the Arthur we know, and he **slew** monsters and wicked giants. Folk heroes are sometimes based on history. But was this Arthur real?

(The next piece) of written evidence comes from the early ninth century, when Arthur was named by the Welsh monk Nennius in his *History of the Britons*. According to Nennius, Arthur was a British war leader who fought a series of twelve battles against the Angles and Saxons, of which Badon was the last. The similarities with Ambrosius are unmistakable.

And that, together with poems and a few other writings of the same time, is all of the written evidence we have for King Arthur. All of the details—Lancelot, Guinevere, the sword in the stone, Camelot and the Round Table, Merlin the magician—appear only in literature. Much of it was written long after the Norman Conquest of 1066.

(For hundreds of years after that,) people were **content** to leave Arthur as a legend. Then, in the early twentieth century, some historians began to wonder. Could Arthur possibly be real after all? One popular view held by many scholars was that Arthur was actually a late-Roman **cavalry commander** who had led British forces against the invading Anglo-Saxons.

Archaeologists have also been looking around Britain for evidence of the real Arthur. One such **investigation** took place in 1976 in the city of Winchester in southern England. Hanging there, in the Great Hall of Winchester Castle, is an enormous round table-top. It is made of solid oak, is eighteen feet (5.4 meters) in diameter, weighs one-and-a-quarter tons (1,138 kilograms), and has places for twenty-five people marked on it. Many argued that it was the actual Round Table of legend. Historically, Winchester had become the capital of the Saxon kings of Wessex in the seventh century. Could the Saxons possibly have turned Arthur's capital into their own?

Unfortunately, the belief did not stand up to modern scientific investigation. **Tree-ring and radiocarbon dating**, plus a study

---

Interact with the Text

5. Text Structures
Look at the beginning of each paragraph in column one. Which text structure is the author using in this section? Why? Circle the signal words the author uses.

Possible response: The author uses sequence/ time order to explain how the legend of Arthur may have developed through the centuries.

6. Interpret
Highlight at least three details about the table-top in the Great Hall of Winchester Castle. Explain why the author includes these details.

Possible response:

These facts explain why some people may have believed the table-top was the famous Round Table used by Arthur.

According to the

time line, Arthur, or

Ambrosius, led Britain

c. 500. Arthur's round

table was built in the

1270s.

of **medieval carpentry practices**, revealed that the table was actually constructed in the 1270s at the start of Edward I's **reign**. This was during a time when the king himself was taking a great interest in everything associated with Arthur. Experts now think that the table at Winchester was probably made to be used at the many knightly tournaments that Edward himself liked to hold.

Although no **genuine** Arthurian objects have ever been discovered, many possible Arthurian places have been investigated. Geoffrey of Monmouth, an author of the 1100s, said that Tintagel in Cornwall was Arthur's birthplace, and there is even a suitably ruined castle perched on a cliff there. But, unfortunately, the castle is no older than Geoffrey himself. Writers choose places as settings for their books for many different reasons. Geoffrey may have added the reference to Tintagel simply to please a rich local nobleman.

In the 1960s, the search for Camelot heated up when archaeologists **excavated** an **Iron Age hill fort** at Cadbury Castle in southern England. Local legend held that Arthur and his knights lay sleeping under the hill. John Leland, a historian writing during King Henry VIII's reign, had stated that the local people often called the **fortified remains** "Camalat—King Arthur's palace."

Exhaustive excavations conducted by the archaeologist Leslie Alcock yielded evidence dating from about Arthur's time of a wall encircling an extensive hilltop

"Arthur's Round Table,"
Winchester Castle, c. 1270

Key Vocabulary
  genuine adj., real, true

In Other Words
medieval carpentry practices ways carpenters worked in the Middle Ages
reign rule, time as king
excavated dug up
Iron Age hill fort fort built c. 1000 B.C.E.
fortified remains ruins

Local legends held that Arthur and his knights lay sleeping under the hill at Cadbury Castle (left). Geoffrey of Monmouth claimed that Tintagel Castle (right) was Arthur's birthplace.

compound. At its center was a large aisled hall. Some see the remains of a stout defensive wall around a great feasting hall such as might befit a king named Arthur. But **skeptics** see only a moderately sized barn surrounded by walls barely able to contain horses and cattle, let alone keep determined enemies away.

So King Arthur remains a mystery. Though archaeologists can find no evidence for Arthur, this fact alone does not disprove his existence. Archaeologists are the first to explain that lack of proof is not a convincing argument against the existence of a person, place, or event. All it takes is one small piece of evidence—one small "voice"—to overcome the **accumulated** weight of silence. Such a discovery may well lie in the future.

Key Vocabulary
skeptic *n.*, person who doubts facts and beliefs that are generally accepted by others

In Other Words
compound group of buildings in an enclosed space
accumulated piled up

8. Interpret
Highlight the most important ideas in the second column. Summarize the author's argument.

Possible response: Just because archaeologists haven't found evidence of Arthur's existence, does not mean Arthur wasn't real.

Underline the signal words and phrases in the last two paragraphs. Choose one of the words. Explain how this word helps you follow the author's thinking and find the information you need to know.

Possible response: The word *But* signals that the author is about to provide new information about the topic.

Why Do We Need Arthur?

But there is another Arthurian mystery. Why is it that we so much want King Arthur to be real? Why do historians and archaeologists continue this search? One of the great attractions of the Arthur story is that it contains something for everyone—action, mystery, romance, the struggle between good and evil. And the tales **have a ring of truth** because some have their roots in genuine ancient traditions.

And the idea of a once and future king, sleeping somewhere, awaiting his time to return, is not **unique to** the Arthur story. In Denmark, the knight Holger Danske sleeps. In Spain it is El Cid. In Germany it is Frederick Barbarossa. Arthur **embodies** real human needs and desires. We *want* him to be real. ❖

In Other Words
have a ring of truth sound like they might be true
unique to found only in
embodies represents, stands for

Selection Review   Was There a Real King Arthur?

A. Choose one of the text features below. Explain how the text features help you understand the information about King Arthur.

| Text Feature 1: | Cause and Effect |
| Text Feature 2: | Compare and Contrast |

The author uses text feature _2_ to

Possible response: compare historical evidence about Arthur's existence. He uses signal words, such as *at the same time* and *however*, to compare events that point toward the legend's plausibility.

B. Answer the questions.

1. Return to the inference you made in Question 4 on page 94. How does the evidence in the article support or change this inference as you read?

Possible response: The text supports my inference because I found out that more books were written by historians that name Arthur as a war leader at Badon. This seems like more evidence that Arthur was famous in his time.

Reflect and Assess

WRITING: Write About Literature

A. Why do many cultures tell legends about heroes like King Arthur? Plan your writing. List examples from both texts that might provide an answer.

The Sword in the Stone	Was There a Real King Arthur?
Arthur is an example of someone who is honest and hardworking.	The story of Arthur can be easily adapted for different people in different time periods.

B. What is your opinion? Write an opinion statement that answers the question. Use examples from both texts to support your opinion.

Students should support their answers with examples from the selections.

_____

_____

_____

_____

_____

_____

_____

_____

_____

_____

LITERARY ANALYSIS: Compare Characters' Motives and Traits

Readers get to know a character in a story through the character's **actions**, **dialogue**, **motives**, and **traits**.

A. List details that you find out about Arthur, using information from "The Sword in the Stone." *Answers will vary. Possible responses are shown.*

Character	Arthur
Actions	He searches for a replacement sword for his brother. He tells the truth about where he found the sword.
Dialogue	"If I am really King, then I swear to serve God and my people, to put right any wrongs, and to bring peace to the land."
Motives	He wants to do what is right.
Traits	honest, loyal, patient

B. Characters' motivations affect story events. Imagine Arthur is motivated by greed. How might each event have a different outcome than what you read in the story? *Answers will vary. Possible responses are shown.*

1. Kay forgets his sword.

Arthur keeps the sword he finds instead of offering it to his brother.

2. The nobles refuse to believe that Arthur should be king.

Arthur wages a battle against the nobles because he wants to be king immediately.

3. Arthur becomes king.

Arthur keeps the land for himself and forces everyone to leave his kingdom.

C. How do your actions, words, motives, and traits show people what you are like? Write a description of yourself that includes each element.

Answers will vary.

VOCABULARY STUDY: Word Families

Word families are groups of words that are related by meaning. Knowing the meaning of one part of an unfamiliar word can help you understand what the entire word means. *Answers will vary.*

A. Read the Key Vocabulary words in the chart below, and write a new word that is from the same family.

Key Vocabulary	New Word
conscientiously	conscience
endure	
evidence	
historian	
investigation	
just	

B. Write what you think each word that you listed above means. Use a dictionary to confirm the meaning.

1. _____
2. _____
3. _____
4. _____
5. _____
6. _____

C. Write sentences containing the new words.

1. _____
2. _____
3. _____
4. _____
5. _____
6. _____

Prepare to Read

▷ **A Job for Valentín**
▷ **In the Heart of a Hero**

Key Vocabulary

A. How well do you know these words? Circle a rating for each word. Check your understanding of each word by circling *yes* or *no*. Then complete the sentences. If you are unsure of a word's meaning, refer to the Vocabulary Glossary, page 852, in your student text.

	Rating Scale
1	I have never seen this word before.
2	I am not sure of the word's meaning.
3	I know this word and can teach the word's meaning to someone else.

Key Word	Check Your Understanding	Deepen Your Understanding
❶ anxiety (ang-**zī**-ut-ē) *noun* **Rating:** 1 2 3	Someone with **anxiety** about flying would look forward to a ten-hour plane ride. Yes (**No**)	I feel anxiety about *Possible response:* taking tests _____ _____ _____ .
❷ distracted (di-**strakt**-id) *adjective* **Rating:** 1 2 3	People who drive are often **distracted** by their cell phones. (**Yes**) No	I get distracted by *Possible response:* phone calls when I'm studying _____ _____ _____ .
❸ inherent (in-**hair**-unt) *adjective* **Rating:** 1 2 3	Good study skills must be learned; therefore, they are **inherent**. Yes (**No**)	I am someone with an inherent talent for _____ *Possible response:* being good with children _____ _____ _____ .
❹ inhibit (in-**hib**-it) *verb* **Rating:** 1 2 3	Fear of driving could **inhibit** travel. (**Yes**) No	People can inhibit others when *Possible response:* they criticize or are mean _____ _____ _____ .

102   Unit 3: The Hero Within

Key Word	Check Your Understanding	Deepen Your Understanding
⑤ prejudiced (**prej**-u-dist) *adjective* **Rating:** 1 2 3	People who accept others for their differences are **prejudiced.** Yes (No)	I don't like it when people are prejudiced toward _____ *Possible response:* senior citizens _____ _____ _____ .
⑥ protest (**prō**-test) *verb* **Rating:** 1 2 3	Laborers sometimes **protest** unfair pay and working conditions. (Yes) No	I would protest if *Possible response:* my boss fired me without a reason _____ _____ _____ _____ .
⑦ survivor (sur-**vī**-vur) *noun* **Rating:** 1 2 3	A **survivor** of a natural disaster is a lucky person. (Yes) No	I know a survivor of *Possible response:* cancer _____ _____ _____ _____ .
⑧ tragedy (**tra**-ju-dē) *noun* **Rating:** 1 2 3	An event that causes thousands of people to lose their homes is a tragedy. (Yes) No	A tragedy that affected many people was _____ *Possible response:* Hurricane Katrina _____ _____ _____ .

B. Use one of the Key Vocabulary words to write about someone you admire.

Answers will vary. _____

_____

Before Reading A Job for Valentín

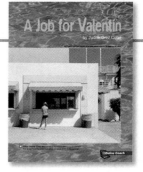

LITERARY ANALYSIS: Point of View

In **first-person point of view**, the narrator tells the story as he or she experiences it and uses the pronouns *I* and *me.* The information is limited because the reader sees it through the narrator's eyes.

A. Read the passage below. Write the clues in the chart that reveal first-person point of view.

> **Look Into the Text**
>
> Bob Dylan laughs and kisses (my) hand.
>
> "My Chiquita banana," he says, "stay true to me. Don't give my whereabouts out to the enemy. I shall return."
>
> "Bye," (I) say. I am such a great conversationalist, inside my own head.
>
> But he's already looking away. We have both heard familiar giggles. It's Clarissa and Anne. I see him waving to them, letting them get a view of his entire, glorious self. He looks over his shoulder at (me) and winks, covering all the bases.

Elements of First-Person Narrator Point of View	Text Clues
First-person pronouns	*I, me, my*
What the narrator sees	I see him waving to them, letting them get a view of his entire, glorious self.
What the narrator hears	We have both heard familiar giggles.
What the narrator feels	I am such a great conversationalist, inside my own head.

B. Answer the question.

What is the narrator's point of view about Bob Dylan? __He flirts with all the girls, including her, but the__ narrator likes him anyway.

READING STRATEGY: Make Inferences

HOW TO MAKE INFERENCES

1. **Record Information and Ideas** Note what the narrator thinks, says, and does. Think about your own experience.

2. **Connect the Inferences** Add up what you know to form big ideas about the narrator.

3. **Read On** Revise your inferences as you learn more information.

A. Read the passage. Use the strategies above to make inferences. Answer the questions below.

Look Into the Text

(The only thing I don't really like) is that Mrs. O'Brien expects to be told if I ever see Bob Dylan messing around on the job.

"People's lives, children's lives, are in that young man's hands," she says. "Keep an eye on him, Teresa, and use that phone to call me, if you need to."

I say, "Yes, ma'am," even though (I feel funny about being asked) (to spy) on Bob Dylan. He's a senior at my school and, yeah, a crazy man sometimes. But if they gave him the job as a lifeguard, they ought to trust him to do it right.

1. How does Teresa feel about Mrs. O'Brien? How do you know?

   Possible response: Mrs. O'Brien makes Teresa feel uncomfortable. She doesn't like it when Mrs. O'Brien

   asks her to spy on Bob Dylan, but she agrees to do it anyway.

2. How does thinking about your own experiences help you infer how Teresa feels?

   Possible response: As I read, I thought about how I would feel in her situation. I might have felt funny, too. It

   should not be Teresa's responsibility to spy on an older boy.

B. Return to the passage above. Circle words and phrases that helped you answer question 1.

Selection Review A Job for Valentín

 What Makes a Hero?
Consider the everyday heroes in your community.

A. In "A Job for Valentín," you found out how Valentín became a hero in unexpected ways. Make inferences about Valentín and Teresa by completing the Inference Chart below.

Inference Chart

Event	What the Narrator Says, Feels, or Thinks	What You Know
Teresa is told she must work with Valentín for the summer.	Teresa thinks her summer will be bad.	The mentally disabled are not bad to work with. Teresa and Valentín may even become friends.
Teresa does not tell on Bob Dylan.	Teresa likes looking at Bob Dylan.	Teresa wants Bob Dylan to like her, so she decides she won't spy on him.
Valentín laughs when Teresa yells at Marciela.	Teresa thinks that Valentín is laughing while he plays with his toy animals.	Valentín is actually laughing at what Teresa says.

B. Use the information in the chart to answer the question.

1. As you were reading, what inference did you make about Valentín and Teresa?

   Possible response: I knew that even though Valentín is mentally disabled, he might be fun to work with and that he understands more than Teresa thinks he does.

2. How may Teresa have been prejudiced toward Valentín before he helped save Pablito? Use **prejudiced** in your answer.

   Possible response: Teresa may have been prejudiced because she formed opinions about Valentín before she met him. She finds him annoying, makes judgments about his physical appearance, and does not see him for who he is.

3. How will Teresa treat Valentín from now on?

   Possible response: She will be more respectful toward him and will learn how to communicate with him.

In the Heart of a Hero

by Johnny Dwyer

Connect Across Texts

In "A Job for Valentín," the hero is not who we expect. This feature article explores why some people act as heroes when others cannot.

On a sunny Sunday last month, the glass-like surface of Lake George, in New York's Adirondack Mountains, was dotted with boats. Just before three, the afternoon's **tranquility shattered**. The *Ethan Allen*, a tour boat carrying almost fifty senior citizens, tipped crazily. Within thirty seconds, it had **capsized** and its passengers were struggling for their lives.

Brian Hart was on the lake that day, paddling a canoe with Brianna, his youngest daughter, and three of her cousins. When he saw the boat overturn, <u>he didn't hesitate, immediately calling 911</u>—"Get to the lake real quick"—even as he headed for the nearest dock. There, he dropped the girls and phoned his brother, Eric. Two minutes later, Eric, 42, and his son, E.J., scooped up Brian in the family fishing boat, and the three of them <u>sped to the scene</u>. Brian and Eric <u>dove straight in</u> and <u>started **hauling survivors**</u> onto life preservers, seat cushions— anything that would float. When other boats arrived, the Hart brothers <u>**hoisted** victims into them</u> for nearly half an hour.

Onlookers gasped in horror, watching the **tragedy unfold**; many

It was a calm, beautiful day before the *Ethan Allen* capsized on Oct. 2, 2005.

Interact with the Text

1. Make Inferences
Underline words that describe Brian's and Eric's actions. What can you infer about what the two men are like?

Possible response:

They are good people

who care about helping

others. They act quickly

and efficiently.

Key Vocabulary
• **survivor** *n.*, person who lives through a hardship or disaster
  tragedy *n.*, terrible disaster

In Other Words
tranquility shattered calmness was wrecked
capsized turned upside down
hauling pulling
hoisted lifted
unfold happen over time

called for help. Those who saw the brothers' actions surely wondered at their uncommon courage: *Do they know what they're doing? Will they be able to save anyone? Will they die trying?* Later—over dinner, perhaps, or just before they drifted off to sleep—these **bystanders** likely pondered another set of questions both simple and complex: *What makes a hero? Why do some of us dive in when others simply cannot?*

In Brian's case, the answer may lie in his **biological makeup**. "I guess my boys were always fearless," says Donald Hart, 71, Brian and Eric's father. "Not only that day, but in childhood, with the motorbikes, snowmobiles. I wasn't surprised they would do something like that."

Dr. Frank Farley, a psychologist who has studied heroic behavior, says that something literally in a hero's **DNA** may contribute to brave actions. Heroes, he says, often have what he calls "Big T"—or thrill-seeking, risk-taking personalities. "They're not satisfied with normal levels of **stimulation**, so they seek out more of it," says Farley.

Recovery divers prepare to search for the *Ethan Allen* after it sank in Lake George, New York, in October 2005.

▲ **Interpret the Visuals** What additional information do the map and caption give you about the photo?

In Other Words
bystanders people who stood by and watched
biological makeup nature
DNA genetic code
stimulation excitement

When Brian plunged into the lake and swam into the crowd of struggling passengers, he remained calm and focused. "Situational heroes," as Farley refers to regular people who **rise to the occasion** in emergencies, simply aren't **inhibited** by "**uncertainty**, which is one of the biggest sources of human fear."

Brian had something else, too, that **complemented** his **inherent** fearlessness: his comfort in the water, particularly this water. As a boy, he'd learned to paddle and fish on Lake George, and later scuba dived and piloted his first motorboat there. "We always used to horse around, brothers grabbing you in the water. I'm sure a lot of people who came [to the scene] in boats didn't jump in because they didn't have the comfort level I had."

And beyond that? Perhaps empathy.

Is it **a coincidence** that this man who dove into the water had once been rescued on Lake George? In 1978, Brian was thrown from a motorboat. He floated dazed—but uninjured—for fifteen minutes until a boater fished him out.

Donald wonders about the circumstances of rescues—a man with the heart of a hero finding himself in the right place at the right time—and **speculates on** what his boys might have taken from hearing about his own experience: "Something like this, it's a series of events that happens, and if there's

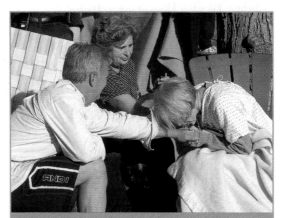
Ethan Allen survivor Carol Charlton holds Brian Hart's hand.

Key Vocabulary
- **inhibit** *v.*, to stop or hold a person back from doing something
- **inherent** *adj.*, natural, basic

In Other Words
rise to the occasion do more than they thought they could
uncertainty doubt
complemented added to
a coincidence just chance
speculates on guesses about

5. Feature Article

Mark an *X* next to each line of dialogue. Explain how this conversation is an effective way to end the article.

Possible response:

The quotes show that

Hart is sensitive to his

daughter's ability to

understand tragedy

and his commitment to

helping. It is effective in

that it ends the article

on a note of hope.

a lesson, maybe it's that there's an outside source, a God above."

Whether **Providence** or circumstance, when Hart, exhausted, finally returned to shore, Brianna asked, X"Did you save everybody?"

X "Yes," he lied. She's 8 years old; there's time yet for truth.

X "Daddy, why did you go back?" she asked.

X "The people needed my help."

For some—for heroes—it's as simple as that. ❖

In Other Words
Providence God's plan

Selection Review In the Heart of a Hero

A. Newspaper articles mainly report the basic facts. Give two examples of things this feature article addressed that a news story might not have.

1. The article provides background information about Brian Hart's life and suggests reasons for his actions.

2. It includes dramatic details about the rescue and quotes from the people who know Brian and from Brian himself.

B. Answer the questions.

1. How do you think other people might feel toward Brian Hart?

Possible response: Brian's father might be proud of his son for risking his life to save others. A survivor of the *Ethan Allen* might feel gratitude that Brian saved his or her life.

2. In your opinion, which of the author's explanations for heroic behavior is most convincing? Give examples from the text to support your answer.

Possible response: I think the author's most convincing explanation for heroic behavior is the idea that people's DNA contributes to being brave. Biology has a big role to play.

Reflect and Assess

WRITING: Write About Literature

A. Plan your writing. Think about your definition of a real hero. Then list the qualities that Valentín and Brian Hart have that make them real heroes. Answers will vary.

Valentín	Brian Hart
considerate of others	

B. Imagine that you can nominate a Hero of the Year. Choose Valentín or Brian Hart. Write a letter to the prize committee describing why the person fits your definition of a real hero.

Students should support their letters with ideas or qualities they listed above.

_____

_____

_____

_____

_____

_____

_____

_____

_____

_____

Integrate the Language Arts

LITERARY ANALYSIS: Multiple Themes in a Text

A **theme** is a main idea or lesson in a story. The author uses characters, dialogue, and plot events to make a general statement about people or life.

A. Read each example from "A Job for Valentín." List possible themes.
Answers will vary. Possible responses are shown.

Example	Possible Theme
"I got assigned a 'mentally challenged' assistant by the city. There's a new program to put retarded people to work at simple jobs so they can make some money, learn a skill, or something."	tolerance or learning to work with others
"I feel scared that I may drown, but I have to reach Pablito."	overcoming fear or sacrifice
"I also expect to get fired for not reporting that Bob Dylan was not at his post."	responsibility or loyalty

B. What do the plot events tell you about the story's theme? Read each plot event and write a possible theme. *Answers will vary. Possible responses are shown.*

Plot event: Valentín saves Pablito and Terry from drowning.

A person who helps other people is selfless and thoughtful.

Plot event: Terry learns to communicate in Valentín's language.

Patience and understanding are important to understanding one another.

Plot event: Mrs. O'Brien offers Valentín and Terry a year-round job.

Hard work and dedication are often rewarded.

C. Think about someone you know, have read about, or have seen on TV who is an everyday hero. Write a brief paragraph explaining why.

Answers will vary.

VOCABULARY STUDY: Borrowed Words

Borrowed words come into one language from another language. Dictionaries tell you the language or languages a word has been borrowed from.

Answers will vary. Possible responses are shown.

A. Read the list of some common abbreviations that you will see in the dictionary and that tell you the language a word has been borrowed from. Look up the words in the chart below and identify the language of origin. Then write the definition of each word.

Language of Origin Key

Fr: French	*Gk:* Greek
ME: Middle English	*MF:* Middle French
It./Ital: Italian	*L:* Latin
Sp./Span: Spanish	*Pg/Port:* Portuguese

Word	Origin	Definition
astronomy	Greek	the study of the universe
dictionary	Latin	a book of word meanings
evacuate	Latin	to remove the contents of
podiatrist	Greek	a doctor who treats feet

B. Use a dictionary to look up the borrowed words below. Write the languages from which they originated.

flute   ME from Middle French origin

money   ME from MF from Latin origin

music   ME from L from Greek origin

pizza   It. from Latin origin

C. Find four more words in the dictionary that have been borrowed from the languages listed below. *Answers will vary.*

French _____

Spanish _____

Italian _____

Portuguese _____

Prepare to Read

▶ **The Woman in the Snow**
▶ **Rosa Parks**

Key Vocabulary

A. How well do you know these words? Circle a rating for each word. Check your understanding of each word by circling *yes* or *no.* Then complete the sentences. If you are unsure of a word's meaning, refer to the Vocabulary Glossary, page 852, in your student text.

Rating Scale	
1	I have never seen this word before.
2	I am not sure of the word's meaning.
3	I know this word and can teach the word's meaning to someone else.

Key Word	Check Your Understanding	Deepen Your Understanding
1 authority (u-**thor**-u-tē) *noun* **Rating:** **1 2 3**	A principal has **authority** in a school. (**Yes**) No	Parents have the authority to *Possible response:* make rules for their children to follow _____ _____ _____ .
2 boycott (**boi**-kot) *noun* **Rating:** **1 2 3**	If you plan a **boycott** of a restaurant, you plan to eat there every day. Yes (**No**)	People can start a boycott of a company _____ *Possible response:* if the company is polluting the environment _____ _____ .
3 compassion (kum-**pash**-un) *noun* **Rating:** **1 2 3**	People who give money to charities show no **compassion** for those in need. Yes (**No**)	I show compassion for others when _____ *Possible response:* I do volunteer work at the hospital _____ _____ .
4 desperately (**des**-pur-it-lē) *adverb* **Rating:** **1 2 3**	Some people act **desperately** when they are afraid. (**Yes**) No	I would act desperately if I had to *Possible response:* get help for an injured family member _____ _____ .

Key Word	Check Your Understanding	Deepen Your Understanding
5 **discrimination** (di-skrim-u-**nā**-shun) *noun* **Rating:** 1 2 3	Allowing all citizens to vote is an example of **discrimination**. Yes **(No)**	I experienced discrimination when _____ *Possible response:* a shop owner made me and my friends leave because he disliked teens _____ _____ .
6 **persistent** (pur-**sis**-tunt) *adjective* **Rating:** 1 2 3	A **persistent** person gives up easily. Yes **(No)**	I am persistent when *Possible response:* I want something badly enough _____ _____ _____ .
7 **provoke** (pru-**vōk**) *verb* **Rating:** 1 2 3	It is possible to **provoke** a person who dislikes you. **(Yes)** No	When people act meanly, they provoke *Possible* *response:* an argument _____ _____ .
8 **segregation** (seg-ri-**gā**-shun) *noun* **Rating:** 1 2 3	**Segregation** brings people together. Yes **(No)**	In the past, segregation in the United States _____ *Possible response:* forced African Americans to sit at the back of the bus and go to separate schools _____ _____ .

B. Use one of the Key Vocabulary words to tell how you could improve a situation in your community.

Answers will vary. _____

_____

Before Reading The Woman in the Snow

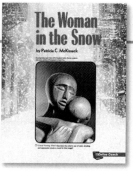

LITERARY ANALYSIS: Point of View

Third-person omniscient point of view is told by a narrator who is not a character in the story. The narrator is omniscient, or all-knowing. This kind of narrator can reveal the thoughts and feelings of all the characters.

A. Read the passage below. Look for clues that tell you the text is told by a third-person omniscient narrator. Paraphrase the text clues in the chart.

> **Look Into the Text**
>
> Grady Bishop had just been hired as a driver for Metro Bus Service. When he put on the gray uniform and boarded his bus, nothing mattered, not his obesity, not his poor education, not growing up the eleventh child of the town drunk. Driving gave him power. And power mattered.
>
> One cold November afternoon Grady clocked in for the three-to-eleven shift. "You've got Hall tonight," Billy, the route manager, said matter-of-factly.

Elements of Third-Person Omniscient	Text Clues
Events are told by narrator	Grady Bishop is hired by the bus service.
Narrator is all-knowing	Wearing the uniform makes Grady forget his alcoholic father, Grady's poor education, and that Grady is obese.
Narrator tells thoughts and feelings of characters	Driving a bus gives Grady power.

B. Answer the question about Grady.

1. What does the narrator know about Grady?

The narrator knows that Grady has been hired by a bus service and that wearing the gray uniform makes him feel important and powerful.

2. Which information would Billy, the route manager, most likely not know? Why?

Billy doesn't know that Grady thinks driving a bus gives him power and that Grady likes power. The narrator is all-knowing and knows Grady's thoughts and feelings, but Billy doesn't know them.

READING STRATEGY: Make Inferences

HOW TO MAKE INFERENCES

1. **Make an Initial Inference** Make an inference about a character or story event.

2. **Add New Information** Include information from the story that supports your inference.

3. **Make a New Inference** Revise your inference based on new ideas and information from the text.

A. Read the passage. Use the strategies above to make inferences as you read. Answer the questions below.

Look Into the Text

> Most Metro drivers didn't like the Hall Street assignment in the best weather, because the road twisted and turned back on itself like a retreating snake. When slick with ice and snow, it was even more hazardous. But Grady had his own reason for hating the route. The Hall Street Express serviced black domestics who rode out to the fashionable west end in the mornings and back down to the lower east side in the evenings.
>
> "You know I can't stand being a chauffeur for a bunch of colored maids and cooks," he groused.

1. What inference can you make about Grady?

Possible response: Grady doesn't like African-American passengers because he is prejudiced and poorly educated.

2. Which strategies did you use to answer question number 1?

Possible response: I made my first inference about Grady's feelings toward African Americans based on what I know about prejudiced people. Then, I used Grady's exact words in the last sentence to support my inference.

B. Make a new inference. Underline the new information that helps you make the new inference. *Answers will vary.*

Selection Review The Woman in the Snow

 What Makes a Hero?
Explore how heroes change the world around them.

A. In "The Woman in the Snow," you learn how people can change the world around them with their attitudes and choices. List the choices the characters make, and how these choices affect other people in the Character Description Chart.

Character Description Chart

Character	Character's Attitudes and Choices	Effect the Character Has on Others
Grady	Grady is a racist. He likes the power he has over people.	He leaves Eula Mae and her baby to die in the snow.
Ray	Ray is kind and generous and believes in being compassionate to everyone.	He is kind to Eula Mae's ghost; she finally makes it to the hospital.
Eula Mae	Eula Mae does not argue with Grady when he tells her to get off the bus.	She dies and continues to haunt Grady, even after she is dead.

B. Use the information in the chart to answer the questions.

1. Why does Ray make the decision to help Eula Mae, even though he doesn't believe she's real?

Ray has heard the ghost story, so he believes that he should be compassionate even to a ghost like Eula Mae.

2. Why does Grady lack compassion? Use **compassion** in your answer.

Possible response: Grady lacks compassion because he is uneducated and likes the power he has over people. He is also a racist and believes he is better than others.

3. What heroic qualities does Ray have? Cite two examples from the text.

Possible response: Ray is generous because he pays Eula Mae's fare and asks for nothing in return. He is also courageous, because he is frightened to pick up Eula Mae but does it anyway.

Connect Across Texts
In "The Woman in the Snow," an ordinary person makes an extraordinary choice. Read this profile about another person's extraordinary choice.

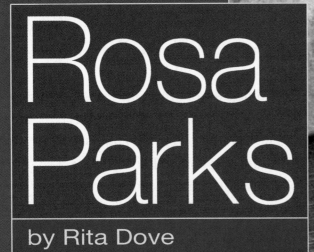

Rosa Parks

by Rita Dove

"Our mistreatment was just not right, and I was tired of it."

—Rosa Parks

Interact with the Text

1. Interpret
Look at the photo and read the quote. What do you predict this magazine profile will be about?

Possible response: I predict this profile will be about the consequences of Rosa Parks's decision to fight her mistreatment.

Circle the people that Parks is compared to in the second paragraph. What do these people all have in common?

Possible response: They

overcame challenges

and achieved something

that had positive effects

in their community.

3. Magazine Profile
Write two details about how African American bus passengers were treated in Montgomery. Highlight the place in the text on page 121 where you found your answer.

Possible response:

African Americans were

required to give up their

seats and move to the

back if a white person

wanted to sit down.

African Americans were

not allowed to sit across

the aisles from whites.

We know the story. One December evening, a woman left

work and boarded a bus for home. She was tired; her feet ached. But this was Montgomery, Alabama, in 1955. As the bus became crowded, the woman, a black woman, was ordered to give up her seat to a white passenger. When she remained seated, that simple decision eventually led to the end of **segregation** in the South, **ushering in** a new era of the civil rights movement.

This, anyway, was the story I had heard from the time I was curious enough to **eavesdrop on** adult conversations. I was 3 years old when a white bus driver warned Rosa Parks, "Well, I'm going to have you arrested," and she replied, "You may go on and do so." As a child, I didn't understand how doing nothing had caused so much activity, but I recognized the **template**: David slaying the giant Goliath, or the boy who saved his village by sticking his finger in the **dike**. And perhaps it is the **lure of fairy-tale retribution** that colors the lens we look back through. Parks was 42 years old when she refused to give up her seat. She has insisted that her feet were not aching; she was, by her own testimony, no more tired than usual. And she did not plan her fateful act: "I did not get on the bus to get arrested," she has said. "I got on the bus to go home."

Montgomery's segregation laws were complex. Blacks were required to pay their fare to the driver, then get off and reboard through the back door. Sometimes the bus would drive off before the paid-up customers made it to the back entrance. If the white section was full and another white customer entered, blacks were

In Alabama in the 1950s, by law if the white section of the bus was full, blacks had to give up their seat to allow whites to sit down.

Key Vocabulary
segregation *n.*, the act of separating or keeping apart

In Other Words
ushering in introducing, beginning
eavesdrop on listen secretly to
template pattern, model
dike barrier to prevent flooding
lure of fairy-tale retribution appeal of evil people being punished

required to give up their seats and move farther to the back. A black person was not even allowed to sit across the aisle from whites. At the time, two-thirds of the bus riders in Montgomery were black.

Parks was not the first to be **detained for this offense**. Eight months earlier, Claudette Colvin, 15, refused to give up her seat and was arrested. And then in October, a young woman named Mary Louise Smith was arrested. Smith paid the fine and was released.

Six weeks later, the time was ripe. The facts, rubbed shiny for retelling, are these: On December 1, 1955, Mrs. Rosa Parks, **seamstress** for a department store, boarded the Cleveland Avenue bus. She took a seat in the fifth row—the first row of the "Colored Section." The driver was the same one who had put her off a bus twelve years earlier for refusing to get off and reboard through the back door. ("He was still mean-looking," she has said.) Did that make her stubborn? Or had her work in the N.A.A.C.P. sharpened her **sensibilities** so that she knew what to do—or more precisely, what not to do: Don't frown, don't struggle, don't shout, don't pay the fine?

After her first arrest in December, 1955, Rosa Parks was arrested again in February, 1956. This time the charge was helping organize a bus boycott.

She was arrested on a Thursday; **bail was posted** by Clifford Durr, the white lawyer whose wife had employed Parks as a seamstress.

4. Make Inferences
Underline phrases that show how the community responded to Parks's arrest. What does the reaction tell you about the community's attitude?

Possible response:

They were tired of being

mistreated and were

ready to stand up as a

group to make a change.

5. Magazine Profile
Biographies show events in sequence, or time order. Summarize the events of the day Parks appeared in court, in your own words.

Possible response: The

trial lasted one-half

hour. That afternoon

the Montgomery

Improvement

Association formed and

elected Martin Luther

King, Jr. as their leader.

That night King spoke to

a crowd.

That evening, after talking it over with her mother and husband, Rosa Parks agreed to challenge Montgomery's segregation laws. <u>Thirty-five thousand handbills were distributed to all black schools the next morning.</u> The message was simple:

"We are . . . asking every Negro to stay off the buses Monday in protest of the arrest and trial . . . You can afford to stay out of school for one day. If you work, take a cab, or walk. But please, children and grown-ups, don't ride the bus at all on Monday. Please stay off the buses Monday."

Monday came. Rain threatened, yet the black population of <u>Montgomery stayed off the buses,</u> either <u>walking or catching one of the black cabs stopping at every **municipal** bus stop</u> for ten cents per customer—standard bus fare. Meanwhile, Parks was scheduled to appear in court. As she made her way through the <u>throngs at the courthouse,</u> a girl in the crowd caught sight of her and cried out, "Oh, she's so sweet. They've messed with the wrong one now!"

Yes, indeed. The trial lasted thirty minutes, with the expected **conviction and penalty**. That afternoon, the Montgomery Improvement Association was formed. The members elected as their president a **relative newcomer to** Montgomery, the young minister of Dexter Avenue Baptist Church: the Reverend Martin Luther King Jr. That evening, addressing a crowd, King declared in that ringing voice millions the world over would soon thrill to: "There comes a time that people get tired." When he was finished, Parks stood up so the audience could see her. She did not speak; there was no need to. Here I am, her silence said, among you.

And she has been with us ever since—a **persistent** symbol of human dignity in the face of brutal **authority**. The famous **U.P.I.** photo (actually taken more than a year later, on December 21, 1956, the day

Key Vocabulary
- **persistent** *adj.*, continuing in spite of challenges, unchanging
- **authority** *n.*, people with power over others

In Other Words
municipal city
conviction and penalty decision and punishment
relative newcomer to person who hadn't lived long in
U.P.I. United Press International (a news agency)

Montgomery's public transportation system was legally integrated) is a study of calm strength. She is looking out the bus window, her hands resting in the folds of her checked dress. A white man sits calmly in the row behind her. That clear profile, the neat eyeglasses and sensible coat—she could have been my mother, anybody's favorite aunt. History is often portrayed **as a grand opera, all baritone intrigues and tenor heroics**. Some of the most **tumultuous** events, however, have been **provoked** by **serendipity**—the assassination of an archduke spawned World War I, a kicked-over lantern may have sparked the Great Chicago

Rosa

How she sat there,
the time right inside a place
so wrong it was ready.

That trim name with
its dream of a bench
to rest on. Her sensible coat.

Doing nothing was the doing:
the clean flame of her gaze
carved by a camera flash.

How she stood up
when they bent down to retrieve
her purse. That courtesy.

—Rita Dove

Key Vocabulary
provoke *v.*, to force a person or thing to act

In Other Words
as a grand opera, all baritone intrigues and tenor heroics as if it were an exciting drama played out on a stage
tumultuous wild and noisy
serendipity a lucky accident

6. Make Inferences
The author describes the U.P.I. photo of Rosa Parks as "a study of calm strength." What can you infer about Parks, and about heroes, from the picture?

Possible response:

Parks looks like a

dignified, but an

ordinary, woman. I

think this means that

anyone can be a hero

and that most heroes

are ordinary, everyday

people.

7. Interpret
Read the poem by the author. In your own words, summarize the main idea.

Possible response:

The time was right for

a hero to step forward,

and Parks was the

appropriate hero.

8. Make Inferences

Why does the story of Parks continue to inspire people?

Possible response:

Parks set an example

of bravery. She also

showed how one person

has the power to stand

up for what is right and

the power to make a

difference in the world.

Fire. One cannot help wondering what role Martin Luther King Jr. would have played in the civil rights movement if the opportunity had not presented itself that first evening of the boycott—if Rosa Parks had chosen a row farther back from the outset, or if she had missed the bus altogether. Today, it is the modesty of Rosa Parks's example that **sustains us**. It is no less than the belief in the power of the individual, that **cornerstone** of the American Dream, that she inspires, along with the hope that all of us—even the least of us—could be that brave, that **serenely** human, when crunch time comes. ❖

In Other Words
sustains us gives us hope and support
cornerstone foundation
serenely calmly

Selection Review Rosa Parks

A. Choose one of the story events. How did the action change the world?

> **Event 1:** Rosa Parks refuses to give up her seat on the bus.
> **Event 2:** African Americans boycott the city buses.

Possible response: Event 2; By boycotting the Montgomery buses, African Americans showed

that they could affect the community and change what was unfair. This action eventually led to

integration.

B. Answer the questions.

1. How does the sequence of events in the magazine profile of Rosa Parks help you understand her influence on the civil rights movement?

Possible response: Rosa Parks played an important part in changing the laws of segregation. The

events that led up to Parks's arrest, and the events that happened after, show how Parks inspired

so many people.

2. Why were Rosa Parks's actions on the bus so important?

Possible response: Parks's actions brought notoriety to Montgomery and the unfairness of

segregation. The civil rights movement grew stronger because people took notice of the

inequalities in the segregated South.

Reflect and Assess

WRITING: Write About Literature

A. Plan your writing. List examples from both selections that support the theme overcoming prejudice. Answers will vary.

The Woman in the Snow	Rosa Parks

B. What do both selections say about the struggle to overcome prejudice? Write a brief theme statement. Use examples from both selections to support your statement.

Students should support their answers with examples from both selections.

_____

_____

_____

_____

_____

_____

_____

_____

_____

_____

Integrate the Language Arts

LITERARY ANALYSIS: Compare Themes

A **theme** is the most important idea in a work of literature. Themes usually deal with issues that all people can relate to, such as looking for love or experiencing loss.

A. Compare the themes of "Hero" by Mariah Carey and "The Woman in the Snow." In the chart, list examples from each selection that deal with the universal theme of heroism. Answers will vary. Possible responses are shown.

Hero	The Woman in the Snow
Every person has the ability to be a hero.	Ray Hammond became the first African American driver that Metro hired.

B. Describe what the examples for each selection say about the universal theme of heroism.

"Hero": Each person has the ability to be a hero and a hero can change a person's life for the better.

"The Woman in the Snow": An ordinary person can be a hero with one simple act and make a change for the better.

C. How is the theme of heroism similar in both selections? What do you think the authors say about heroism in each selection? Use examples from the text to support your response.

Answers will vary.

VOCABULARY STUDY: Word Families

Knowing the meaning of one word can help you understand other words that belong in the same **word family**.

A. The following words are in the same word family as words found in the selections. Write what you think each word means. Then use a dictionary to confirm the definition. *Answers will vary. Possible responses are shown.*

Word	What I Think It Means	What It Means
discriminate	to treat people in a certain group unfairly	to show a difference in treatment
hazard	something that causes destruction	danger
provocation	something that forces a person to act	something that angers or irritates
segregate	divide	to separate people or things
sensible	showing good sense	showing good reason and judgment
tumult	violent and noisy commotion	a violent disturbance or disorder

B. List related words that belong to each word's family below.
Answers will vary. Possible responses are shown.

hero	differ	depend
heroic, heroine	difference, different, differential, indifferent	dependable, dependent, independent

C. Look through each of the selections. Find three words. Brainstorm related words that belong to the word's family. *Answers will vary.*

1. _____

_____

2. _____

_____

3. _____

_____

Key Vocabulary Review

A. Read each sentence. Circle the word that best fits into each sentence.

1. You might start a(n) (**investigation**/ **boycott**) to learn the truth about something.

2. A (**survivor** /**skeptic**) questions what other people believe.

3. A (**persistent**/ **prejudiced**) person does not give up.

4. You might behave (**conscientiously** /**desperately**) in a crisis.

5. (**Segregation**/ **tragedy**) does not allow people from different races to live together.

6. A judge is required to be (**genuine** /**just**) in his or her courtroom.

7. Siblings often (**protest** /**provoke**) each other to do silly things.

8. Some people have a(n) (**inherent**/ **distracted**) sense of loyalty.

B. Use your own words to write what each Key Vocabulary word means. Then write a synonym for each word. *Answers will vary. Possible responses are shown.*

Key Word	My Definition	Synonym
1. authority	a power over others	control
2. compassion	caring about other people's troubles	pity
3. conscientiously	to work with a lot of attention	carefully
4. endure	to last for a long time	survive
5. inhibit	to not allow	prevent
6. prejudiced	having negative opinions about others	intolerant
7. protest	to show that you're against something	object
8. tragedy	something terrible and unexpected	disaster

Unit 3 Key Vocabulary

anxiety	conscientiously	endure	• inherent	• persistent	segregation
• authority	desperately	• evidence	• inhibit	prejudiced	skeptic
boycott	• discrimination	genuine	• investigation	protest	• survivor
compassion	distracted	historian	just	provoke	tragedy

• Academic Vocabulary

C. Complete the sentences. *Answers will vary. Possible responses are shown.*

1. I am easily **distracted** when <u>TV is on while I try to read</u>
   _____.

2. **Evidence** is important to police because <u>it will help them arrest the person who committed the crime</u>
   _____.

3. I feel **anxiety** when <u>I am about to make a speech</u>
   _____.

4. Something I would like to see a **boycott** of is <u>the local grocery store because it does not recycle</u>
   <u>plastic bags</u>_____.

5. A **survivor** of a serious illness might feel <u>grateful to be alive</u>
   _____.

6. A **genuine** emerald is valuable because <u>it is a rare gem</u>
   _____.

7. Some things that a **historian** might do are<u>do research and study ancient objects</u>
   _____.

8. Someone I know experienced **discrimination** when <u>she was not hired for a job because she is a girl</u>
   _____.

Prepare to Read

▶ **Curtis Aikens and the American Dream**
▶ **Go For It!**

Key Vocabulary

A. How well do you know these words? Circle a rating for each word. Check your understanding of each word by circling the correct synonym. Then complete the sentences. If you are unsure of a word's meaning, refer to the Vocabulary Glossary, page 852, in your student text.

Rating Scale

1	I have never seen this word before.
2	I am not sure of the word's meaning.
3	I know this word and can teach the word's meaning to someone else.

Key Word	Check Your Understanding	Deepen Your Understanding
❶ ambitious (am-**bi**-shus) *adjective* **Rating:** 1 2 3	An **ambitious** person is _____. satisfied (**determined**)	My friend is ambitious because *Possible response:* she wants to own her own business someday _____ _____ _____ .
❷ cause (**kawz**) *noun* **Rating:** 1 2 3	A **cause** is a _____. difficulty (**idea**)	A cause I think is important is *Possible response:* animal rights _____ _____ _____ .
❸ confession (kun-**fe**-shun) *noun* **Rating:** 1 2 3	A **confession** is a _____. denial (**declaration**)	One reason someone might make a confession is _____ *Possible response:* if he or she feel guilty about something he or she has done _____ _____ .
❹ discourage (dis-**kur**-ej) *verb* **Rating:** 1 2 3	To **discourage** people is to _____ them. (**dissuade**) inspire	A person should discourage a friend from _____ *Possible response:* cheating on a test _____ _____ _____ .

Key Word	Check Your Understanding	Deepen Your Understanding
5 fate (fāt) *noun* **Rating:** 1 2 3	The **fate** of something is its _____. (destiny) past	I believe it is my fate to _Possible response: get a_ great job working with wildlife _____ _____ _____ _____.
6 literacy (**li**-tu-ru-sē) *noun* **Rating:** 1 2 3	**Literacy** is a kind of _____. ignorance (knowledge)	Literacy is important because _Possible response:_ people need to read and write in order to get good jobs _____ _____ _____.
7 profession (pru-**fe**-shun) *noun* **Rating:** 1 2 3	A **profession** is a _____. hobby (career)	A profession I would like to know more about is _____ *Possible response:* the law profession _____ _____ _____.
8 reputation (re-pyu-**tā**-shun) *noun* **Rating:** 1 2 3	A **reputation** is an _____ others have about you. (opinion) enthusiasm	I have a reputation for being _Possible response: a_ good student _____ _____ _____ _____.

B. Use one of the Key Vocabulary words to write about a time your knowledge about something gave you power.

Answers will vary. _____

_____

Before Reading Curtis Aikens and the American Dream

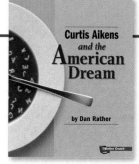

LITERARY ANALYSIS: Text Structure (Chronology)

A biography tells the true story of someone's life, including information about important events and people. Authors often describe events in the order they happened using sequence words, dates, and times. This organization is called **chronological order.**

A. Read the passage below. Find clues that show you this is a biography written in chronological order. Write the clues in the chart.

> **Look Into the Text**
>
> In the third grade, Curtis made a decision that would determine the course of his life. As he sat through a parent-teacher conference, he heard his teacher praise him: "'I just love having your boy in my class,'" Curtis remembers her saying. "'He's a great kid, he's sweet,' and then I heard a 'but.' And I thought, 'Oh no. What's this? But he's dumb? He's stupid?'" Well, no. She didn't say anything close to that, but she did say that he had some reading trouble, and she thought it would be best for him to repeat the third grade.

Type of Clue	Examples in Passage
Dates and times	*third grade*
Sequence words	*as, then*
Important event	Curtis's teacher wanted Curtis to repeat the third grade, because he had trouble reading.
Important people	Curtis, his teacher, Curtis's parent

B. Complete the sentence.

The most important event in Curtis's life was <u>hearing his teacher say he should repeat third grade</u>

<u>because he had difficulty reading</u>

READING STRATEGY: Self-Question

Reading Strategy
Ask Questions

HOW TO SELF-QUESTION

1. **Ask Yourself Questions** Asking questions as you read is a good way to find new information or solve problems.

2. **Make a Question-Answer Chart** Ask *Who, What, Where, When, Why,* and *How* questions.

3. **Reread the Passage** to find the answers. If you can't find the answers in the text, ask a classmate or teacher.

A. Read the passage below. Use the strategies above to self-question as you read. Complete the Question-Answer Chart. Use the 5W/How questions.

Look Into the Text

"I was shocked. I was floored. I'm thinking to myself, 'Well, I'm not gonna let anyone ever call me dumb or stupid again.' So instead of learning to read, I learned to hide the fact that I couldn't read." Bad choice, as Curtis would find out. Faking it took a good deal more effort than if he had simply asked for help. As he grew older, he felt that if anyone found out his secret, the label "stupid, dumb" would be much bigger and harder to shake. So he dug himself deeper and deeper into a hole.

Question-Answer Chart

My Questions	My Answers
Possible response: Why didn't Curtis ask for help once he realized pretending to read was difficult?	*Possible response:* He didn't ask for help because he was afraid people would think he was dumb.
Possible response: What would happen if someone discovered Curtis couldn't read?	*Possible response:* I don't know yet. I might find the answer later in the biography, or I could ask my teacher.

B. Describe how self-questioning helped you understand the passage.

Possible response: Asking questions kept me interested in the reading. I wanted to keep reading in order to find the answers to my questions.

Selection Review Curtis Aikens and the American Dream

Curtis Aikens and the American Dream

by Dan Rather

EQ ### How Can Knowledge Open Doors?
Consider how learning can give you power.

A. In "Curtis Aikens and the American Dream," you found out how knowledge gave Curtis power. Complete the T Chart with the events in Curtis's life before and after he learned to read and write.

T Chart

Before Curtis Learned to Read and Write	After Curtis Learned to Read and Write
Watching TV and listening to music helped Curtis develop a strong vocabulary and self-confidence to fool people into thinking he could read and write.	His self-confidence increased and was no longer an act.
Curtis took classes in high school that did not require much reading or writing.	Curtis took French lessons. Curtis became a food columnist.
Curtis dropped out of college.	Curtis decided to reach out to others who could not read.
Curtis had to trust that people were not cheating him out of money.	People across the nation reacted positively to Curtis's story.

B. Use the information in the chart to answer the questions.

1. How did Curtis's life change after he learned to read and write?

    Possible response: Curtis decided that helping others who could not read and write was important. He was more self-confident and tried new things.

2. Why does Curtis support the cause of literacy? Use **cause** in your answer.

    Possible response: He supports the cause of literacy because learning to read and write changed his life, and he knows literacy can change other people's lives, too.

3. How might your life be different if you could not read or write?

    Possible response: I would not be able to read the comics in the newspaper every morning. School would be very difficult.

Connect Across Texts

"Curtis Aikens and the American Dream" describes how one person reaches for success by learning. In this essay, what does basketball star Magic Johnson say to people about success in life?

Go For It!

by Earvin "Magic" Johnson
with William Novak

Basketball was my ticket to success. But if I hadn't been good enough at basketball, I would have been successful in something else.

Magic Johnson at the 1992 Olympics in Barcelona, Spain.

1. Nonfiction Text Features
Look at the photo and caption on page 135. How do they help you understand what the main idea of the selection might be?

Possible response: The

caption tells who is in

the photograph and

where and when the

photo was taken. The

photo and caption tell

me that this selection

will be about Magic

Johnson.

2. Question the Author
Underline two sentences that show some of the author's beliefs. What question could you ask about the author or his opinion?

Possible response: What

reason does the author

give to explain why there

are not enough nurses

or pilots? How does he

know?

I would have gone to college, and worked hard, and made something of myself. You can do that, too. Basketball is not the best way to get ahead. It's probably the most difficult path you could take. There are thirty teams in the **NBA**, and each team has twelve players. That makes 360 players who are in the league at any one time. In a country as big as ours, that's not a big number. There are about 1,800 college seniors who play ball, and only a few of them are good enough to be **drafted**. So even if you're good enough and fortunate enough to play in college, what makes you think you're going to play in the NBA? You have to understand that your chances of playing basketball for a living are **miniscule**.

The black community already has enough basketball players. And enough baseball players, and football players. But there are a lot of other people we could really use. We need more teachers. We need more lawyers. We need more doctors. We need more accountants. <u>We need more nurses. We need more pilots.</u> And more scientists.

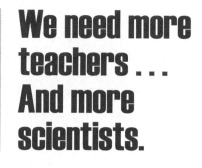

We need more teachers . . . And more scientists.

And more carpenters. And more professors. And more police officers. And more bankers. And more computer programmers. And more mechanics. And more **social workers**. And more car dealers. And more politicians.

And every single one of these **professions**—*including doctor and lawyer—is easier to get into than the NBA.*

If you can possibly go to college, go! I know it's hard. I know that some kids you know will **discourage** you. If you're **ambitious**, if you

Key Vocabulary
• **profession** *n.*, job that requires education or training
discourage *v.*, to make someone not want to do something
ambitious *adj.*, having big goals

In Other Words
NBA National Basketball Association
drafted chosen to play on a professional team
miniscule tiny
social workers people who work for a city or state to help other people

Magic lives up to his name.

Earvin "Magic" Johnson got his nickname in high school after a local sportswriter saw him in action on the basketball court. Johnson went on to play basketball for two years at Michigan State University in East Lansing. Then in 1979, he was drafted by the NBA to play for the Los Angeles Lakers. From there, he went on to make NBA history. He was named to the NBA All-Star team twelve times and was voted both league and NBA Finals Most Valuable Player three times. He retired from the NBA in 1991. Johnson was a member of the USA's famous "Dream Team," which won a gold medal at the 1992 Olympics. He was voted into the Naismith Memorial Basketball Hall of Fame in 2002.

Magic Johnson spends time with students at his computer center in Philadelphia, PA.

His basketball career over, Johnson continues to amaze. He is the head of Magic Johnson Enterprises, a company that tries to bring business to urban areas. It is estimated that he is worth $800 million from his post-basketball activities. But Johnson gives back to the community through his charity, The Magic Johnson Foundation. He provides scholarships and develops community centers and technology training centers. Johnson lives up to his own advice: Go for it!

study hard, if your goals are high, some people may tell you you're "acting white." Stay away from these people! They are not your friends. If the people around you aren't going anywhere, if their dreams are no bigger than hanging out on the corner, or if they're **dragging you down**, get rid of them. Negative people can **sap your energy** so fast, and they can take your dreams from you, too.

In Other Words
dragging you down making it harder for you to succeed
sap your energy take away your desire to reach your goals

Interact with the Text

3. Nonfiction Text Features
Look at the photo and the caption on this page. What information do they provide? Why is a photo a good way to show this information?

Possible response:

I always see photos

of Magic playing

basketball, but this

photo shows him doing

something he thinks is

more important.

4. Interpret
Do you agree that you should not spend time with people who have no dreams for their lives? Why or why not?

Possible response:

I disagree because

sometimes those people

are your family. I do

agree that you shouldn't

let these people

discourage you.

5. Question the Author
Underline a sentence that you find confusing or that you think others may find confusing. Ask a question about the author to help you understand his opinion or belief.

Possible response:

What does the author

think people are making

excuses about?

I don't mean to tell you it's easy. It's *not* easy. Growing up today is hard. I know that. It's much harder than when I was your age. <u>We've got to quit making excuses.</u> Quit feeling sorry for ourselves. We have to go to college. Think about business. Work hard. Support one another, like other groups do.

The government will not save you.

The black leadership will not save you.

You're the only one who can make the difference.

Whatever your dream is, go for it. ❖

Selection Review Go For It!

A. Choose one of the questions you provided in your answer to question 2 on page 136 or question 5 on this page. Answer the questions below.

1. What was your question?

Possible response: What reason does the author give for why there are not enough nurses or pilots?

2. What answer did you find?

Possible response: People think it is difficult to become a nurse or a pilot. Also, it is easy to believe people who tell you that a job like that is an impossible dream.

3. What evidence in the text supports your answer?

Possible response: The author says it is easier to become a nurse or a pilot than a basketball player in the NBA. He explains that the African American community needs more people in professions like medicine.

B. Answer the questions.

1. How did the photos and captions help support the author's opinions and beliefs?

Possible response: The essay is about being successful, and the photos and captions show two very different ways the author has been successful in his life.

2. The author lists things that help people achieve their goals. Which one of these has influenced your life?

Possible response: I refuse to be friends with people who do not take my goals seriously.

Reflect and Assess

WRITING: Write About Literature

A. Plan your writing. List examples from both texts that describe how knowledge can open doors to success in the future. *Answers will vary.*

Curtis Aikens and the American Dream	Go For It!

B. Write a public service announcement that encourages high school students to go to a technical school or college. Include information and quotes from each selection.

Encourage students to read aloud their announcements.

_____

_____

_____

_____

_____

_____

_____

_____

_____

LITERARY ANALYSIS: Text Structure (Chronology)

Chronology is the order in which events happen. Authors often organize biographies in chronological order. *Answers will vary. Possible responses are shown.*

A. List sequence words that show chronological order.

Sequence Words	
1. first	**5.** next
2. then	**6.** before
3. later	**7.** previously
4. after	**8.** subsequently

B. The following events from "Curtis Aikens and the American Dream" are presented out of order. Use the sequence words from the chart to write a paragraph about Aikens and his life in chronological order.

Events:

Curtis learned to read. Curtis started a produce company in California. Curtis dropped out of college. Curtis decided to become a celebrity to promote the cause of literacy. Curtis heard a public service announcement from Literacy Volunteers of America.

First, Curtis dropped out of college. Then Curtis started a produce company in California. After Curtis heard a public service announcement from Literacy Volunteers of America, Curtis learned to read. Subsequently, Curtis decided to become a celebrity to promote the cause of literacy.

C. Think about what you or someone you know did yesterday. Recount those events in chronological order. Use at least five different sequence words.

Students should use a variety of sequence words in their recount.

VOCABULARY STUDY: Dictionary and Jargon

Many English words have an everyday meaning and a specialized meaning. **Jargon** is the specialized language of a career field. Meanings of words also vary according to their parts of speech. Word meanings and parts of speech can be found in a **dictionary**.

A. The words in the chart below are all related to baseball. Look up each word in the dictionary and write the specialized and the everyday meaning. *Answers will vary. Possible responses are shown.*

Word	Specialized Meaning	Everyday Meaning
bat	*a solid stick used for hitting a ball*	a type of mammal that flies
hit	to strike the ball without fouling or getting out	to strike something
out	a player who throws the ball to the batter	a container used to hold and pour liquids
run	a point made by a runner	to move quickly

B. Brainstorm words that have both a specialized meaning and an everyday meaning, and list each in the chart. *Answers will vary.*

Word	Specialized Meaning	Everyday Meaning

C. Write a sentence for each word in Activity B using one of the meaning types. *Answers will vary.*

1. _____

2. _____

3. _____

4. _____

▶ **Superman and Me**
▶ **A Smart Cookie**
▶ **It's Our Story, Too**

Prepare to Read

Key Vocabulary

A. How well do you know these words? Circle a rating for each word. Check your understanding of each word by circling *yes* or *no*. Then write a definition. If you are unsure of a word's meaning, refer to the Vocabulary Glossary, page 852, in your student text.

Rating Scale	
1	I have never seen this word before.
2	I am not sure of the word's meaning.
3	I know this word and can teach the word's meaning to someone else.

Key Word	Check Your Understanding	Deepen Your Understanding
❶ arrogant (**ar**-u-gunt) *adjective* **Rating:** **1 2 3**	A person who is **arrogant** would never brag. Yes (No)	My definition: *Answers will vary.*
❷ assume (u-**sūm**) *verb* **Rating:** **1 2 3**	You might **assume** a very old car will not run. (Yes) No	My definition: *Answers will vary.*
❸ constant (**kon**-stunt) *adjective* **Rating:** **1 2 3**	There is usually **constant** noise at a football game. (Yes) No	My definition: *Answers will vary.*
❹ disgusted (di-**skus**-tid) *adjective* **Rating:** **1 2 3**	Someone might feel **disgusted** by a respectful comment. Yes (No)	My definition: *Answers will vary.*

Key Word	Check Your Understanding	Deepen Your Understanding
5 prodigy (**prah**-du-jē) *noun* **Rating:** 1 2 3	A **prodigy** might be able to play the piano before learning to tie his or her shoes. (Yes) No	My definition: *Answers will vary.*
6 recall (rē-**kawl**) *verb* **Rating:** 1 2 3	Someone who loves music might **recall** his or her favorite song. (Yes) No	My definition: *Answers will vary.*
7 shame (**shām**) *noun* **Rating:** 1 2 3	A person might feel **shame** after lying to a friend. (Yes) No	My definition: *Answers will vary.*
8 standard (**stan**-durd) *noun* **Rating:** 1 2 3	A restaurant with a high **standard** for excellence would use the best ingredients in its food. (Yes) No	My definition: *Answers will vary.*

B. Use one of the Key Vocabulary words to write about what you have discovered from reading a favorite book.

Answers will vary.

_____

Before Reading Superman and Me

LITERARY ANALYSIS: Text Structure (Cause and Effect)

Authors use **cause and effect** to explain how one event (the cause) leads to another event (the effect).

A. Read the passage below. In the Cause-and-Effect Chart, list examples of cause-and-effect relationships in the text.

Look Into the Text

In a fit of unemployment-inspired creative energy, my father built a set of bookshelves and soon filled them with a random assortment of books about the Kennedy assassination, Watergate, the Vietnam war, and the entire twenty-three-book series of the Apache westerns. My father loved books, and since I loved my father with an aching devotion, I decided to love books as well.

Cause-and-Effect Chart

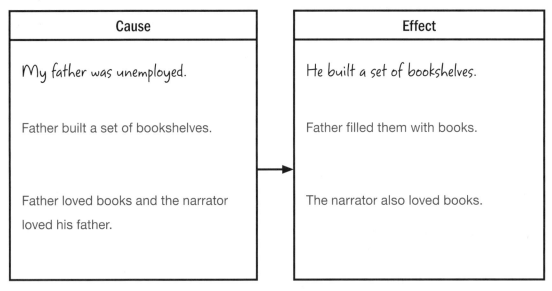

Cause	Effect
My father was unemployed.	He built a set of bookshelves.
Father built a set of bookshelves.	Father filled them with books.
Father loved books and the narrator loved his father.	The narrator also loved books.

B. Complete the sentences.

The narrator developed a love for books because _he loved his father, who also loved books_ .

The narrator's father built a set of bookshelves because _he was unemployed, and he loved books_ .

READING STRATEGY: Find Question-Answer Relationships

How to FIND QUESTION-ANSWER RELATIONSHIPS

1. **Ask Questions** As you read, ask *Who, What, Where, When, Why* and *How* questions to learn how important events are related.

2. **Reread** Go back to find answers that are "right there" in the text.

3. **Read On** Keep reading to find answers later if the answer cannot be found in this section.

A. Read the passage. Use the strategies above to find question-answer relationships as you read. Then answer the questions below.

Look Into the Text

> I was three years old, a Spokane Indian boy living with his family on the Spokane Indian Reservation in eastern Washington state. We were poor by most standards, but <u>one of my parents usually managed to find some minimum-wage job or another, which made us middle-class by reservation standards.</u> I had a brother and three sisters. We lived on a combination of irregular paychecks, hope, fear, and government-surplus food.

1. Why was the narrator's family considered to be middle-class by reservation standards?

   One of his parents usually had a minimum-wage job, which must not have been common on the
   reservation.

2. Which of the three strategies did you use to answer question 1? Explain.

   Possible response: Reread; the answer was right there.

B. Return to the passage above and underline the words or sentences that gave you the answer to the first question. Then ask another 5W or H question. Which strategy did you use to find the answer?

Question: *Possible response:* What makes reservation standards different from other standards?

Strategy: *Possible response:* Read On; I can't find the answer in the text.

Selection Review Superman and Me

EQ How Can Knowledge Open Doors?
Discover how books can take you places.

A. In "Superman and Me," you found out how reading changed Sherman Alexie's life and opened up doors for him. In the Goal-and-Outcome Chart, list the events that had an effect on the outcome of Alexie's goal.

Goal-and-Outcome Chart

> **Goal:** To not be like the other Native Americans who felt that to be a failure was the only option.

⬇

> **Event 1:**
> Constantly read books or anything with words and paragraphs.
>
> **Event 2:**
> Began to write novels, short stories, and poems.
>
> **Event 3:**
> Visited schools to teach creative writing to Native American kids who otherwise would never learn how.

⬇

> **Outcome:** Alexie saved his life through reading and did not become like the other Native American kids who felt that failure was the only option.

B. Use the information in the chart to answer the questions.

1. How did reading affect Alexie's life?

Reading gave Alexie the skills to become a writer and teacher. He strived for success even though other Native American kids felt that failure was the only option.

2. What did other people assume about Alexie because he was Native American? Use **assume** in your answer.

Others would always assume that because Alexie is Native American, he would fail.

3. In the end, Alexie describes students who have given up. Why do you think those students resist learning?

Possible response: The students are afraid of failure. Some students hate to be forced to go to school, and some are simply not interested in learning.

Connect Across Texts

In "Superman and Me," Sherman Alexie describes how a comic book changed his life. Read "A Smart Cookie" and "It's Our Story, Too" to learn how Cisneros's book changed the life of one of her readers.

A Smart Cookie

by Sandra Cisneros

Do words have the power to change lives? Author Sandra Cisneros's characters (and her readers) certainly think so.

I could've been somebody, you know? my mother says and sighs. She has lived in this city her whole life. She can speak two languages. She can sing an opera. She knows how to fix a T.V. But she doesn't know which subway train to take to get downtown. I hold her hand very tight while we wait for the right train to arrive.

She used to draw when she had time. Now she draws with a needle and thread, little knotted rosebuds, tulips made of silk thread. Someday she would like to go to the ballet. Someday she would like to see a play. She borrows opera records from the public library and sings with **velvety lungs powerful as morning glories**.

Today while cooking oatmeal she is **Madame Butterfly** until she sighs and points the wooden spoon at me. I could've been somebody, you know? Esperanza, you go to school. Study hard. That Madame Butterfly was a fool. She stirs the oatmeal. Look at my *comadres*. She means Izaura whose husband left and Yolanda whose husband is dead. Got to take care all your own, she says shaking her head.

Then out of nowhere:

Shame is a bad thing, you know. **It keeps you down.** You want to know why I quit school? Because I didn't have nice clothes. No clothes, but I had brains.

Yup, she says **disgusted**, stirring again. I was a smart cookie then.

The Dreamer, 2002, Patssi Valdez. Acrylic on canvas.

△ **Critical Viewing: Design**
What is the title of this work? How do the colors and light contribute to its meaning?

Key Vocabulary
shame *n.*, a painful feeling that is caused by embarrassment or guilt
disgusted *adj.*, feeling very upset

In Other Words
velvety lungs powerful as morning glories a strong and beautiful voice
Madame Butterfly a famous opera character
comadres very good friends (in Spanish)
It keeps you down. It keeps you from being happy and doing what you want to do.

It's Our Story, Too

by Yvette Cabrera

The Orange County Register (Santa Ana, California)
April 15, 2002

Growing up, I studied books my high school English teachers said were must reads for a well-rounded education. Books like J. D. Salinger's *Catcher in the Rye*, Fyodor Dostoyevsky's *Crime and Punishment*, and Thomas Hardy's *Tess of the d'Urbervilles*.

It was literature with great meaning that taught important lessons. But still, I **felt a disconnection**. *Beowulf* was an epic poem. But as my high school teacher went into great detail explaining what **a mail shirt** was, I wondered what that had to do with my life.

It was that way all through high school. Then one day in college I was assigned to read *The House on Mango Street*.

Mango. The word alone **evoked memories** of childhood weekends. Back then my family and I would pile into our sky-blue Chevrolet Malibu and head to **Olvera Street's plaza** in downtown Los Angeles.

For my sisters and me, the treat for behaving ourselves was a juicy mango on a stick sold at a fruit stand in the plaza. We would squeeze lemon and sprinkle chile and salt over the bright yellow slices.

As an adult, whenever I had a reporting assignment near Olvera Street, I'd always take a minute to stop. Standing amid the smell of sizzling **carne asada**, the sounds of **vendors negotiating** prices in Spanish, and children licking a rainbow of *raspados* (shaved ice treats), I would bite into my mango and feel at home.

That's what *The House on Mango Street* did for me.

Fresh fruit from a fruit stand at the Olvera Street plaza in Los Angeles, California

Interact with the Text

1. Text Structure (Chronology)

Highlight the phrase the author uses to show a flashback. Then highlight a phrase that signals another time shift. Explain how these words signal how time changes.

Possible response: The author uses *Back then* as a clue that this event took place farther back in the past. The author then shifts forward to a time in her adult life by using *As an adult.*

In Other Words

felt a disconnection couldn't relate to the stories
a mail shirt armor in old battles
evoked memories reminded me

Olvera Street's plaza an outdoor shopping area that is famous for its Hispanic products
carne asada grilled steak (in Spanish)
vendors negotiating sellers arguing about

2. Interpret

How did reading *The House on Mango Street* remind the author of her childhood? How do you think the author feels about her childhood?

Possible response:

The author compares reading the book to her childhood memory of eating a mango. She had a happy childhood and has many good memories.

3. Find Question-Answer Relationships

Underline words and phrases that show why the author felt so connected to Cisneros's book. Explain how you found your answer.

Possible response: The author finally read a book that described a life experience similar to her own. I found the answer by considering how the information and ideas fit together.

East on the 10, 2001, Frank Romero. Oil on wood, private collection.

▲ **Critical Viewing: Effect** What mood do the colors and lines create? How might this reflect the feeling of a large city like Los Angeles?

On the first page, Esperanza explains how at school they say her name funny, "as if the syllables were made out of tin and hurt the roof of your mouth." I was **hooked**.

I knew nothing of the East Coast **prep schools** or the English **shires** of the books I had read before. But like Esperanza, I could remember how different my last name sounded when it was **pronounced melodically** by my parents but **so haltingly** by everyone else.

Cisneros's hometown of Chicago may have been hundreds of miles away from the palm-tree lined streets of Santa Barbara, California, where I grew up. But in her world I was no longer **the minority**.

In Other Words

hooked so interested I couldn't stop reading it
prep schools expensive private schools
shires villages
pronounced melodically said in a musical way

so haltingly said in a jerky, ugly way
the minority part of the small group that no one seemed to notice or care about

That was a dozen years ago. Today, Latinos are the **majority** in cities like Santa Ana, California, where Cisneros spoke at Valley High School.

Today, these students can pick from bookstore shelves filled with authors such as Julia Álvarez, Victor Villaseñor, and Judith Ortiz Cofer. These are authors who go beyond **census numbers** to explain what U.S. Latino life is about.

Cisneros provided an hour of humorous storytelling that had the students busting with laughter. They crowded in line afterward, **giddily** waiting to get her autograph.

"Everything she explains, what she says is true," Jessica Cordova, a 10th-grader at Valley High School, says of *The House on Mango Street.* "She puts a lot of emotion, feeling, and thought into the book."

Later, as I talk to Cisneros, she explains how much **the literary world** has changed since she finished writing *The House on Mango Street* twenty years ago. Back then, forget trying to get *The New York Times* to review your book if you were Latino—or getting a major bookseller to carry it, she says.

One thing has remained **constant**, something that Cisneros can see by the question that's most asked by students.

The House on Mango Street is a book by Sandra Cisneros. The narrator is a Latina girl named Esperanza, who describes people and events in her neighborhood.

Key Vocabulary
- **constant** *adj.*, the same, without any change

In Other Words
majority group which has the most people
census numbers the official number of people who live in the country
giddily excitedly
the literary world the book-selling and publishing businesses

---

4. Interpret
Underline the words that show how much time has passed since Cisneros wrote *The House on Mango Street.* What can you conclude about the influence Latino authors have had since then?

Possible response:

Latinos have had a big

influence on modern

culture. Today, more

people know about

Latino culture, and

Latino authors have

become more popular

with a wider audience.

5. Text Structure (Chronology)

Underline the signal words and phrases that show this is taking place in the present. Explain why the author chose to conclude the memoir in the present tense.

The author wants to

stress that Cisneros's

book still affects

readers. Readers

connect to the story and

feel better knowing that

someone else has had

similar experiences.

"<u>They want</u> to know, 'Is this real? Did this happen to you?'" <u>Cisneros says.</u> "They're so concerned and want to make sure this is my story, because it's their story, too." ❖

Selection Review   A Smart Cookie; It's Our Story, Too

A. Write a question that you would like to ask either Cisneros or Cabrera about these selections.

Question: *Possible response:* Why does Esperanza's mother quit school?

Describe how you can find the answers to your questions in the text.   *Possible response:*

Some answers might be found "right there," but if not, I can look at how the information and ideas in the text fit together, and see if I can find an answer. If I still don't find an answer I will keep reading.

B. Answer the questions.

1. Why do the authors use flashbacks to tell their stories? How are they effective?

Signal words and flashbacks clearly describe what happened in the past. Signal words shift the chronology of the events clearly so that the reader does not become confused.

2. Reread page 148. Describe one way that Esperanza's mother's advice might have opened doors for Esperanza.

Possible response: Esperanza might have decided that she will stay in school and learn how to support herself.

Reflect and Assess

WRITING: Write About Literature

A. Plan your writing. List examples of advice that each author gives to struggling students. *Answers will vary.*

Sherman Alexie	Sandra Cisneros	Yvette Cabrera
read whenever possible		

B. Choose one of the struggling students you have read about—one of Alexie's students, Esperanza's mother, or young Yvette Cabrera. Write an e-mail message offering advice about how the student can change his or her attitude toward school and reading. Use examples from each selection.

Students should support their answers with examples from the selections.

_____

_____

_____

_____

_____

_____

_____

Integrate the Language Arts

LITERARY ANALYSIS: Analyze Imagery

Imagery is language that appeals to the five senses. It helps readers picture what is being described. *Answers will vary.*

A. Read the excerpt below from "Superman and Me." On a separate sheet of paper, draw a picture of the image.

> . . . Our house was filled with books. They were stacked in crazy piles in the bathroom, bedrooms, and living room. In a fit of unemployment-inspired creative energy, my father built a set of bookshelves and soon filled them with a random assortment of books about the Kennedy assassination, Watergate, the Vietnam War, and the entire twenty-three-book series of the Apache westerns.

B. Choose words or phrases from all three selections that appeal to the five senses. Complete the chart below with the imagery. Cite the page number and the selection.

Sense	Page Number / Selection	Imagery
Sight	page 341, "It's Our Story, Too"	"palm-tree lined streets of Santa Barbara, California"
Taste		
Smell		
Sound		
Touch		

C. Use imagery to describe a place you know well or an experience you have had. Include how things taste, smell, look, feel, or sound.

Students should use language that appeals to the five senses.

_____

_____

_____

_____

VOCABULARY STUDY: Multiple-Meaning Words

Many English words are **multiple-meaning words**, or words that have more than one meaning. You can study the context clues near the word to figure out the word's meaning.

A. Read the sentences in the chart. Use context clues to figure out the meaning of each underlined word.

Sentence	Word Meaning
The large crowd at the concert added to my excitement.	a large number of people
My parents keep a record of every grade I receive on a test.	something that recalls or relates past events
My mom asked me to go to the store to buy milk.	a business where things are sold
In order to sew a shirt, you need thread.	a group of fibers twisted together

B. Write a second meaning for each of the words. *Answers will vary. Possible responses are shown.*

1. crowd _to push together or press close_

2. record _to set down in writing_

3. store _to place in a location for later use_

4. thread _to pass into or through something_

C. Write two sentences for each multiple-meaning word. Use a different meaning for each sentence. *Answers will vary.*

batter _____

_____

practice_____

_____

tense _____

_____

tire _____

_____

Prepare to Read

▶ **The Fast and the Fuel-Efficient**
▶ **Teens Open Doors**

Key Vocabulary

A. How well do you know these words? Circle a rating for each word. Check your understanding of each word by marking an *X* next to the correct definition. Then complete the sentences. If you are unsure of a word's meaning, refer to the Vocabulary Glossary, page 852, in your student text.

Rating Scale

1	I have never seen this word before.
2	I am not sure of the word's meaning.
3	I know this word and can teach the word's meaning to someone else.

Key Word	Check Your Understanding	Deepen Your Understanding
1 aggressive (u-**gre**-siv) *adjective* **Rating:** 1 2 3	☐ motivated ☒ overly energetic or forceful	A situation when you would choose to be aggressive would be when *Possible response:* you are playing a sport like football .
2 assemble (u-**sem**-bul) *verb* **Rating:** 1 2 3	☒ to put together ☐ to move something	If you have wood, nails, and a hammer, you can assemble a *Possible response:* bookshelf .
3 device (di-**vīs**) *noun* **Rating:** 1 2 3	☐ a decoration ☒ a tool used for a particular job	A device that makes communication easier is _____ *Possible response:* a cell phone .
4 efficient (i-**fi**-shunt) *adjective* **Rating:** 1 2 3	☐ working at a slower speed than normal ☒ working well without wasting energy	Traveling to a distant place is more efficient when you *Possible response:* fly instead of drive .

Key Word	Check Your Understanding	Deepen Your Understanding
5 **environment** (in-**vī**-ru-munt) *noun* **Rating:** 1 2 3	[X] the things that surround you [ ] the things within each person	People can help the environment by _____ *Possible response:* recycling _____ _____ _____ .
6 **obstacle** (**ahb**-sti-kul) *noun* **Rating:** 1 2 3	[ ] something that can be used as a tool [X] something that gets in your way	An obstacle you might have when you try to get to class on time is *Possible response:* a locker you cannot open _____ _____ .
7 **solution** (su-**lū**-shun) *noun* **Rating:** 1 2 3	[X] an answer that solves a problem [ ] a way of forgiving a person	One solution to an allergy problem might be _____ *Possible response:* taking medicine _____ _____ _____ .
8 **technology** (tek-**nah**-lu-jē) *noun* **Rating:** 1 2 3	[ ] a resolution to a problem or difficulty [X] scientific knowledge as it is used in the world	Examples of modern technology that I use most often are *Possible response:* cell phones, computers _____ _____ _____ .

B. Use one of the Key Vocabulary words to describe a time when you had to solve a difficult problem. How did you solve it?

Answers will vary. _____

_____

Before Reading The Fast and the Fuel-Efficient

LITERARY ANALYSIS: Text Structure (Problem and Solution)

Some nonfiction authors use a **problem and solution** text structure. The author introduces a problem and then explains how it is solved.

A. Read the passage below. In the Sequence Chart, write the steps the students took to solve the problem.

> **Look Into the Text**
>
> A student got under the car to pop the axle in and Kinsler yanked on the suspension to create clearance. But, after many tries, it hadn't connected.
>
> Quietly, Calvin Cheeseboro . . . took over.
>
> First, the wheel-facing side popped into place. Then, with Kinsler again pulling on the suspension, the inboard side connected with the transmission with a satisfying clunk . . .
>
> The team had hopefully resolved their most difficult problem. They'd find out soon if their solution had worked.

Sequence Chart

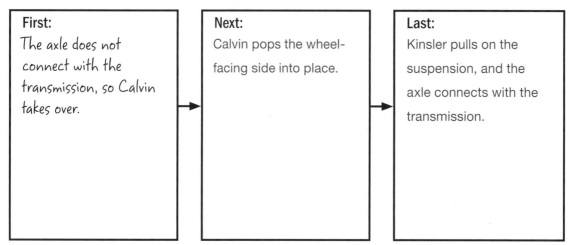

First:	Next:	Last:
The axle does not connect with the transmission, so Calvin takes over.	Calvin pops the wheel-facing side into place.	Kinsler pulls on the suspension, and the axle connects with the transmission.

B. Answer the question about the team's solution to their problem.

What was the team's problem, and how did they solve it?

The team could not connect the axle. First, Calvin took over and popped the wheel into place from the wheel-facing side. When Kinsler pulled on the transmission, the axle popped easily into place.

READING STRATEGY: Find Question-Answer Relationships

How to FIND QUESTION-ANSWER RELATIONSHIPS

1. **"Right There" or "Think and Search" Questions** These are the types of questions you can find right in the text.

2. **"Author and You" Questions** Use what you have already read to figure out an answer. Check that your answers make sense with the rest of the author's ideas.

A. Read the passage. Use the strategies above to find question-answer relationships. Then answer the questions below.

> **Look Into the Text**
>
> The ideas that come out of West Philly's auto shop aren't rocket science, Hauger says, but they do require imagination and some risk-taking—traits he thinks Detroit could use. He dreams of the high school program sharing the team's know-how of building hybrid cars cheaply. No major automaker sells a performance car that gets such outrageously high mileage. With oil prices high and demand for hybrids soaring, the timing could not be better.
>
> Developing a car model costs automakers about $1 billion. Even adding back the discounts and freebies the school team received—such as carbon-fiber body panels and custom wheels— the Attack would still have clocked in well under $100,000. Hauger estimated their two-seater, if mass-produced, could sell for about $50,000.

1. What is the auto shop trying to accomplish?

The auto shop wants to build a hybrid car that is more affordable for consumers.

2. Which of the two strategies did you use to answer question 1?

Possible response: I used the first strategy. The answer to the question was "right there" in the text.

B. Return to the passage above and underline the words or sentences that gave you the answer to the question.

Selection Review The Fast and the Fuel-Efficient

EQ **How Can Knowledge Open Doors?**
Explore how knowledge changes the world.

A. In "The Fast and the Fuel-Efficient," you learned how a group of students overcame many problems and discovered that knowledge and hard work can open doors. Write the events of the competition and the final outcome in the chart.

Goal-and-Outcome Chart

Goal: Teachers wanted to instill the values of hard work and responsibility to a group of students whose environment outside of school encouraged the opposite.

↓

Event 1:
The team had to figure out how to raise money for the competition.

Event 2:
The car's axle kept breaking, and the team had to figure out a permanent solution.

Event 3:
On the day of the competition, the weather and bad drivers made things dangerous and difficult.

↓

Outcome: The team won the competition, and the students on the team learned the value of hard work and responsibility.

B. Use the information in the chart to answer the questions.

1. How did the team's problems along the way eventually help them?

Possible response: Fixing the smaller problems only made the team's car better and the teamwork stronger. In the end, the problems helped them achieve their goal of winning the competition.

2. Explain how the students' environment was or was not an obstacle to winning the competition. Use **environment** and **obstacle** in your answer.

Possible response: For many students, their environment outside of school was an obstacle to future success because there was no one to instill the values of hard work and responsibility.

3. How might this high-school experience benefit these students in the future?

Possible response: The students have learned the value of hard work and how working together as a team can lead to success. These students will probably go on to apply what they've learned in college and in their future careers.

Teens Open Doors

by Richard Thompson

Interactive

NEWS ARTICLE

Connect Across Texts

The students in "The Fast and the Fuel-Efficient" found that the **technology** *they used could change the world. As you read this article, consider how technology can open all sorts of doors.*

Getting through high school can be challenging for any teenager. For junior Molly Rizk, who has **cerebral palsy**, one of the most difficult tasks is not taking tests at Whittier Regional Vocational Technical High School. It's opening her locker.

That should change in the fall, thanks to the skill of four classmates who have designed and produced a locker remote control. It will allow Rizk to get into her locker as quickly as other students.

Assistive Technology: Resources that help people with disabilities to become more independent.

Examples:
- wheelchairs, crutches, and other equipment
- hearing aids, text phones, and captioned TV

The wheels of the iBot wheelchair can lift a person to standing height.

The remote control took less than two months to complete. It was one of four entries last month at the University of Massachusetts-Lowell's Assistive Technology Design Fair. The fair is a noncompetitive event that gives **engineering experience** to high school students who complete projects that help people with special needs or disabilities.

Since it began in 2002, the fair has grown. Now it includes more than 100 students from a dozen schools across the country.

Key Vocabulary
- **technology** *n.*, scientific knowledge as it is used in the world

In Other Words
cerebral palsy a condition that affects the central nervous system
engineering experience experience in designing, building, and using machines

---

Interact with the Text

1. Interpret

Highlight the sentence that tells what the students in the school did for Molly. How do you think this made her feel?

Possible response: This

probably made Molly

feel good. It shows that

others care, and it will

also make opening her

locker much easier.

2. Nonfiction Text Features

Underline the exact words that someone said about the benefits of the project. How does this quotation elaborate on the ideas in the article?

The idea is that a lot

of students worked

together on the project,

and the quotation shows

that the teacher feels

many of the students are

very talented.

3. Find Question-Answer Relationships

What other school departments were involved in this project? Circle the answer in the text. Then tell which strategy you used to answer this question.

Possible response: I

used the "Right There"

strategy because the

answer was right in the

text.

For juniors Zachary Drapeau and Tom Smallwood, and seniors Casey Hansen and Nathan Lindberg, their work could make getting through college easier to afford. If they choose to **enroll** at University of Massachusetts-Lowell, each student will be able to apply for a $2,000 grant for each of the four years.

"We tried to run this like it was a real-world project that an engineering company would go through," said Paul Moskevitz, a machine technology instructor who was a **mentor** to the group.

More than a dozen students at Whittier contributed to the final product, Moskevitz said. He added that he liked how a variety of the school's programs, including carpentry, electronics, robotics, and metal fabrication were involved.

"We have lots of capabilities at this school, and it was good for folks to see the other **disciplines**," Moskevitz said.

Students must use keys to unlock their lockers at Whittier. The **device** developed by the four students lets Rizk use a remote control. It automatically slides the bolt out of the lock. They have also given her a specially designed key. It is molded to fit her grasp, in case the batteries in the remote stop working.

The remote control uses **an infrared signal**. It ensures that if more than one is used in a hallway, the signal will only be able to open the locker **programmed to the same encryption**.

Assistive Technology:
Resources that help people with disabilities to become more independent.

More examples:
- voice recognition, Braille, and other touch technology
- symbols-based computer software, switch technology, speech-generators
- prosthetic limbs

High school senior Ryan Patterson invented a glove that deaf people can wear to send messages to a screen for others to read.

Key Vocabulary
- **device** *n.,* machine or tool that is used to do a particular job

In Other Words

enroll go to school
mentor teacher and guide
disciplines types of classes and studies
an infrared signal a powerful beam of light
programmed to the same encryption that has the same code

Molly Rizk tests the new device.

4. Interpret
Why do you think the author chose to write about this project?

Possible response: I think the author wrote this article because what these students created will help many people. It is an amazing accomplishment.

"There was a lot of **trial and error** along the way," Smallwood said. "Especially trying to fit the parts together and trying to get things to work and to have everything centered so the **deadbolt** would come across and strike the plate at the right time."

In the last few weeks, the students have been in the process of **patenting** their device. David Cunningham, the school's technology chairman, said he hopes that the device could have **broader application**. It's a realistic possibility, he said, given that the setup can be easily **duplicated and maintained**.

Next year, school officials plan to "check with local **nursing homes** . . . to see if this device could be used" to help **their residents**, Cunningham said.

Mike Hart, president of the Haverhill Rotary Club, saw the remote control in action last month when the students sat in on one of his

5. Find Question-Answer Relationships
Who else do the students hope to help with their invention? Underline the answer in the text. Which strategy would help you determine how this product might help those people?

Possible response: The students hope to help the residents of local nursing homes. I could use the "Right There" strategy because I can find the answer right in the text.

In Other Words

trial and error testing new ideas and then fixing them if they didn't work
deadbolt metal bar in the lock
patenting getting ownership of
broader application many more uses

duplicated and maintained made again and taken care of
nursing homes homes for people with very serious health problems
their residents the people who live there

6. Nonfiction Text Features
Highlight Molly's words on this page. What do her words tell you about her previous experiences with people, especially her peers?

Possible response:

Molly's peers may have

ignored her in the past.

They may have showed

her that they did not

care.

group's weekly meetings. Hart said he was "very impressed." The presentation "really added a lot to the meeting . . . I was amazed at **the sophistication and the complexity of** the device," he said. "It was just beyond what you would've expected their achievements to be."

Rizk said she was moved by the commitment of her classmates. "When I first saw the actual locker, I was touched that the kids had built this for me," said Rizk. "I really appreciated that they took the time out of their busy schedules to do this for me, and I've learned that people can be very caring once you get to know them." ❖

In Other Words
the sophistication and the complexity of the professional quality and hard work that was shown in

Selection Review Teens Open Doors

A. Choose one of the questions below, and answer it by using one of the question-answer strategies. Next to your answer, write the strategy you used.

Question 1: Why did the students want to build this device for Molly?
Question 2: How will the students benefit from this project?

Possible response to question 1: The students built the device because they saw how difficult it was for Molly to use a traditional locker. I used the "Right there" strategy.

Possible response to question 2: They may get grants to help pay for college. They also get satisfaction in helping someone. I used the "On my own" strategy.

B. Answer the questions.

1. What did the quotations in the text help you understand?

Possible response: Some quotations helped me understand what the students and their instructors went through because they shared their own thoughts and words about the topic.

2. What are other challenges that Molly might face at school? What are ways that these might be solved?

Possible responses: Molly might have a difficult time getting from class to class in crowded hallways. She might have a hard time if the school has stairs. It might help if she left class early so she can go through the hallways with fewer students. The school could build a ramp for her or install an elevator.

WRITING: Write About Literature

A. Plan your writing. Think about the work that the West Philly team and the students at Whittier High School did as described in these selections. Write which project you think is more important in the center oval. Then support your choice with examples from the text in the outer ovals.

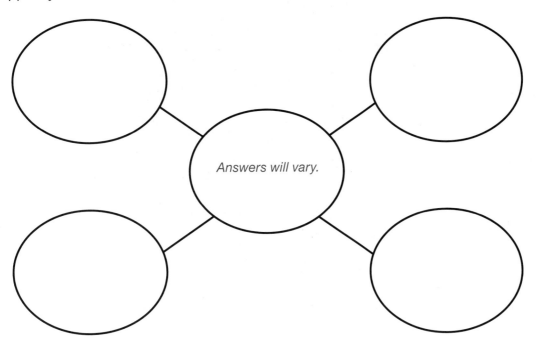

Answers will vary.

B. What is your opinion? Which group's work is more important? Write an opinion statement. Explain your opinion and support it with examples from both selections.

Students should support their answers with examples from the selections.

Integrate the Language Arts

LITERARY ANALYSIS: Text Structure (Problem and Solution)

Some nonfiction authors use a **problem and solution** text structure. The author introduces a problem and then describes how the problem is solved.

A. Write the main problem in "The Fast and the Fuel-Efficient." Then list the smaller problems that had to be solved along the way.

Main Problem	Smaller Problems
West Philadelphia High School's Electric Vehicle Team wanted to win the Tour de Sol in 2006. Winning a third time would mean scholarships and well-paying jobs for the students and badly needed funding for the school.	The car's axle broke in two. The instructors had to instill the value of hard work, responsibility, and a passion for learning in their students. The team needed money to support what they were doing.

B. Write a brief paragraph describing how the main and the smaller problems were solved in "The Fast and the Fuel-Efficient."

Possible response: The team won the Tour de Sol in 2006. Calvin Cheeseboro was able to reattach the car's welded axle. The students were excited about the work they were doing, so they worked hard and acted responsibly. Because the team won, they got the scholarship money and funding that they needed.

C. Describe a problem that the students in "Teens Open Doors" struggled with. What was their solution?

Answers will vary.

VOCABULARY STUDY: Multiple-Meaning Words

Many **multiple-meaning words** have specialized meanings in different subject areas.

A. For each word, look in a dictionary to find a specialized definition in two subject areas. Write the subject areas and the definitions below.

1. area

a region or district (Social Studies); a measurement of surface (Math)

2. difference

a significant change (Social Studies); an answer to a subtraction equation (Math)

3. formula

a solution to a problem (Math); a chemical composition (Science)

B. Brainstorm words you know that have two or more multiple meanings, and write them in the chart below. Then write two or more specialized definitions. Use a dictionary to help you, if needed. *Answers will vary.*

Word	Specialized Meanings

C. Write two sentences for each word in the chart above using each meaning. *Answers will vary.*

1. _____

_____

2. _____

_____

3. _____

_____

Key Vocabulary Review

A. Read each sentence. Circle the word that best fits into each sentence.

1. It may be your (**fate** / device) to work with children in the future.

2. The (disgusted / **ambitious**) woman worked long hours and went to night classes so she could get a promotion.

3. Without (**literacy** / technology) it is nearly impossible to get a good job.

4. You should not let other people (recall / **discourage**) you from trying new things.

5. The man chose law as a (**profession** / solution), so he could help other people.

6. The (reputation / **prodigy**) could solve complex math problems when she was five years old.

7. You may need to overcome a(n) (**obstacle** / cause) to achieve your goals.

8. She felt (**shame** / fate) after she told the teacher a lie.

B. Use your own words to write what each Key Vocabulary word means. Then write a synonym for each word. *Answers will vary. Possible responses are shown.*

Key Word	My Definition	Synonym
1. assemble	to put together	build
2. assume	to believe something is true even if you are not sure	suppose
3. cause	a belief that someone works for	goal
4. confession	telling the truth	admission
5. constant	stays the same	unchanging
6. disgusted	feeling dislike or disapproval	offended
7. efficient	making good use of something	economic
8. standard	a way of judging something	measure

Unit 4 Key Vocabulary

aggressive	• assume	• device	• environment	prodigy	shame
ambitious	cause	discourage	fate	• profession	solution
arrogant	confession	disgusted	literacy	recall	standard
• assemble	• constant	efficient	obstacle	reputation	• technology

• **Academic Vocabulary**

C. Answer the questions using complete sentences. *Answers will vary. Possible responses are shown.*

1. How does **technology** make your life easier?

Computers and cell phones allow me to communicate quickly with people.

2. Name one **solution** to a problem in your community.

We could build an animal shelter for stray animals.

3. How might an **arrogant** person treat other people?

He or she might tell other people they are inferior.

4. What happy memory do you **recall** from the past?

I remember visiting my grandparents.

5. What is your **reputation**?

I have the reputation for being kind and sensitive.

6. Describe a **device** you use every day.

I use a hair dryer in the morning to dry my hair.

7. What can you do to improve the **environment**?

I can conserve water and recycle newspapers and cans.

8. Why might **aggressive** people achieve their goals?

They might not stop until they get what they want.

Prepare to Read

▶ **The Interlopers**
▶ **An Interview with the King of Terror**

Key Vocabulary

A. How well do you know these words? Circle a rating for each word. Check your understanding of each word by circling *yes* or *no*. Then complete the sentences. If you are unsure of a word's meaning, refer to the Vocabulary Glossary, page 852, in your student text.

Rating Scale	
1	I have never seen this word before.
2	I am not sure of the word's meaning.
3	I know this word and can teach the word's meaning to someone else.

Key Word	Check Your Understanding	Deepen Your Understanding
❶ boundary (**bown**-du-rē) *noun* **Rating:** **1 2 3**	A fence is sometimes a **boundary** between two houses. **(Yes)** No	An example of a boundary is *Possible response:* a fence or a hedge _____ .
❷ feud (**fyūd**) *noun* **Rating:** **1 2 3**	Friends who have a **feud** get along well with each other. Yes **(No)**	One time I had a feud with *Possible response:* my younger sister _____ .
❸ grant (**grant**) *verb* **Rating:** **1 2 3**	Many organizations **grant** money to people who need help. **(Yes)** No	My parents grant me permission to *Possible response:* go out with my friends _____ .
❹ identification (i-den-tu-fu-**kā**-shun) *noun* **Rating:** **1 2 3**	People have trouble feeling an **identification** with others who are like them. Yes **(No)**	I feel a sense of identification with *Possible response:* the people in my family _____ .

Key Word	Check Your Understanding	Deepen Your Understanding
⑤ obvious (**ob**-vē-us) *adjective* **Rating:** 1 2 3	Solutions to problems are always **obvious.** Yes (No)	It is obvious that I *Possible response:* have brown hair _____ _____ _____ _____ .
⑥ reconciliation (re-kun-si-lē-**ā**-shun) *noun* **Rating:** 1 2 3	An argument usually comes after a **reconciliation.** Yes (No)	Once, I had a reconciliation with *Possible response:* a friend after a terrible fight _____ _____ _____ .
⑦ release (rē-**lēs**) *verb* **Rating:** 1 2 3	A careless person could accidentally **release** a bird from its cage. (Yes) No	I release stress by *Possible response:* exercising _____ _____ _____ .
⑧ terror (**ter**-rur) *noun* **Rating:** 1 2 3	News of a tornado could spread **terror** through a small town. (Yes) No	I felt great terror when *Possible response:* I watched a scary movie _____ _____ _____ .

B. Use one of the Key Vocabulary words to write about a scary experience you have had because of an unexpected situation.

Answers will vary. _____

_____

Before Reading The Interlopers

LITERARY ANALYSIS: Plot Structure

Plot structure is the pattern of events in fiction: exposition (the introduction, or the part of the story where the characters and setting are introduced), conflict, climax (the turning point), and resolution (how the story ends).

A. Read the passage below. Find the characters, setting, and plot in this introduction. Then complete the chart.

> **Look Into the Text**
>
> In a forest of mixed growth somewhere in the eastern Carpathian Mountains, a man stood one winter night. He was watching and listening, as though waiting for some beast of the woods to come within the range of his vision . . . and his rifle. But the game he sought could not be found in any sportsman's guide. Ulrich von Gradwitz searched the dark forest on the hunt for a human enemy.

Elements of Exposition	Text Clues
Characters	Ulrich von Gradwitz
Setting	a forest in the Carpathian Mountains
Plot	a man hunts for a human enemy

B. Answer the question about the exposition.

In what ways does the author create a frightening introduction?

Possible response: The author introduces a character who is alone in a dark forest. The character is waiting for

his enemy to come out of the dark.

READING STRATEGY: Make Connections

How to MAKE CONNECTIONS

1. **Pause to Ask Questions** How does the story relate to your experience?

2. **Make Connections** Connect things to your own thoughts and experiences.

3. **Add More Connections** Ask yourself how they help you understand the story.

A. Read the passage. Use the strategies above to make connections as you read. Then answer the questions below.

> **Look Into the Text**
>
> The narrow strip of woodland around the edge of the Gradwitz forest was not remarkable, but its owner guarded it more jealously than all his other possessions. Long ago, the court had granted the land to his grandfather, taking it away from the illegal possession of a neighboring family. The family who had lost the land had never agreed with the court's decision. Over time, they began poaching trips and caused scandals that started a feud between the families which had lasted for three generations.

1. How does Gradwitz, the owner, feel about his land?

   Gradwitz is jealous and possessive about his land. He feels hateful toward the neighboring

   family, even though the land is not really valuable.

2. How does relating the story to your experience help you answer the question?

   Possible response: I know how it feels to have something stolen or to be afraid that it will be. I

   also know what it is like to feel jealous.

B. Return to the passage above and circle the words and phrases that helped you to answer the first question.

Selection Review The Interlopers

EQ **What Makes Something Frightening**
Think about the power of the unexpected.

A. In "The Interlopers," you found out how two enemies reconciled because of an unexpected natural event. Complete the Plot Diagram by describing the conflict, the climax, and the resolution.

Plot Diagram

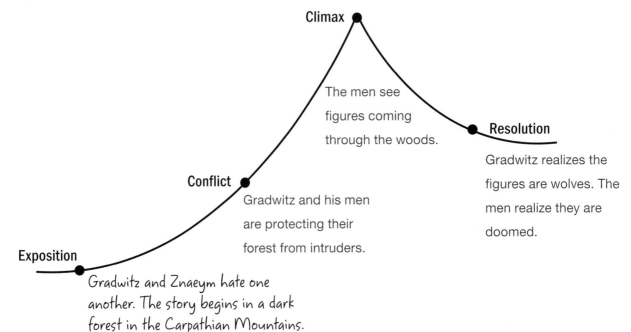

Climax

The men see figures coming through the woods.

Resolution

Gradwitz realizes the figures are wolves. The men realize they are doomed.

Conflict

Gradwitz and his men are protecting their forest from intruders.

Exposition

Gradwitz and Znaeym hate one another. The story begins in a dark forest in the Carpathian Mountains.

B. Use the information in the Plot Diagram to answer the questions.

1. What is the climax of the story? Why is it the most important event?

Figures are rushing toward the trapped men. This is the most important event because the men think it

means rescue, but it doesn't.

2. In what way is terror an important part of the plot of the story?
Use **terror** in your answer.

Possible response: The climax and the resolution build suspense because the men feel terror

when they realize the figures coming toward them are wolves.

3. Do you think the story would be more or less frightening if the author had described what happens to the men after the wolves reach them? Why?

Possible response: I think the story would be less frightening because the unknown, or what I imagine, is

always more frightening.

An Interview with the King of Terror

by Bryon Cahill

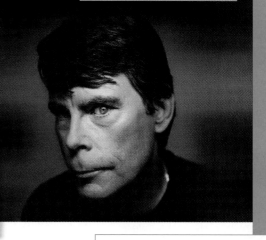

Connect Across Texts

In "The Interlopers," two enemies come face to face with the unexpected. As you read this interview, think about how writers can use the unexpected to reach our greatest fears.

Stephen King is one of the world's most famous horror writers. Over his career he has sold more than 80 million copies of his spine-tingling books, and the movies based on his stories chill audiences in their seats. His subjects range from the outright **terror** of *Carrie* and *The Shining* to the mysteries of the **supernatural** in *The Dead Zone* and *The Green Mile*. The "King of Terror" has said, "I am Halloween's answer to Santa Claus." What makes him so popular?

Q: What makes a scary story really scary?

A: I don't know. That's a really tough question. That's like asking someone: "What makes a funny story really funny?" Scary things are personal. People come up to me sometimes and say, "You know I really love that book *IT* because I was always terrified of clowns." But other people come up to me and say, "Why would you say such mean things about clowns? I'm married to a guy who's a clown. Children love [them]! It's so mean to say that about clowns." When I was a kid, clowns just scared me and I've seen other kids cry about clowns and to me there's something scary, something **sinister** about such a figure of happiness and fun being evil. **Lon Chaney** once said,

Key Vocabulary
terror *n.*, feeling of great fear

In Other Words
supernatural things that are not part of this world, like unusual powers and abilities
sinister threatening and evil
Lon Chaney An actor who starred in many classic horror movies

Interact with the Text

1. Analogy
Highlight the author's analogy. Why did he make this analogy? What does it mean?

Possible response: He wants to describe the way he is viewed by his readers. It means that he is the best writer of the scary and spooky genre.

2. Make Connections
Circle the two different views of clowns that King mentions. Which view is most like your own? Explain.

Possible response: The first view is like mine. I like clowns. I think clowns are funny and entertaining to watch.

3. Make Connections

Underline what King believes makes something scary. Describe something you have seen or know from personal experience that supports King's belief.

Possible response:

King's description reminds me of my brother. He looks sweet, but he is actually a little monster.

4. Interpret

Highlight King's main point on this page. In your own words, summarize what King means by this statement.

Possible response:

Things that are different or unknown are scary because we don't know if they will be harmful or not.

"Nobody laughs at a clown at midnight." So I guess that sometimes what makes a scary thing scary is that when we realize <u>there's something sinister behind a nice face.</u>

I think things are scarier when there's some sensory deprivation, when we take away our ability to sense things, when we take away escape—that makes things scary. <mark>We're afraid of things that are different than we are.</mark> A lot of times what somebody does when they're writing scary stories is they're giving us permission to **be politically incorrect**, to say, "It's all right to be afraid of things that are different than you are." And people will say, "You have to be nice to people that are different than you are." And we understand that that's true and we try to do it but **nevertheless**, there's always that little bit of fear that says, "Maybe they're going to eat us up." And the person who writes a scary story says that it's all right to feel that way because you have to find a place to get rid of that.

Friendly or scary? The clown from the movie *IT* may change your mind.

Q: What, if anything, scares you?

A: Well clowns **freak me out** and scare me. I think that any kind of situation that I'm trapped in, certainly

In Other Words
be politically incorrect say or do things that might insult other people
nevertheless even though we know it's wrong
freak me out terrify me

claustrophobia or turbulence at 40,000 feet, freaks me out a lot. I hate that. Any kind of a situation where I'm not in control and somebody else is. Those things freak me out.

Q: Would you like to talk about building suspense in a book?

A: The most important thing about building suspense is building **identification** with character. You have to take some time and make your reader care about the characters in the story. There's a difference between horror and terror. You can go to a movie and you can be horrified because you don't know what terrible things are going to happen or who's going to get their head chopped off and that's horrible. But you don't necessarily know any of those people. They're very **two-dimensional**.

But if you take somebody and you put them in a situation . . . and <u>little by little you get to know this guy and you get to understand him a little bit and you get to see different **aspects** of him and you start to feel for him . . . this person. Then you start to **empathize with** him and you start to put yourself in his shoes and then you start to be very, very afraid because you don't want anything to happen to him.</u> It isn't a question anymore of *when* will something happen to him. It's a question that you're saying, "I don't want anything to happen." But because it's the kind of story that it is, you know that something **is gonna**, so one by one you close off the exits and things get more and more nerve wracking until finally there's an explosion. You know that's going to

> There's a difference between horror and **terror.**

Key Vocabulary
identification *n.*, feeling that you know and understand someone else's experiences and feelings

In Other Words
claustrophobia or turbulence feeling trapped on a small, bumpy plane ride
two-dimensional unrealistic
aspects sides
empathize with care about and understand
is gonna is going to happen

5. Make Connections
Underline King's statement about identifying with characters. What connection can you make to this statement that helps you understand what he means?

Possible response: I know what it feels like to care for people I know, so that must be similar to caring about the characters in a scary movie or book.

happen. The other thing is that there's a **format to** these stories where we all understand that things are going to build up to some kind of climax. And that adds to the suspense.

Q: What is the most important element of storytelling to you?

A: They all have their part to play but for me the most important thing is I want the reader to turn the page. So I would say that it's **an almost intangible thing that adds up to readability**. That makes somebody want to sit down and read the story that you wrote. It's a kind of modesty almost where you say to yourself this is not about me, this is about the person who reads my stories. It's not **psychoanalysis**, it's not about showing off (although it always is, we know that). You just hope that it goes out to somebody who's going to connect with what you said. And that you're going to tell them the story that makes them want to continue to read. Different writers feel different ways about this. I want to make a connection with them that's emotional. I want them to read the story and I want to make them sweat a little bit, laugh, and cry. I'm less interested in their thought processes than I am **their lower emotion**.

> I want the reader to **turn the page.**

Q: You once said, "I am the literary equivalent of a Big Mac and fries."

A: Yeah, and I'm still paying for that. What I meant by that is I'm tasty. I go down smooth. And I don't think that a steady diet of Stephen King

In Other Words

format to set pattern for
an almost intangible thing that adds up to readability something about a good story that is hard to describe
psychoanalysis figuring out how the mind works

their lower emotion in how they feel
the literary equivalent of a writer who is like

would make anybody a healthy human being. I think that you **oughtta** eat your vegetables, and you oughtta find other things, you oughtta **find some Dickens, some Ian McEwan**... you oughtta range widely and read all kinds of different stuff. You shouldn't just settle on one thing. I'd feel the same way about people that said they didn't read anything but *Harry Potter*. I'd say, "There's something wrong with you, buddy." If you're gonna read fiction, read all kinds of things and challenge yourself, read some stuff that's really tough.

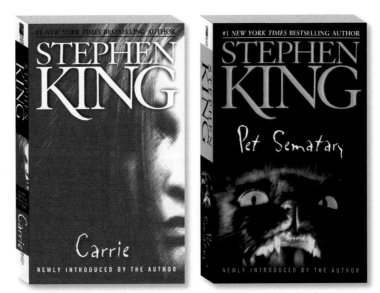

Many of King's books have been made into movies and TV shows.

Q: If you were a teacher, what is the most important lesson you would impart to your students? What writing advice do you have for our readers?

A: As writers, I'd say write every day. If you want to write and you want to write well, do it a lot. Practice it. The same way that you would anything else that you want to do all the time. Baseball players know about it, trombone players know about it, swimmers know about it. Use it or lose it. Get better. Work at it. Feel comfortable with it. Feel comfortable with sentences, feel comfortable with paragraphs until those things just roll off your fingertips. And the better you feel about it, the better it's going to go for you.

In Other Words
oughtta should (slang)
find some Dickens, some Ian McEwan read a mix of classics and good modern books
Harry Potter popular books for young people
impart teach, share with

8. Interpret

Underline the words and phrases on page 179 that describe King's view on reading fiction. Do you agree or disagree with King?

Possible response: I

agree with King that it is

important to challenge

yourself by reading a

variety of authors and

to read fiction that is

difficult, too.

Q: After you were hit by a van in '99, rumors were circulating that you would never write again. If that tragedy couldn't stop you, do you think you'll ever retire?

A: Sure, I'll die. Or I'll get a horrible disease, or something. You see, I'm a horror writer, I can think of all sorts of nasty reasons to stop. ❖

In Other Words
rumors were circulating people were saying
retire stop writing as your job

Selection Review An Interview with the King of Terror

A. In this interview, King says he turns nice things, like clowns, sinister. What connection can you make to this statement and how is this useful to you in understanding the text?

Possible response: It is scarier when nice things become frightening, like clowns. The statement makes me think about how true it is that we are often frightened by things we don't expect.

B. Answer the questions.

1. Why do you think King uses analogies to discuss the process of writing about terror?

Possible response: It seemed hard for King to describe how to write scary stories. King often compared scary stories to other things so he could explain his writing process.

2. What are three strategies King uses to write his stories? Give specific examples from the interview.

King creates characters that readers like. He takes away control and the ability to sense things. He brings in something the character is afraid of; something different from him or her.

Reflect and Assess

WRITING: Write About Literature

A. Plan your writing. Read the story starter in your student text on page 415. Complete the Plot Diagram with details about a scary story that you can write that begins with the story starter.

Plot Diagram

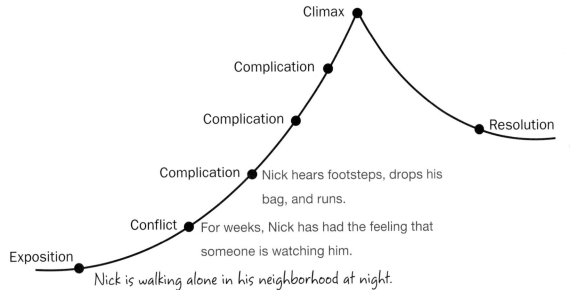

Climax

Complication

Complication

Resolution

Complication ● Nick hears footsteps, drops his bag, and runs.

Conflict ● For weeks, Nick has had the feeling that someone is watching him.

Exposition

Nick is walking alone in his neighborhood at night.

B. Now write your own tale of terror. Use the ideas you listed in the Plot Diagram to tell your story.

Students' stories should include ideas from their Plot Diagrams.

_____

_____

_____

_____

_____

_____

_____

_____

_____

LITERARY ANALYSIS: Analyze Irony

Verbal irony contrasts what a character says with what he or she really means. **Situational irony** contrasts what we expect to happen with what really happens.

A. Read the examples from "The Interlopers" that show how Saki uses verbal irony. Then explain how the underlined dialogue is ironic.

Examples of Verbal Irony	How the Dialogue is Ironic
"Trapped. What a joke! Ulrich von Gradwitz trapped in his stolen forest. That's justice for you."	He says "justice," but really means that it's not fair.
"What a useful idea," said Ulrich fiercely. "My men have orders to follow me. When they get me out, I will remember your idea."	He means, "I will make sure that you are crushed by the tree instead of me."

B. Find examples from "The Interlopers" that show how Saki uses situational irony. Then explain how each situation is ironic.

Examples of Situational Irony	How the Situation is Ironic
"He was watching and listening, as though waiting for some beast of the woods to come within the range of his vision."	The wolves are the beasts watching and listening.
"Ulrich and his men were on the lookout— not for four-footed game, but for thieves prowling across the boundary."	Ulrich should have been on the lookout for wild animals.
Ulrich asks Georg to bury the old quarrel and be his friend.	The two men finally become friends before they are eaten by wolves.

C. Write about a TV show or film you have seen that used verbal or situational irony. Explain why you think the writer or director used it.

Answers will vary.

_____

_____

VOCABULARY STUDY: Synonyms

Synonyms are related words that have the same, or nearly the same, meaning. Knowing the exact meaning of a synonym helps you use words more precisely. *Answers will vary.*

A. Use a dictionary to find the meanings of these synonyms for the word *fear.* Write the definition in your own words in the chart below. Then rank the words from 1 (most intense) to 4 (least intense).

Synonyms	Meaning	Rank
dread		
fright		
panic		
terror		

B. Use a thesaurus to find synonyms for the words in the chart.

Word	Synonyms
answer	
drink	
gloomy	
misfortune	
silent	

C. Write sentences using the synonyms you listed in the chart above. Make sure the synonym you choose fits the precise meaning of your sentence.

answer _____

drink _____

gloomy _____

misfortune _____

silent _____

Prepare to Read

▶ **The Baby-Sitter**
▶ **Beware: Do Not Read This Poem**

Key Vocabulary

A. How well do you know these words? Circle a rating for each word. Check your understanding of each word by marking an *X* next to the correct definition. Then complete the sentences. If you are unsure of a word's meaning, refer to the Vocabulary Glossary, page 852, in your student text.

Rating Scale	
1	I have never seen this word before.
2	I am not sure of the word's meaning.
3	I know this word and can teach the word's meaning to someone else.

Key Word	Check Your Understanding	Deepen Your Understanding
1 capable (**kā**-pu-bul) *adjective* **Rating:** 1 2 3	☒ able to do something ☐ easily influenced	If I work hard, I am capable of *Possible response:* running a marathon
2 precision (pri-**si**-zhun) *noun* **Rating:** 1 2 3	☐ confusion or error ☒ exactness or accuracy	One thing I do with precision is *Possible response:* keep track of how much money I spend
3 rely (ri-**lī**) *verb* **Rating:** 1 2 3	☐ to complete something ☒ to depend on something	One person I rely on for help is *Possible response:* my mom
4 resist (ri-**zist**) *verb* **Rating:** 1 2 3	☒ to fight against something ☐ to focus on something	It is hard for me to resist *Possible response:* chocolate

Key Word	Check Your Understanding	Deepen Your Understanding
5 **ritual** (**ri**-chu-wul) *noun* **Rating:** 1 2 3	[X] a formal way of doing something [ ] the wrong way to do something	My morning ritual is *Possible response:* waking up and taking a shower, then making breakfast _____ _____ _____ .
6 **subside** (sub-**sīd**) *verb* **Rating:** 1 2 3	[ ] interpret [X] to become less strong	To make my anger subside, I *Possible response:* exercise _____ _____ _____ _____ .
7 **trace** (**trās**) *noun* **Rating:** 1 2 3	[ ] a tool that helps a person to do their job [X] a small sign or evidence	If you are at a campsite, you might find a trace of _____ *Possible response:* a campfire _____ _____ _____ .
8 **vulnerable** (**vul**-nu-ru-bul) *adjective* **Rating:** 1 2 3	[X] helpless or easily hurt [ ] tired and lazy	People are vulnerable when *Possible response:* they walk alone at night _____ _____ _____ _____ .

B. Use one of the Key Vocabulary words to write about a fear you have overcome.

Answers will vary. _____

_____

Before Reading The Baby-Sitter

LITERARY ANALYSIS: Mood and Tone

Mood is the feeling of a story. Sometimes, the mood of a story will change.
Tone is how the author feels about the subject, the characters, or you,
the reader.

A. Read the passage below. Find details that create a mood and reveal the
author's tone. Write the details in the T Chart below.

> **Look Into the Text**
>
> Hilary hated baby-sitting at the Mitchells' house, though she
> loved the Mitchell twins. The house was one of those old, creaky
> Victorian horrors, with a dozen rooms and two sets of stairs . . .
>
> There was a long, dark hallway upstairs, and the twins slept
> at the end of it. Each time Hilary checked on them, she felt as if
> there were things watching her from behind the closed doors of
> the other rooms or from the walls. She couldn't say what exactly,
> just *things*.

T Chart

Mood	Tone
The Mitchells' house is an old, creaky, Victorian horror.	Hilary hates babysitting at the Mitchells' house.
The house has long, dark hallways.	When Hilary goes down the hallway to check the twins, she can't describe why she feels odd.
Hilary feels like things are watching her in the dark hallways.	The closed doors and walls make Hilary feel afraid.

B. Use the information in the T Chart to complete the sentence.

The author's tone creates a mood of *Possible response:* horror and fear. The reader feels afraid

because of the description of the house and the author's serious tone   .

READING STRATEGY: Make Connections

HOW TO MAKE CONNECTIONS

1. **Read aloud** with a partner.

2. **Pause** to make connections to the text.

3. **Talk** with your partner about your connections.

4. **Discuss and evaluate** whether or not your connections help you understand the story.

A. Read the passage. Use the strategies above to make connections as you read. Answer the questions below.

Look Into the Text

After she smoothed the covers over the sleeping boys, Hilary always drew in a deep breath before heading down the long, uncarpeted hall. It didn't matter which stairs she headed for, there was always a (strange echo) as she walked along, each (footstep articulated with precision,) and then a slight (tap-tapping) afterward. She never failed to turn around after the first few steps. (She never saw anything behind her.)

1. Why does Hilary feel nervous?

   Hilary hears strange sounds as she walks down the hall. Her footsteps make strange sounds. She feels

   like someone or something is following her.

2. What connections did you make when you read about Hilary walking through the hallway?

   Possible response: I have been in someone's dark house, and it is scary because you don't know

   another's house as well as your own. The sound of creaking floors scares me when I am alone.

B. Return to the passage above and circle the words or phrases that gave you the answer to the first question.

What Makes Something Frightening?
Explore how fears can become reality.

A. In "The Baby-Sitter," you found out how Hilary's fears about the Mitchells' old house become reality. Complete the Sequence Chart with the events of the story.

Sequence Chart

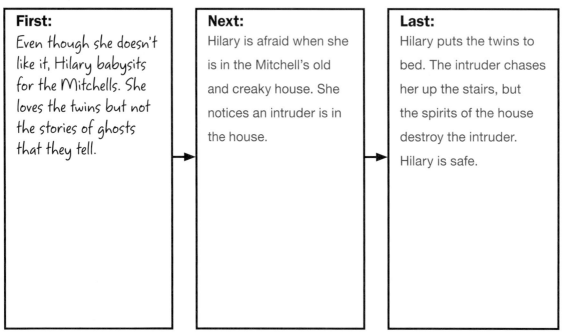

First:	**Next:**	**Last:**
Even though she doesn't like it, Hilary babysits for the Mitchells. She loves the twins but not the stories of ghosts that they tell.	Hilary is afraid when she is in the Mitchell's old and creaky house. She notices an intruder is in the house.	Hilary puts the twins to bed. The intruder chases her up the stairs, but the spirits of the house destroy the intruder. Hilary is safe.

B. Use the information in the Sequence Chart to answer the questions.

1. How does the mood of the story change by the end?

Possible response: The mood changes from terrifying to one of relief.

2. Why do the man's screams subside? Use **subside** in your answer.

Possible response: Hilary notices the intruder's screams subside because the spirits or ghosts from inside the house destroy him somehow.

3. How might Hilary feel about babysitting at the Mitchell house in the future?

Possible response: She may still feel strange or a bit scared, but I think she will also feel that the spirits will protect her and the boys.

Connect Across Texts

In "The Baby-Sitter," some of Hilary's deepest fears come to life. As you read this poem, consider how poetry has the power to bring our fears to life.

BEWARE:
Do Not Read This Poem
by Ishmael Reed

tonite, *thriller* was
abt an ol woman, so <u>vain</u> she
<u>surrounded her self w/</u>
<u>many mirrors</u>

5   It got so bad that finally she
<u>locked herself indoors</u> & her
whole life became the
        mirrors
one day the villagers broke

10 into her house, but she was too
swift for them. <u>she disappeared</u>
        <u>into a mirror</u>
each tenant who bought the house
after that, lost a loved one to
15   the ol woman in the mirror:
        first a little girl
        then a young woman
        then the young woman/s husband
the hunger of this poem is legendary

20 it has taken in many victims

In Other Words

thriller the spooky TV show
vain pleased with herself, focused on her looks
swift quick
tenant person living there
legendary so famous, well-known

Interact with the Text

1. Repetition and Word Choice

Underline the words that tell you about the woman. What mood does the poet's word choice create?

Possible response: The poet creates a disturbing mood. It is disturbing because it seems like the woman is crazy or obsessed.

2. Make Connections

Circle a phrase that tells how the woman affects people in the house. What connections can you make to this part of the poem?

Possible response:

I have seen a movie where people who move into a scary house are never seen again.

3. Interpret

List words and phrases that describe the image. Then explain how this image adds to the poem's mood.

Possible response:

a hand reaching out

shattered glass

desperate

alone

The image creates

a frightening mood

because it makes me

think the hand belongs

to the old woman

reaching out to take

another life.

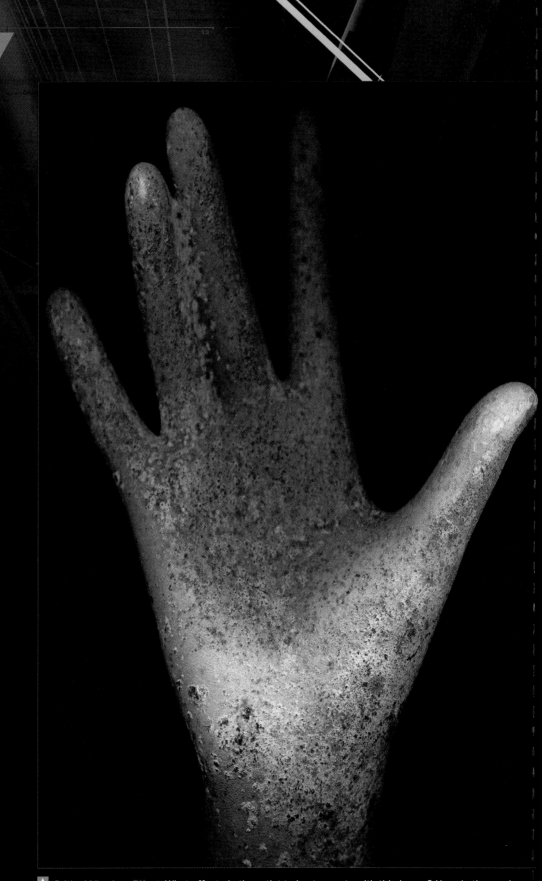

▲ Critical Viewing: Effect What effects is the artist trying to create with this image? How do they make you feel? Explain your response.

back off from this poem
it has drawn in yr feet
back off from this poem
it has drawn in yr legs
25 back off from this poem
it is a greedy mirror
you are into this poem. from
   the waist down
nobody can hear you can they?
30 this poem has had you up to here
     belch
this poem aint got no manners
you cant call out frm this poem
relax now & go w/ this poem
35 move & roll on to this poem

    do not resist this poem
    this poem has yr eyes
    this poem has his head
    this poem has his arms
40   this poem has his fingers
    this poem has his fingertips

(this poem is the reader & the
   reader this poem)

  statistic: the us bureau of missing persons reports

45   that in 1968 over 100,000 people disappeared
    leaving no solid clues
      nor trace   only
  a space   in the lives of their friends

Key Vocabulary
resist *v.*, to fight against
• **trace** *n.*, small sign that something or someone was in a place

In Other Words
belch burp
us bureau of missing persons government agency that looks for people who have disappeared
no solid clues no evidence that would tell people where they were

4. Interpret
Circle the metaphor that explains the relationship between the reader and the poem. What is the poem capable of doing? Use the word **capable** in your response.

Possible response: The poem is capable of coming to life and taking the reader.

5. Interpret
Highlight the phrases that include facts. Why does the poet use this statistic? What effect does this have?

Possible response: The poet wants me to know that people go missing every day and that this is very common. It is a very disturbing thought.

Selection Review Beware: Do Not Read This Poem

A. In the chart, list the lines of the poem you made connections to. Then tell how your connections helped you understand the poem.

Lines from the Poem	My Connection	My Understanding
"she disappeared / into a mirror"	I once read about a girl who entered another world through a wardrobe.	The connection reminds me to use my imagination to find meaning.
Possible response: "it has taken in many victims"	*Possible response:* Victims makes me think of criminals.	*Possible response:* I understand this poem is about danger.
Possible response: "nobody can hear you can they?"	*Possible response:* I feel as if I'm in a horror movie and a monster is getting close.	*Possible response:* The poet wants me to feel really scared.
Possible response: "over 100,000 people disappeared"	*Possible response:* I hear reports on the news about people who are missing.	*Possible response:* I know this statistic is true. This makes the poem even scarier.
Possible response: "leaving no solid clues/nor trace"	*Possible response:* I have seen TV shows about people who disappear.	*Possible response:* I understand that this should scare me like a horror story does.

B. Answer the questions.

1. How did the poet's words, repetition, or syntax help create the mood of the poem?

   Possible response: Words like *back off* and then *relax now & go w/ this poem* make me question which side the poet is on. It creates a very frightening mood.

2. How might this poem bring people's fears to life?

   Possible response: This poem creates the ideas that a house can take a person's life and that a person can disappear. This is scary, especially to someone living in an old house.

Reflect and Assess

WRITING: Write About Literature

A. Plan your writing. Read the opposing opinions. Put an *X* next to the opinion you agree with. Then list examples from each text to support it. *Answers will vary.*

☐ **Opinion 1:** Scenes that are shown are the most frightening.

☐ **Opinion 2:** Scenes that rely on the reader's imagination are the most frightening.

Selection	Events That Are Shown	Events That Aren't Shown
"The Baby-Sitter"		
"Beware: Do Not Read This Poem"		

B. Which events are more frightening—scenes that are shown, or scenes that rely on the reader's imagination? Write an opinion statement. Remember to use the text evidence you listed in the chart to support your statement.

Students should support their answers with examples from the selections.

_____

_____

_____

_____

LITERARY ANALYSIS: Analyze Foreshadowing

Authors use **foreshadowing** when they give hints or clues about events that will happen later in the story.

A. Jane Yolen foreshadows events in "The Baby-Sitter" by giving clues. Write one clue for each of these events.

Event	Clue
the attack by "Them"	The boys tell Hilary about the spell and about "Them."
The intruder gets in the house.	Cookies are missing.

B. Read each clue below from "The Baby-Sitter." Write what the clue foreshadows.

Clue	What the Clue Foreshadows
Hilary feels as if there are things watching her.	There are spirits or powers in the house, and they attack the intruder.
Hilary is a stubborn girl.	She would continue to babysit despite her fear.
She counts what cookies remain—there are thirteen.	Several cookies would mysteriously disappear.
The twins have a ritual their grandma taught them.	The ritual saves their lives.

C. Choose one detail from "Beware: Do Not Read This Poem," and write a brief paragraph explaining how it foreshadows later events.

Answers will vary.

_____

_____

_____

VOCABULARY STUDY: Thesaurus

A **thesaurus** lists words with their synonyms and antonyms. Using a thesaurus helps writers avoid repeating the same words.

A. Use a thesaurus and write two synonyms for each word. *Possible responses are shown.*

creaky _____ squeaky, rusty _____

imagine _____ picture, visualize _____

ritual _____ custom, ceremony _____

strange _____ odd, bizarre _____

stubborn _____ difficult, hard-headed _____

B. Complete the chart below by writing one synonym and one antonym for each word. *Answers will vary. Possible responses are shown.*

Word	Synonym	Antonym
disappeared	missing	discovered
legendary	famous	unknown
nuzzle	snuggle	push away
rapidly	quickly	slowly
screaming	screeching	whispering

C. Write sentences using either the synonym or antonym for the words in the chart above. *Answers will vary.*

1. _____

   _____

2. _____

   _____

3. _____

   _____

4. _____

   _____

5. _____

   _____

Unit 5
Pages 446–469

Prepare to Read

▶ **The Tell-Tale Heart**
▶ **The Raven**

Key Vocabulary

A. How well do you know these words? Circle a rating for each word. Check your understanding of each word by circling the synonym. Then write a definition. If you are unsure of a word's meaning, refer to the Vocabulary Glossary, page 852, in your student text.

Rating Scale	
1	I have never seen this word before.
2	I am not sure of the word's meaning.
3	I know this word and can teach the word's meaning to someone else.

Key Word	Check Your Understanding	Deepen Your Understanding
❶ burden (**bur**-din) *noun* **Rating:** 1 2 3	A **burden** is a _____. (**load**) secret	My definition: *Answers will vary.*
❷ cease (**sēs**) *verb* **Rating:** 1 2 3	To **cease** making noise is to _____ making noise. start (**stop**)	My definition: *Answers will vary.*
❸ dread (**dred**) *noun* **Rating:** 1 2 3	If you feel **dread,** you feel _____. funny (**fear**)	My definition: *Answers will vary.*
❹ ominous (**ah**-mu-nus) *adjective* **Rating:** 1 2 3	An **ominous** sky is a _____ sky. (**dangerous**) clear	My definition: *Answers will vary.*

Key Word	Check Your Understanding	Deepen Your Understanding
5 ponder (**pon**-dur) *verb* **Rating:** 1 2 3	To **ponder** carefully is to _____ carefully. speak (think)	My definition: *Answers will vary.* _____ _____ _____ _____
6 prophet (**pro**-fut) *noun* **Rating:** 1 2 3	A **prophet** is a person who is a _____. poet (predictor)	My definition: *Answers will vary.* _____ _____ _____ _____
7 relevance (**re**-lu-vents) *noun* **Rating:** 1 2 3	When something has **relevance**, it has _____. (importance) insignificance	My definition: *Answers will vary.* _____ _____ _____ _____
8 suspect (su-**spekt**) *verb* **Rating:** 1 2 3	To **suspect** something means to _____ it. know (suppose)	My definition: *Answers will vary.* _____ _____ _____ _____

B. Use one of the Key Vocabulary words to write about a time you or someone else imagined something that frightened you.

Answers will vary.

_____

Before Reading The Tell-Tale Heart

LITERARY ANALYSIS: Suspense

Writers often build **suspense** in their stories to keep readers interested.
Techniques include raising questions, slowing down or speeding up the
action, putting characters in dangerous situations, hinting that the narrator
is not trustworthy, and giving clues about things that may happen later.

A. Read the passage below. Find examples that the narrator is not
trustworthy, and list them in the chart. Then explain how each example
makes you feel.

Look Into the Text

> True! I had been and still am very nervous—very, very
> dreadfully nervous. But why *will* you say that I am mad? The
> disease had made my senses sharper. It had not destroyed or
> dulled them. Above all, my sense of hearing was sharp. I heard all
> things in the heaven and in the earth. How, then, can you say I
> am mad? Listen! You shall see how healthy and calm I am as I tell
> you the whole story.

Example	My Feelings
The narrator is very nervous.	This makes me feel worried. What bad thing does the narrator think will happen?
Other people think the narrator is mad, or crazy.	*Possible response:* This makes me a little suspicious of the narrator. Can he really be trusted? Maybe he is crazy.
The narrator explains that he can hear unbelievably well.	*Possible response:* The narrator might be put into a dangerous situation where he might have to hear something.
The narrator is determined to prove that he is not crazy.	*Possible response:* This makes me wonder if he really is crazy, because he's denying it too much.

B. Complete the sentence.

This text was suspenseful because   *Possible response:* I am very suspicious of this narrator. He is trying
  too hard to prove he is not crazy. I want to read more about the danger he has put himself in.   .

READING STRATEGY: Make Connections

HOW TO MAKE CONNECTIONS

1. **Look** for words, phrases, and ideas that are important to understanding the story.

2. **Make a connection** between these ideas and your own life, other texts, and the world.

3. **Explain** how these connections help you to understand the text.

A. Read the passage. Use the strategies above to make connections as you read. Then answer the questions below.

Look Into the Text

> I smiled—for what did I have to fear? I greeted the officers warmly. The scream, I said, was my own. I had had a bad dream. The old man, I said, was on vacation in the country. I took my visitors all over the house. I told them to search—search *well*. Finally, I took them to his room. I showed them his belongings, safe and undisturbed. Feeling very confident, I even brought chairs into the room. I told the officers to rest for a while. Quite sure of myself, I even put my own chair right over the old man's body.

1. How does this text compare to things you may have seen in movies, television, or read in other books?

   Possible response: The narrator has either committed a crime or is covering up a crime. Many of the

   criminals in TV shows act this confident because they believe they will not be caught.

2. What does making this connection help you understand about the narrator's actions?

   Possible response: I think the narrator is crazy because he knows where the man's body is, but he won't

   tell the police.

B. Return to the passage above and circle the words, phrases, or ideas that describe what the narrator does to convince the officers that he is innocent.

Selection Review The Tell-Tale Heart

EQ **What Makes Something Frightening?**
Consider the role of imagination.

A. In "The Tell-Tale Heart," you learned how a writer can use suspense to make a story frightening. Complete the chart below with examples of each technique the author uses and the effect each example had on you as you read.

Technique	Example	Effect
Raising questions	The narrator questions why others think he is mad.	I knew there must be a reason why others thought he was crazy.
Slowing down or speeding up the action	The narrator waits patiently to kill the old man. He repeats his actions every night.	I knew that something really bad was going to happen. This built the suspense.
Putting characters in dangerous situations	The old man is being watched by the narrator every night.	I knew that eventually the old man would be murdered.
Hinting that the narrator is not reliable	The narrator keeps saying that he is not crazy.	I believed that the narrator was crazy, especially as I read about his actions.
Giving clues about things that may happen later	The author uses a vulture to describe the man's eye.	I know that this bird often symbolizes death. This was a clue that someone was going to die.

B. Use the information in the chart to answer the questions.

1. Which technique worked best to make this story suspenseful? Why?

Possible response: Hinting that the narrator is not trustworthy or reliable worked best. I questioned what

the narrator was saying and thinking, which left me wondering what would happen next.

2. Why does the narrator believe the officers suspect him? Use **suspect** in your answer.

Possible response: The narrator believes the officers suspect him because he believes they are making fun

of him.

3. Imagine that the police officers suspect the narrator. How might the ending be different?

Possible response: The narrator may not have confessed because he would have focused more on

avoiding capture and less on what he thought he heard.

Connect Across Texts

In "The Tell-Tale Heart," Edgar Allan Poe brings readers into the narrator's twisted imagination. As you read this classic poem by Poe, consider the role of the imagination on our deepest fears.

The Raven
by Edgar Allan Poe

Once upon a midnight dreary, while I pondered, weak and weary,
Over many an old and curious book filled with forgotten lore—
While I sat there, nearly napping, suddenly there came a tapping,
As of someone gently rapping, rapping at my bedroom door.
5 "It is some visitor," I muttered, "tapping at my bedroom door—
                Only this, and nothing more."

Ah, clearly I remember it was in cold and dark December,
And each separate dying ember formed a ghost upon the floor.
Eagerly I wished for tomorrow—I had tried but failed to borrow
10 Help from books to cease my sorrow—sorrow for the lost Lenore—
For the rare and beautiful maiden whom the angels name Lenore—
                Nameless here for evermore.

Key Vocabulary
ponder v., to think carefully about
● **cease** v., to stop

In Other Words
dreary that was gloomy, dark, and sad
forgotten lore knowledge that was taught long ago
rapping knocking
ember glowing coal
for evermore forever

Interact with the Text

1. Imagery and Repetition
Highlight words and phrases that help to create a picture in your mind. Describe the picture.

Possible response: I picture a lonely and sad person in a dark, depressing room.

2. Make Connections
Why do you think the poet repeats the name Lenore?

Possible response: I think the poet is grieving for Lenore. People who are sad sometimes repeat things to show their grief.

3. Interpret

What is the speaker trying to convince himself of in the first stanza? Underline the phrase that helps you figure out the answer.

The speaker is afraid and is trying to convince himself that the noise is a visitor at his door.

4. Imagery and Repetition

Circle the words or phrases in lines 25–35 that create pictures in your mind. Describe the image the poet is creating.

Possible response: The poet wants the reader to feel desperate and alone like the speaker in the poem.

And the silken, sad, uncertain rustling of each purple curtain
Thrilled me—filled me with fantastic terrors never felt before;
15 So that now, to still the beating of my heart, I stood repeating,
"It's some visitor entreating entrance at my bedroom door—
Some late visitor entreating entrance at my bedroom door—
            That is it and nothing more.

Very soon my soul grew stronger; hesitating then no longer,
20 "Sir," said I, "or Madam, truly your forgiveness I ask for;
The fact is that I was napping, and so gently you came rapping,
And so faintly you came tapping, tapping at my bedroom door,
That I was not sure I heard you." Then I opened wide the door—
            Darkness there and nothing more.

25 Deep into that darkness peering, long I stood there wondering, fearing,
Doubting, dreaming dreams no man had ever dared to dream before;
But the silence was unbroken, and the stillness gave no token,
And the only word there spoken was the whispered word, "Lenore!"
This I whispered, and an echo murmured back the word "Lenore!"
30   Only this and nothing more.

Back into the bedroom turning, all my soul within me burning,
Soon again I heard a tapping somewhat louder than before.
"Surely," I said, "surely that is something at my glass pane;
Let me see, then, what could be there, and this mystery explore—
35 Let my heart be still a moment and this mystery explore—
            It is the wind and nothing more!"

In Other Words
entreating asking for
hesitating pausing, waiting
peering looking and searching
token hint of what was out there

Open wide I flung the shutter, when, with many a flit and flutter,
In there stepped a noble Raven from the ancient days of yore.
Not the smallest greeting made he; not a minute stopped or stayed he;
40 But, with look of lord or lady, perched above my bedroom door—
Perched upon a bust of Pallas just above my bedroom door—
                 Perched, and sat, and nothing more.

Then this ebony bird beguiling my sad spirit into smiling,
By the serious appearance of the expression that it wore,
45 "Though your crown is short and shaven, you," I said, "are sure no craven,
Terrible, grim, and ancient Raven wandering from the Nightly shore—
Tell me what your lordly name is on the Night's so ghostly shore!"
                 Said the Raven, "Nevermore."

I was amazed by this ungainly bird to hear it speak so plainly,
50 Though its answer little meaning—little relevance it bore;
For we cannot help agreeing that no living human being
Ever yet was blessed with seeing bird above his bedroom door—
Bird or beast upon the sculptured bust above his bedroom door,
                 With such name as "Nevermore."

Interact with the Text

5. Imagery and Repetition

Underline the words and phrases that describe the raven. How does the description of the raven create suspense?

Possible response: It is odd for a bird to be described as noble and ancient with a serious look on its face. This makes me question what the speaker is thinking. He might be crazy, or the raven might have come for a reason.

Key Vocabulary
- **relevance** *n.*, importance that connects to something else

In Other Words
days of yore past
bust of Pallas statue of the head of the Greek goddess, Athena
beguiling charming
craven coward
Nevermore Never again

Australian Raven, 2005, Kate Breakey. Handcolored silver gelatin photograph, Courtesy of Stephen Clark Gallery.

▲ **Critical Viewing: Mood** Study the artist's use of color, shadow, and light. What mood do these elements make you feel?

55   But the Raven, sitting lonely on the silent bust, spoke only

That one word, as if his soul in that one word he did outpour.

Nothing further then he uttered—not a feather then he fluttered—

Till I scarcely more than muttered "Other friends have flown before—

On the morrow *he* will leave me, as my hopes have flown before."

60   Then the bird said, "Nevermore."

Startled at the stillness broken by reply so clearly spoken,

"Surely," I said, "what it utters is a trick and nothing more,

Caught from some unhappy master whom a terrible Disaster

Followed fast and followed faster till his songs one burden bore—

65   Till the sad songs of his Hope that even sadder burden bore

              Of 'Never—nevermore.'"

But the Raven still beguiling all my spirit into smiling,

Soon I wheeled a cushioned seat in front of bird and bust and door;

Then, while into the cushion sinking, in my mind I started linking

70   Idea to idea, all the time thinking what this ominous bird of yore—

What this grim, ungainly, ghastly, gaunt and ominous bird of yore

            Meant in croaking, "Nevermore."

So I sat engaged in guessing, but without a word expressing

To the bird whose fiery eyes now burned into my spirit's core;

75   This and more I sat divining, with my head at ease reclining

On the cushion's velvet lining which the lamp-light shined all over,

But whose velvet violet lining with the lamp-light shining o'er,

           She shall touch, ah, nevermore!

Key Vocabulary
burden *n.*, something heavy or difficult that one has to carry
ominous *adj.*, threatening

In Other Words
uttered said
On the morrow Tomorrow
bore carried
divining guessing

6. Make Connections
Reread this page. What connection can you make? Underline the text you made a connection to. Then explain the connection.

Answers will vary.

7. Interpret
Reread the last line. What is the speaker upset about?

He is sad about Lenore.

He loves her and now

she is gone.

8. Imagery and Repetition
Underline the repeated phrase on this page. What kind of mood does Poe create by repeating this phrase?

Possible response:

Poe creates a mood of

urgency or suspense.

9. Make Connections
Reread the last two stanzas on this page. The speaker asks the raven to tell him if he will ever see Lenore again. Have you ever wanted something so badly that you would not take *no* for an answer? How does this help you understand the text?

Answers will vary.

Then, I thought, the air grew denser, perfumed from an unseen censer
80   Swung by angels whose soft foot-falls tapped so lightly on the floor.
"Wretch," I cried "your God has lent you—by these angels he has sent you
Relief—relief and cure from your memories of Lenore;
Drink, oh drink this kind cure and forget this lost Lenore!"
                    Said the Raven, "Nevermore."

85   <u>"Prophet!" I said, "thing of evil!—still a prophet, bird or devil!</u>—
Did the Tempter or the tempest storm toss you to this shore?
All alone yet all undaunted, on this desert land enchanted—
On this home by Horror haunted—tell me truly, I ask for—
Is there—is there relief from sorrow? tell me—truth, I ask you for!"
90   Said the Raven, "Nevermore."

  <u>"Prophet! I said, "thing of evil!—still a prophet, bird or devil!</u>
By that Heaven that bends above us—by that God we both adore—
Tell this soul with sorrow laden if, within the distant Aidenn,
It shall clasp again a maiden whom the angels name Lenore—
95   Clasp a rare and beautiful maiden whom the angels name Lenore."
                    Said the Raven, "Nevermore."

"Be that word our sign of parting, bird or fiend!" I yelled, upstarting—
"Then get yourself back into the tempest and the Night's ghostly shore!
Leave no feather as a token of that lie your soul has spoken!
100 Leave my loneliness unbroken!—leave the bust above my door!
Take your beak out of my heart, and take your form off of my door!"
                    Said the Raven, "Nevermore."

Key Vocabulary
prophet *n.*, someone who predicts what will happen in the future

In Other Words
censer container for burning incense
Wretch Poor, unhappy person
all undaunted not discouraged
distant Aidenn long-ago Garden of Eden
fiend evil creature, devil
tempest storm

And the Raven, never flitting, still is sitting, *still* is sitting

On the pale bust of Pallas just above my bedroom door;

105 And his eyes have all the seeming of a demon's that is dreaming,

And the lamp-light over him streaming throws his shadow on the floor;

And my soul from out of that shadow that lies floating on the floor

Shall be lifted—nevermore!

10. Interpret

Underline the words and phrases that the poet uses to describe what the raven does to him. What can you conclude about the speaker?

Possible response: The speaker is frightened and depressed. He has allowed the raven to make him crazy. He believes the raven is the cause of his sorrow.

Selection Review   The Raven

A. Choose and answer one question about "The Raven." Give examples from the poem to support the connections you make. Then explain how making this connection helps you understand the text better.

Question 1:   **How does the poem remind you of "The Tell-Tale Heart"?**

Question 2:   **How does the situation the speaker finds himself in remind you of your own life?**

I chose question   *Possible response:* Question 1; Both texts are written about people who imagine things that frighten them. In "The Tell-Tale Heart," the narrator is crazy and his imagination leads to his confession. In "The Raven," the speaker imagines that the raven has power over him. Making this connection helps because I can compare the texts because the two situations are very similar. Understanding the story helped me better understand the poem.

Selection Review, continued

B. In the T-chart, list examples of imagery and repetition from the poem. Then answer the questions.

T Chart

Imagery	Repetition
raven	nevermore
fire	Lenore
cold room	bedroom door
the cushion's velvet lining	burden bore
lamp light shining	ominous bird of yore

1. How does imagery and repetition help to build suspense in the poem? Write a paragraph. Give examples from the poem to support your answers.

Possible response: The imagery in the poem is dark and scary because the poet uses images such as a fire in a cold room with a lamp shining in the darkness. I can also picture the raven sitting above him in a position of power. The raven repeats "nevermore" and is accusatory. This makes me think that something terrible is about to happen.

2. What do you think happened to Lenore? How does imagining what happened to Lenore make this poem more frightening? Support your opinion with examples from the poem.

Possible response: I think that Lenore was murdered. I know she died because the man misses her and knows she is gone forever. I think she was murdered because the encounter with the raven is so dark and threatening. It's almost as if he feels guilty and expects her ghost to appear and blame him.

Reflect and Assess

WRITING: Write About Literature

A. Plan your writing. List the most frightening details from each selection. *Answers will vary.*

The Tell-Tale Heart	The Raven
The old man's eye is like the eye of a vulture.	Someone or something will not stop tapping at the narrator's door.

B. How do you think Poe would answer the question, "What makes something frightening?" Write a short response giving your opinion. Give details from both texts to support your answer.

Students should support their answers with examples from the selections.

_____

_____

_____

_____

_____

_____

_____

_____

_____

_____

_____

_____

Integrate the Language Arts

► The Tell-Tale Heart
► The Raven

LITERARY ANALYSIS: Analyze Mood, Tone, and Symbolism

Mood is the feeling that a reader gets from a story. **Tone** is the author's attitude toward his or her topic. A **symbol** is something that stands for something else. Writers use symbolism to make their stories more interesting. *Answers will vary. Possible responses are shown.*

A. Read the words and phrases from "The Tell-Tale Heart" that help create the mood and tone of the story. Then write how the words and phrases make you feel.

Words and Phrases	How It Makes Me Feel
"I knew he had no idea that every night, just at midnight, I looked upon him while he slept."	This makes me scared. It's creepy that the narrator spies on the old man while he sleeps.
"It was the unseen shadow of Death that made the old man feel my closeness."	This makes me feel afraid. It's obvious the narrator is about to murder the old man.
"The noise grew louder—louder—louder!"	This makes me nervous, because it seems like something terrible is about to happen.

B. Answer the questions.

1. How would you describe the mood of this story?

   The mood is frightening, dark, and disturbing.

2. How would you describe the story's tone?

   The author feels that the narrator is a disturbed man.

3. How does Poe's choice of words create mood and tone?

   Poe uses mysterious words to form creepy phrases like "unseen shadow of Death."

4. What do you think the old man's eye symbolizes? Explain.

   Answers will vary.

C. Sunrise is often used in literature. List more examples of symbols you have read in books or short stories and what they mean.

   raven, death; moon, love; bird, freedom

210   Unit 5: Fear This!

VOCABULARY STUDY: Analogies

An **analogy** is a comparison between two pairs of words to show relationships.

Example: "School is to education as restaurant is to food" can be written as school : education :: restaurant : food.

A. Complete the analogies. Circle the letter of the correct answer.

1. fearful : brave :: _____
   a. cat : mouse
   b. happy : joyful
   c. loud : quiet *(circled)*

2. raven : bird :: _____
   a. oak : tree *(circled)*
   b. skirt : shirt
   c. tall : short

3. month : December :: _____
   a. find : lose
   b. season : summer *(circled)*
   c. snow : rain

4. dreary : gloomy :: _____
   a. first : last
   b. earth : moon
   c. funny : humorous *(circled)*

B. Explain the relationships between the pairs of words for each analogy above.

1. Both word pairs are opposites.

2. The first word is one type of the second word in both pairs.

3. The second word is an example of the first word in both pairs.

4. Both word pairs have the same meaning.

C. Complete each analogy. Then explain the relationship.

1. happy : joyful :: sad : unhappy
   Relationship: The first word has the same meaning as the second word in both pairs.

2. exciting : boring :: hot : cold
   Relationship: The first word is the opposite of the second word in both pairs.

3. desk : office :: sofa : house
   Relationship: Both word pairs are furniture that can be found in each kind of building.

4. write : paper :: type : computer
   Relationship: Both word pairs show forms of communication with the tools used.

Key Vocabulary Review

A. Use the words to complete the paragraph.

dread	ominous	subside	trace
obvious	resist	suspect	vulnerable

Tina began to ____suspect____ something was wrong when it became ____obvious____ that
(1)   (2)

she was alone in the cemetery. She could not find a single ____trace____, or sign, of her friends.
(3)

She was filled with ____dread____ and felt ____vulnerable____ and helpless. When she heard an
(4)   (5)

____ominous____ noise, she could barely ____resist____ the urge to scream. Finally, she saw her
(6)   (7)

friends, and her fear began to ____subside____.
(8)

B. Use your own words to write what each Key Vocabulary word means.
Then write a synonym for each word. *Answers will vary. Possible responses are shown.*

Key Word	My Definition	Synonym
1. boundary	a line that separates places	border
2. cease	to come to an end	stop
3. feud	a long-lasting quarrel	argument
4. grant	to allow something	give
5. release	to let something go	free
6. relevance	a connection to something	significance
7. rely	to depend on something	count on
8. ritual	a formal way of doing something	ceremony

boundary	dread	• obvious	prophet	• rely	suspect
burden	feud	ominous	reconciliation	resist	terror
• capable	• grant	ponder	• release	ritual	• trace
• cease	identification	• precision	• relevance	subside	vulnerable

• **Academic Vocabulary**

C. Answer the questions using complete sentences. *Answers will vary. Possible responses are shown.*

1. If you could meet a **prophet**, what would you ask him or her?

I would ask if there will ever be a cure for cancer.

2. Describe someone from a book or movie whom you feel a strong **identification** with.

I identify with Esperanza in *The House on Mango Street*. Her reactions to things are a lot like mine.

3. What is an example of a task that requires **precision**?

Doing a science experiment requires precision.

4. When have you felt **terror**?

I felt terror when I read a Stephen King novel.

5. Describe one thing you are very **capable** of doing on your own.

I am capable of making dinner.

6. What are two things that people often **ponder** in books and movies?

People often ponder love and death.

7. How do you feel after you have a **reconciliation** with someone?

I feel relieved and happy.

8. Describe a **burden** that some people have in their lives.

Some people have the burden of taking care of a sick family member or friend.

Prepare to Read
▸ Ad Power
▸ What's Wrong with Advertising?

Key Vocabulary

A. How well do you know these words? Circle a rating for each word. Check your understanding of each word by circling *yes* or *no*. Then complete the sentences. If you are unsure of a word's meaning, refer to the Vocabulary Glossary, page 852, in your student text.

Rating Scale	
1	I have never seen this word before.
2	I am not sure of the word's meaning.
3	I know this word and can teach the word's meaning to someone else.

Key Word	Check Your Understanding	Deepen Your Understanding
❶ advertising (**ad**-vur-tīz-ing) *noun* **Rating:** 1 2 3	Commercials are examples of **advertising** on television. (Yes) No	I notice advertising when it appears _Possible_ _response:_ in magazines and on TV _____ _____ .
❷ appeal (u-**pēl**) *verb; noun* **Rating:** 1 2 3	Products that come in unattractive packaging will **appeal** to consumers. Yes (No)	To appeal to teens, a TV commercial should have _____ _Possible response:_ humor and music _____ _____ .
❸ consumer (kun-**sū**-mur) *noun* **Rating:** 1 2 3	A **consumer** is the buyer of a company's product. (Yes) No	A healthy person might be a consumer of _Possible_ _response:_ vitamins or fresh fruits and vegetables _____ _____ .
❹ convince (kun-**vins**) *verb* **Rating:** 1 2 3	It is easy to **convince** a person to buy a bad product. Yes (No)	I want to convince my friends that _Possible response:_ we should go to a concert _____ _____ .

Key Word	Check Your Understanding	Deepen Your Understanding
5 impact (**im**-pakt) *verb* **Rating:** 1 2 3	Advertisers use commercials to **impact** buyers' shopping habits. (Yes) No	I know I impact my grade when I _Possible response:_ study _____ .
6 manipulate (mu-**ni**-pyū-lāt) *verb* **Rating:** 1 2 3	A factual article about wildlife can **manipulate** children. Yes (No)	A salesperson can manipulate a shopper by _____ *Possible response:* promising a discount; or using flattery _____ .
7 persuasive (pur-**swā**-siv) *adjective* **Rating:** 1 2 3	A salesperson uses **persuasive** techniques to sell a product. (Yes) No	I can be very persuasive when I _Possible response:_ feel strongly about an idea _____ .
8 profit (**prah**-fut) *noun* **Rating:** 1 2 3	Businesses make a **profit** when their sales decline. Yes (No)	A student group could use the profit they make in a fundraiser to _Possible response:_ buy new equipment _____ .

B. Use one of the Key Vocabulary words to write about how an advertisement influenced you.

Answers will vary.

_____

Before Reading Ad Power

LITERARY ANALYSIS: Argument and Evidence

An **argument** gives a writer's point of view about an issue or problem. A writer supports an argument with **evidence**, such as facts, statistics, data, and quotations.

A. Read the passage below. Find the evidence that supports the writer's argument. Complete the diagram with the evidence.

> **Look Into the Text**
>
> People in Ghana, a country in West Africa, have a saying: *To the fish, the water is invisible.* In other words, when you're surrounded by something all the time, you don't notice it. . . .
>
> In parts of the world where people have a lot of modern conveniences and up-to-date technology, you could say that advertising has become "the water in which we swim." There's so much of it that we hardly notice it anymore. In fact, some experts estimate that a young person growing up in North America is likely to see between 20,000 and 40,000 TV commercials every year. When you add in all the advertisements from other media— up to 16,000 a day!—it's easy to see how you'd begin to stop noticing, and just keep swimming.

Main-Idea Diagram

> **Argument:** There is so much advertising that we hardly notice it anymore.
>
> > **Evidence:**
> > The writer uses a saying to explain how people don't notice something that always surrounds them.
> >
> > **Evidence:**
> > The writer uses statistics from experts that show how young people see approximately 16,000 ads a day.

B. Answer the question.

Is the author's evidence reliable? Why or why not?

Possible response: The evidence seems reliable because the author uses a saying from Ghana to provide

interest and to make a point, and then she includes statistics from experts.

READING STRATEGY: Draw Conclusions

HOW TO DRAW CONCLUSIONS

1. **Note** the writer's claims.

2. **Add the writer's evidence** that supports each claim.

3. **Add your background knowledge** and experience.

4. **Synthesize** or combine, your ideas with the writer's ideas.

5. **Draw a conclusion** that makes a judgment, gives an opinion, or shows new understanding.

A. Read the passage. Use the strategies above to draw conclusions as you read. Then answer the questions below.

> **Look Into the Text**
>
> Every time you put on a T-shirt or a pair of jeans that shows a company's logo, you become a walking billboard. You're "advertising" the company's products.
>
> Think about the exchange. You get a T-shirt. The company gets the money you paid for the shirt plus the exposure that comes from you wearing it. Your willingness to wear the company's name on your body is the same as you personally endorsing the product.

1. What claim does the writer make about logos?

The writer claims that when you buy a piece of clothing with an obvious logo you are advertising that company whenever you wear the clothing.

2. What is your personal experience with clothes and logos?

Possible response: People notice logos that I wear, especially if they are popular brands. Sometimes people buy clothes with certain logos if a certain person or group is wearing the logo.

B. Draw a conclusion about the author's claim.

Possible response: Companies are smart to put logos on their clothes because they are getting free advertising every time someone wears the clothes.

How Do the Media Shape the Way People Think?

Explore how advertising changes our opinions.

A. In "Ad Power," you learned how advertising influences people. List the facts, statistics, data, and quotations the writer uses to support her argument that ads have become so common that people no longer notice them.

Facts	Statistics/Data	Quotations/Expert Opinions
Ads surround us. They are on the radio, signs, billboards, posters, logos, the Internet, magazines, and TV.	A young person may see or hear up to 16,000 ads a day.	Some experts argue that advertising appeals to people's emotions, not their minds. They think ads trick people into buying products.
TV and radio ads use music and visuals that are hard to avoid. Moviemakers display products for audiences to see.	Twenty-eight percent of teens purchase the products they see in magazines.	The slogan "Diamonds are forever" was used by a diamond company. Ever since, diamonds have been used for engagement rings.

B. Use the information in the chart to answer the questions.

1. How reliable is the writer's evidence? Based on her evidence and your experience, do you agree or disagree with her claim? Why or why not?

   Possible response: Her evidence seems reliable because she uses facts, statistics, expert opinions, and quotations. However, she doesn't include sources for her evidence. I agree with her claim because I know how advertising influences me and my friends.

2. What kind of consumer is the writer trying to convince readers to be? Use **consumer** or **convince** in your response.

   Possible response: The writer wants us to be cautious and informed consumers. She wants to convince us to be aware of ads and not to buy things without thinking about the products or our reasons for buying them.

3. Will you look at advertising differently from now on? Why or why not?

   Possible response: I will probably be more aware of how much advertising I see and when and where I see it. It's true that I often see things I never thought of as advertising before, such as T-shirt logos or a brand in a TV show.

What's Wrong with Advertising?

by David Ogilvy

Connect Across Texts

*"Ad Power" examines how **advertising** **impacts** our lives. In this essay, an ad executive explains how he feels about the work he does.*

David Ogilvy, the "Father of Advertising," began his career by selling kitchen stoves door-to-door. In 1949, Ogilvy only had $6,000, but he used it to open **an advertising agency** with two partners. Their company went on to create advertising for many of the world's largest companies. Forty years later, the Ogilvy Group was sold for $864 million. *Time* magazine called Ogilvy "the most sought-after wizard in the advertising industry."

Ogilvy once said, "Never write an advertisement which you wouldn't want your family to read. You wouldn't tell lies to your own wife. Don't tell them to mine." Here are more of David Ogilvy's ideas from his book *Ogilvy on Advertising*.

Is Advertising Evil?

A professor in New York teaches his students that "advertising is . . . **intellectual and moral pollution**. . . . It is **undermining** our faith in our nation and in ourselves."

Holy smoke, is *that* what I do for a living?

Some of the defenders of advertising are equally guilty of **overstating** their case. Said Leo Burnett, the great Chicago advertising man: "Advertising is not the noblest creation of man's mind . . . It does not,

Interact with the Text

1. Draw Conclusions
Highlight the words and phrases that describe Ogilvy's success. Think about your knowledge and experience. What do you think his position on advertising will be?

Possible response: Ogilvy will probably talk about the positive impact of advertising because he was a successful and famous advertising executive.

2. Persuasive Appeals
Underline the professor's quote. Why do you think Ogilvy begins the essay with a negative quote about advertising?

Possible response: He wants readers to react emotionally and to have something to argue against, like in a debate.

Key Vocabulary
advertising *n.,* work that encourages people to buy, do, or use things
• **impact** *v.,* to influence and affect
persuasive *adj.,* believable
appeal *n.,* request for a good reaction

In Other Words
an advertising agency a company that creates advertisements
intellectual and moral pollution destroying our minds and values
undermining weakening and damaging
overstating exaggerating

3. Persuasive Appeals

Underline the information that makes advertising seem as though it helps people. What ideas does Ogilvy use to appeal to readers' emotions?

Possible response: He

talks about children

and their health,

which appeals to most

people's emotions.

4. Draw Conclusions

Circle the advertising categories in the chart that affect you the most. What conclusion can you draw about the amount of advertising money that is spent in these industries?

Possible response: So

much money is spent

advertising in these

industries because

so many people use

these products. There

also may be a lot of

competition between

brands.

single-handedly, **sustain the whole structure of capitalism and democracy and the free world**. . . . We are merely human, trying to do a necessary human job **with dignity, with decency, and with competence**."

My view is that advertising is no more and no less than a reasonably **efficient** way to sell. Procter & Gamble spends about $600,000,000* a year on advertising. Howard Morgens, their former president, is quoted as saying, "We believe that advertising is the most effective and efficient way to sell to the consumer. If we should ever find better methods of selling our type of products to the consumer, we'll leave advertising and turn to these other methods."

Few of us advertising professionals lie awake nights feeling guilty about the way we earn our living. We don't feel bad when we write advertisements for toothpaste. If we do it well, <u>children may not have to go to the dentist so often</u>.

*This was Proctor & Gamble's advertising **budget** in 1983. Today, the manufacturing company spends about $2 billion a year on advertising.

ADVERTISING DOLLARS SPENT

Large companies spend a large percentage of their budgets on advertising. Look at these products. Do they sound familar to you? Have you bought or used any of them yourself? Maybe these advertising dollars are well spent after all.

Top Advertising Categories *January–September 2005*	
Industry	**Ad Expenditur** (billions)
Automobile (foreign and domestic brands)	$12.4
Financial Services (banks, credit cards, car loans, etc.)	$5.7
Telecommunications (phone, internet)	$5.5
Personal Care Products (cosmetics, shampoo, etc.)	$4.2
Travel and Tourism	$4.0

Source: TNS Media Intelligence Report, December 2005

▲ **Interpret the Chart** Why do you think automobile companies spend more on advertising than companies that sell personal care products?

In Other Words

sustain the whole structure of capitalism and democracy in the free world keep the free world running

with dignity, with decency, and with competence with pride, good taste, and skill

efficient easy and effective

budget cost

I did not feel bad when I wrote advertisements promoting travel to Puerto Rico. They helped **attract industry** and tourists to a country that had been in poverty for 400 years.

I do not think that I am wasting my time when I write advertisements for the World Wildlife Fund.

My children were grateful when I wrote an advertisement that recovered their dog Teddy from **dognappers**.

Nobody suggests that the printing press is evil because it is used to print pornography. It is also used to print the Bible. Advertising is only evil when it advertises evil things.

Some **economists** say that advertising tempts people to waste money on things they don't need. Who are they to decide what you need? Do you *need* a dishwasher? Do you *need* a deodorant? Do you *need* a trip to Rome? I **feel no qualms of conscience** about persuading you that you do. What the economists don't seem to know is that buying things can be one of life's more innocent pleasures, whether you need them or not.

If advertising were **abolished**, what would be done with the money? Would it be spent on public works? Or **distributed to stockholders**? Or given to the media for the loss of **their largest source of revenue**? Perhaps it could be used to reduce prices to the consumer—*by about 3 percent.*

Reports show that Americans spent more money than they earned in 2005. Advertisers fight for their attention—and their money.

Interact with the Text

5. Interpret
Circle both arguments about advertising. Summarize the two-sided argument about consumers. Which argument do you agree with? Why?

Possible response:

Ogilvy thinks buying things makes consumers happy. Economists think ads persuade people to waste money. I agree with economists. We waste our money on products we don't need, but want.

In Other Words

attract industry bring businesses, jobs
dognappers the people who stole him
economists experts who study how people spend money
feel no qualms of conscience don't feel ashamed or guilty

abolished stopped
distributed to stockholders given to people who own parts of a company
their largest source of revenue the way they make most of their money

Highlight the writer's main point in the first paragraph. Based on your experience, do you agree or disagree? Explain.

Possible response: I

agree. I once used a

shampoo because I liked

the ad, but it made my

hair dry. I never bought

it again.

7. Interpret
Underline the main idea behind subliminal advertising. Why would it be wrong for advertisers to use this method?

Possible response:

It would be wrong

because people would

not be able to control

what they were buying.

They would not be aware

of why they were buying

things.

Can Advertising Sell Bad Products?

It is often charged that advertising can persuade people to buy inferior products. So it can—*once*. But the consumer sees that the product is inferior and never buys it again. This is expensive for the manufacturer, whose **profits** come from *repeat* purchases.

The best way to increase the sale of a product is to *improve the product*. This is particularly true of food products. The consumer is amazingly quick to notice an improvement in taste and buy the product more often.

Manipulation?

You may have heard it said that advertising is "**manipulation**." I know of only two examples, and neither of them actually happened. In 1957, a **market researcher** called James Vicary **hypothesized** that it might be possible to flash commands on television screens so fast that the viewer would not **be conscious of** seeing them. However, the viewer's *unconscious* mind *would* see the commands—and obey them. He called this gimmick "subliminal" advertising, but he never even got around to testing it, and no advertiser has ever used it.

I myself once came near to doing something so diabolical

The best way to increase the sale of a product is to improve the product.

Key Vocabulary
profit *n.*, the money a company makes after expenses
• **convince** *v.*, to make someone believe
manipulate *v.*, to control

In Other Words
market researcher man who studied how consumers spend their money
hypothesized guessed
be conscious of realize he or she was

that I hesitate to confess it even now, thirty years later. Suspecting that **hypnotism** might be an element in successful advertising, I hired a professional hypnotist to make a commercial. When I saw it in the projection room, it was so powerful that I had visions of millions of **suggestible consumers** getting up from their armchairs and rushing like **zombies** through the traffic on their way to buy the product at the nearest store. Had I invented the *ultimate* advertisement? I burned it,

TRUTH IN ADVERTISING?

Advertisers want their products tp appear attractive and appealing. Many times, this includes removing distracting objects and "touching up" photos. Which of these photos gives a more appealing glimpse of a vacation getaway?

Original Photo   **Touched-Up Photo**

In Other Words

hypnotism controlling people's unconscious so they will do whatever they are told to do
suggestible consumers buyers who didn't know what they were doing
zombies half-dead people

Interact with the Text

8. Persuasive Appeals
Highlight what Ogilvy did that he describes as "diabolical." Why do you think he confesses this?

Possible response:

Readers will think he's

honest and might be

persuaded to agree with

his opinions.

9. Interpret

Highlight the important words and phrases in the conclusion. What is Ogilvy's final point about advertising?

Possible response:

He claims advertisers

cannot manipulate

consumers even if they

wanted to.

and never told my client how close I had come to **landing him in a national scandal**.

One way or another, the odds against your being manipulated by advertising are now very long indeed. Even if I wanted to manipulate you, I wouldn't know how to get around the **legal regulations**. ❖

In Other Words

landing him in a national scandal making him and his company look bad

legal regulations laws that prevent untruthful or deceptive ads

---

Selection Review What's Wrong with Advertising?

A. List two ways the writer tries to appeal to the reader's emotions. Explain the effect each appeal had on you.

1. *Possible response:* He uses examples of the good things advertising has done. These examples helped me understand that advertising can have positive effects.

2. *Possible response:* He explains how advertising is not manipulation and lists two examples of manipulation that did not happen. This made me think that advertisers are not bad people.

B. Answer the questions.

1. In your own words, state the writer's main idea. Then use your own experience and knowledge to draw a conclusion about his claim.

Possible response: Not all advertising is bad. I agree because I saw an ad for a volunteer group, and I decided to become a volunteer.

2. Imagine you are writing a letter to David Ogilvy. What would you tell him about the conclusions you drew about his essay?

Possible response: I would tell him that his essay is written convincingly, but my experience tells me that advertising does have the power to manipulate people who are not informed.

Reflect and Assess

WRITING: Write About Literature

A. Plan your writing. Collect definitions and other information about
advertising from each selection. *Answers will vary. Possible responses are shown.*

Ad Power	What's Wrong with Advertising?
jingles and slogans	intellectual and moral pollution
art or science of persuasive communication	a reasonably efficient way to sell to the consumer
anything someone does to grab your attention and hold on to it long enough to sell a product	promotes good products
trickery to convince you to spend money	manipulation

B. What is advertising? Use the information given in both texts, add what
you know, and synthesize your own definition. Write your definition below.
Support your definition with examples from the texts.

Students should support their answers with examples from the selections.

_____

_____

_____

C. Use what you have learned about advertising to write your own ad.

Answers will vary.

_____

_____

_____

_____

_____

_____

LITERARY ANALYSIS: Compare Literature

The reason an author writes a selection is known as the **author's purpose**.
An **author's perspective** reflects his or her background, experiences, and
viewpoint. *Answers will vary. Possible responses are shown.*

A. Write what you think the author's purpose and perspective are for
each selection.

Selection	Author's Purpose	Author's Perspective
"Ad Power"	to inform readers about the negative influence of advertising	first-person perspective of someone who has studied advertising
"What's Wrong with Advertising?"	to inform readers about the positive aspects of advertising; to persuade readers that advertising is not bad	first-person perspective of someone who has created advertising

B. Read the excerpt from "Ad Power." Then answer the questions.

> Advertising is basically anything someone does to grab your attention and hold on to it
> long enough to tell you how cool, fast, cheap, tasty, fun, rockin', or rad whatever they're
> selling is. Some people have a different definition. They argue that advertising is trickery
> used to shut down your brain just long enough to convince you to open your wallet!

1. What is the author's purpose?

The author's purpose is to show that there are different perspectives on advertising.

2. Does the author have an agenda?

No, the author seems most interested in informing readers, not persuading them.

3. What effect does the author's purpose have on you?

She made me really think about the issue. Before, I just accepted all the advertising around me. Now, I
question it.

C. Think about an ad that you have read or seen on television. Write two or
three sentences describing the purpose of the ad and if there is a bias
that affects how the ad is presented.

Answers will vary.

VOCABULARY STUDY: Latin and Greek Roots

Many English words are made up of **Latin and Greek roots** with other word parts added. Knowing the meaning of the roots can help you understand the meaning of the entire word.

A. The chart below shows some common Latin and Greek roots and their meanings. Complete the chart by listing words you've used that contain each root. *Answers will vary. Possible responses are shown.*

Root	Meaning	Words I've Used
fin	end	final
sume	to take	assume
uni	one	unisex
voc	call	vocal

B. Read the paragraph below. Underline words you find that contain the Latin and Greek roots from the chart above.

> My friends and I began talking one day about how much energy we <u>consume</u> in our daily lives. Leaving a light on or a stereo playing after you have left the room are ways we waste energy. We started thinking about some ideas that can be used <u>universally</u> to make our planet a better place to live. I decided that my <u>vocation</u> would be to help save our environment. I am so glad that I <u>finally</u> figured out a meaningful way to live my life!

C. Write a meaning for each word with a Latin or Greek root that you found in the paragraph above. Use the root meanings in Activity A to help you.

1. _____
2. _____
3. _____
4. _____

Prepare to Read
▶ A Long Way to Go: Minorities and the Media
▶ The Color Green

Key Vocabulary

A. How well do you know these words? Circle a rating for each word. Check your understanding of each word by marking an X next to the correct definition. Then complete the sentence. If you are unsure of a word's meaning, refer to the Vocabulary Glossary, page 852, in your student text.

Rating Scale	
1	I have never seen this word before.
2	I am not sure of the word's meaning.
3	I know this word and can teach the word's meaning to someone else.

Key Word	Check Your Understanding	Deepen Your Understanding
❶ alternative (awl-**tur**-nu-tiv) *adjective* **Rating:** 1 2 3	[X] different from what is usual [ ] what is expected	I enjoy alternative _Possible response: music_
❷ expand (ik-**spand**) *verb* **Rating:** 1 2 3	[X] to grow larger [ ] to make smaller	I can expand my vocabulary by _Possible response: reading more_
❸ influence (**in**-flū-uns) *verb* **Rating:** 1 2 3	[ ] to ignore something [X] to affect someone or something	People who influence me in a positive way are_____ *Possible response:* my parents and my friends
❹ media (**mē**-dē-u) *noun* **Rating:** 1 2 3	[X] a means of communication [ ] a means of hiding information	For me, two of the most important sources of media are *Possible response:* TV and the Internet

Key Word	Check Your Understanding	Deepen Your Understanding
5 **minority** (mu-**nor**-u-tē) *noun, adjective* **Rating:** **1 2 3**	☐ a large group or crowd ☒ a small group of people	One minority group I would like to know more about is *Possible response:* the hearing impaired _____ .
6 **racism** (**rā**-si-zum) *noun* **Rating:** **1 2 3**	☒ prejudice against a race ☐ a contest	A judge would be accused of racism if she ___*Possible*___ *response:* treated African American lawyers differently than white lawyers _____ .
7 **stereotype** (**ster**-ē-u-tīp) *noun* **Rating:** **1 2 3**	☐ a fact or statistic ☒ an idea about a group of people	One stereotype of teenagers is ___*Possible response:*___ teenagers are reckless drivers _____ .
8 **token** (**tō**-kun) *adjective* **Rating:** **1 2 3**	☒ representing a larger group ☐ representing individuals	A company might hire a token woman if it had _____ *Possible response:* all male employees _____ .

B. Use one of the Key Vocabulary words to write about a TV show that affects your worldview.

Answers will vary.

_____

_____

Before Reading A Long Way to Go: Minorities and the Media

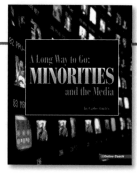

LITERARY ANALYSIS: Evaluate Evidence

Persuasive writers support their claims with **evidence**, such as facts, examples, data, and statistics. Readers should evaluate evidence by asking: *Is it biased? Is it from a trustworthy source? Is it recent?*

A. Read the passage below. Evaluate the evidence that supports the writer's claim that minorities are making slow progress in the media. Complete the chart.

> **Look Into the Text**
>
> Minorities have traditionally had only a small presence in the media. The national popularity of Bryant Gumbel, Connie Chung, and Geraldo Rivera on television is very recent. While these breakthroughs are certainly welcome, progress is slow. For example, only about 40 percent of the nation's 1,600 daily newspapers have *any* minorities as editors.

Writer's Evidence	My Evaluation of the Evidence
The national popularity of Bryant Gumbel, Connie Chung, and Geraldo Rivera is very recent.	*Possible response:* The examples are not recent and represent only three minority groups. The writer could mention some anchors who are less famous.
Only 40 percent of 1,600 daily newspapers have minority editors.	*Possible response:* Statistics are believable, but the writer does not state the source of the statistics.

B. Answer the question.

Why is it important to evaluate the evidence that a writer uses to support his or her opinion?

Possible response: Facts may or may not be completely accurate or from a reliable source. Readers should evaluate the evidence before they believe what they read.

READING STRATEGY: Compare Opinions

Reading Strategy
Synthesize

How to COMPARE OPINIONS

1. **Record Ideas** List each important claim.

2. **Add Texts** Read another selection on the same topic.

3. **Compare** Determine how the claims are alike and different. Combine the ideas.

4. **Read On** Add more claims to your notes.

A. Read the passage. Use the strategies above to compare opinions as you read. Then answer the questions below.

Look Into the Text

The entertainment media have a fascination with Latino gangs. The news media also like to show them often. At the same time, the entertainment media rarely show other Latino characters. And the news media rarely show other Hispanic topics, except for such "problem" issues as immigration and language. The result has been a Latino public image—better yet, a stereotype—in which gangs are an important part.

1. What is the writer's opinion about the media's fascination with Latino gangs?

   The media only show Latinos who are involved in gangs or other negative activities. The media

   stereotype Latinos.

2. Based on your own experience, do you agree with the writer's claim?

   Possible response: Yes. I see a lot of negative stories about Latinos and do not see a lot of Latino actors or

   TV shows about Latinos.

3. How will comparing this author's opinion with another author's opinion help you understand the topic better?

   Possible response: Thinking about how the claims are similar and different will help me decide what I think

   about how the media portray Latinos.

B. Return to the passage above, and underline the words or phrases that helped you answer the first question.

Selection Review A Long Way to Go: Minorities and the Media

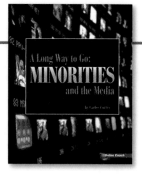

 How Do the Media Shape the Way People Think?
Consider the ways television shapes our worldview.

A. In "A Long Way to Go: Minorities and the Media," you learned how the media can influence the way minorities are portrayed. Complete the diagram below.

Main-Idea Diagram

> **Author's Main Point:**
> The few minorities in the media are shown as stereotypes. Minorities resent the stereotypes and want change.

> **Evidence:**
> People connect the stereotype of Mexican gangs to East L.A.

> **Evidence:**
> Minority groups have protested the way they are portrayed and the lack of good roles that are available to them.

> **Evidence:**
> Minority people have formed their own companies so they can express their own views.

> **Evidence:**
> Only nine black people, three Asians, three Puerto Ricans, and one Chicano have won Academy Awards.

B. Use the information in the chart to answer the questions.

1. What kinds of evidence does the writer use in his essay? Is his evidence reliable? Why or why not?

    Possible response: The writer uses statistics and real examples. Both are reliable because they can be proven.

2. How might racism play a role in how the media portray minorities? Use **racism** in your answer.

    Possible response: Racism might play a role because some people might feel threatened when more minorities start winning important TV and movie roles.

3. Do you think the media have a responsibility to portray minorities fairly? Explain.

    Possible response: Yes. The media should show minorities in a positive way because many people are influenced by media and believe what they see and read.

Connect Across Texts

"A Long Way to Go" describes one writer's concerns about the way the media show **minorities**. *This editorial gives another view of the media—and how people can make a change for the better.*

The Color Green

from *The Daily Bruin*, University of California, Los Angeles

by Mark Punzalan, class of 2000

The Problem

People often forget that television is a business. Good shows get viewers and make money. Bad shows do not. And the ones that make money are the ones that **get renewed** for another season.

With that said, it was sad to see the reaction of cultural groups when the networks announced the current fall **lineup** and the lack of minority representation on the new shows. They didn't blame producers and writers for creating poor television shows. Instead, they blamed the **network executives** for being racially prejudiced.

Almost immediately, **N.A.A.C.P.** president Kweisi Mfume cried "**racism**, racism, racism." He threatened lawsuits and boycotts to get more minorities on television.

Since I watch a lot of TV, I can identify with the problem. I would like to watch more television shows with more people who look like me. But I watch good television shows, and the majority of today's shows featuring minorities just aren't very good. It has been a while since I have seen one that is actually worth watching.

George Lopez, whose show began in 2002, plays the lead in one of the only three hit network sitcoms to star Latinos since 1951. His sitcom's crew includes Latinos, as well as other minorities.

Interact with the Text

1. Compare Opinions

Underline Kweisi Mfume's reaction to the fall lineup. Would Carlos Cortés have supported this reaction? Why or why not?

Possible response: Cortés would agree that low minority representation is a sign of racism. I do not think he would support a lawsuit.

2. Fact and Opinion

Highlight the sentences that show the writer's opinion about minorities on TV. How do you know these are his opinions?

Possible response: He uses the word *good* and shares information about himself.

Key Vocabulary

minority *n.*, a group that has fewer members than most of the people

racism *n.*, belief that some races and ethnic groups are better than others

In Other Words

get renewed are scheduled
lineup schedule of TV shows
network executives people in charge of shows
N.A.A.C.P. National Association for the Advancement of Colored People

3. Compare Opinions

Circle the writer's opinion about color. Combine this idea with Cortés's idea about minorities in the media. Do you think race plays a role in the success or failure of TV shows? Explain.

Possible response: Yes.

If people do not like the

characters because they

are minorities, the show

could fail.

4. Fact and Opinion

Underline one fact in column 1. How do you know this statement is a fact?

Possible response:

There is proof that this

event really happened.

5. Compare Opinions

Highlight what the writer thinks minorities need to do to change how they are represented. Compare his opinions with Cortés's opinion.

Possible response: They

both believe minorities

should work to control the

media and the shows and

stories about them.

The same can be said for many of today's shows with largely white casts. But in the end, the colors black and white are not as important to network executives as the color green. If a show is not very good, it won't make the bucks. And that, not necessarily racism, is why the majority of today's shows fail.

The Wrong Choice

Minority leaders expect everyone to forget this idea. Instead of suggesting that minorities should get into the business and make good shows, many minority leaders cry racism. This may get you the front-page headlines, some **juicy sound bites** and some free publicity in the morning papers. But it really does not solve the minority problem on television.

In some ways, it only makes matters worse. After the threats from the N.A.A.C.P., the networks answered by sprinkling a couple of African Americans, Asian Americans, and Latinos onto a few of their shows. But is that what we really need—more **token** minority characters with no depth, personality, or soul? We have had more than our fair share of token minority characters with nothing more than their skin color to add to shows.

If you want more minorities on television, you find ways to make better minority shows that people will watch. Granted, there is discrimination in the entertainment business. Only the most **naive** person would tell you the entertainment industry is full of people sensitive to every single ethnic group out there.

But good shows are good shows, and even the most prejudiced television executive would support a good show with minorities that is able to attract viewers.

Television shows such as *Good Times*, *The Jeffersons*, *The Cosby Show*, and *In Living Color*, all had largely minority casts. They were able to achieve success, not because of some lawsuit, but because they were great shows that survived on their own excellence. People did not care what color the cast was. They tuned in because they wanted to watch entertaining television.

The television industry is still **an old boys network**. Undoubtedly, a few of those old boys are not very sympathetic to minorities. So what do you do about it? Complain and sue like crazy? Or do you suggest to African Americans, Latinos, and Asian Americans that they work harder to enter the entertainment industry and control it for themselves?

Key Vocabulary
  token *adj.*, included only to represent a larger group

In Other Words
juicy sound bites short quotations that sound good on the news
naive young or inexperienced
an old boys network run by the same powerful people who have always run it

The cast of *Grey's Anatomy,* which premiered in 2005, features minorities in prominent roles.

The Right Solution

Instead of waiting for non-minorities to create minority shows, why not push minorities to enter the industry? That would give them **a greater voice** in television. Not only would there be more minorities on television, but there would be more realistic characters from different groups, instead of a few token non-white characters.

Rarely have I heard any minority leaders suggest to their own people that they take action. They are usually too busy **dwelling on** the problem instead of actually coming up with a solution.

It is fairly easy to blame the entertainment industry for the lack of minority representation on television. But it is another thing to take some responsibility to try to fix the situation. Perhaps the best way to get more minorities on TV is to stop shouting racism all the time. Instead, start pushing television writers and producers to make better minority shows. More importantly, start pushing more minorities to make these shows. This would accomplish a lot more than some lawsuit or boycott. ❖

In Other Words
a greater voice more influence
dwelling on thinking about

Selection Review   The Color Green

A. Complete the T Chart with the facts and opinions the writer uses
in "The Color Green" to support his claims.

T Chart

Facts	Opinions
Good shows make money. Bad shows do not. The shows that make money get renewed.	It was sad to see the reaction of cultural groups when the networks announced the fall lineup.
N.A.A.C.P. president threatened lawsuits and boycotts.	I would like to see TV shows with more people who look like me.
Many minority leaders cry racism.	The majority of today's shows featuring minorities aren't very good.
There is discrimination in the entertainment industry. Some entertainment executives are not sympathetic to minority groups.	We have more than our fair share of token minority characters with no depth, personality, or soul.
People watched *Good Times, The Jeffersons, The Cosby Show,* and *In Living Color* because they were good.	Minorities need to work harder to enter the entertainment industry and control it.

Write your opinion. What fact from the article can you use to support your opinion?   _Possible_
response: I think that there should be more shows on television with minorities. If groups do not speak
out, then no one will be aware of the problem.

B. Think about the two selections. List each writer's claim. Then
compare their opinions, and synthesize the information to draw a
conclusion about the topic.

1. "A Long Way to Go":

The media should represent more minorities and represent them in a more positive way.

2. "The Color Green":

Minorities should create better shows and stop crying racism.

3. My Opinion:

Possible response: Minorities should work to create better shows, but the media should also do a
better job representing and hiring minorities.

Reflect and Assess

WRITING: Write About Literature

A. Plan your writing. List reasons why you think people should care about the way minorities are represented on TV. Then list examples from both texts. *Answers will vary.*

Reasons	Examples from Texts

B. Why should people care about the way minorities are represented on TV? Write an opinion statement. Use your own reasons and examples from both texts to support your opinion.

Students should support their answers with examples from the selections.

_____

_____

_____

_____

_____

_____

_____

_____

_____

_____

_____

_____

Integrate the Language Arts

LITERARY ANALYSIS: Persuasive Text Structures

Persuasive writing is organized into **text structures** that make the writer's ideas easy to follow. Some common structures are strength of arguments, point-counterpoint, and problem/solution.

A. In "The Color Green," the author uses the "point-counterpoint" persuasive text structure. Write two of the author's counterpoints in the chart below. *Answers will vary. Possible responses are shown.*

Point	Counterpoint
The lack of minorities on TV is the fault of racially prejudiced network executives.	The network executives care about whether or not a show is making money, not the ethnicity of the cast members. If the show isn't making money, the executives will probably recommend canceling it.
	In the past, there have been many successful shows with all-minority casts. Similarly, there are many successful shows today that have a diverse cast.

B. Using information from the selections, write a solution to each problem listed below. *Answers will vary. Possible responses are shown.*

Problem: Many minority roles on television promote stereotypes.

Solution: Minorities should be encouraged to enter the media industry to gain some control over how minorities are portrayed. People should protest stereotypes and point out these stereotypes.

Problem: Minorities do not have much say in the media.

Solution: Minority groups can form their own media. Many newspapers, magazines, and radio programs today are focused on primarily minority markets.

C. Choose a topic from one of the selections and write the central argument. Restructure the author's points using a "strength of argument" text structure. *Answers will vary.*

Argument: _____

Idea 1: _____

Idea 2: _____

Idea 3: _____

VOCABULARY STUDY: Latin and Greek Roots

Many English words are made up of **Latin and Greek roots** with other word parts added. Knowing the meaning of the roots can help you figure out the meaning of the entire word. *Answers will vary.*

A. *Meter* is a common Greek root that means "measure." Write what you think each word means. Confirm the definition for each word in the dictionary.

Word	What I Think It Means	Definition
barometer		
geometry		
pentameter		
thermometer		

B. The chart below shows some common Latin and Greek roots and their meanings. Complete the chart by listing words you've heard that contain each root.

Root	Meaning	Words I've Used
cred	believe	
graph	write	
oper	work	
pop	people	

C. Write sentences using the words you listed in Activity B.

1. _____

2. _____

3. _____

4. _____

Unit 6
Pages 542–561

Prepare to Read
▶ What Is News?
▶ How to Detect Bias in the News

Key Vocabulary

A. How well do you know these words? Circle a rating for each word. Check your understanding of each word by circling the correct synonym. Then write a definition. If you are unsure of a word's meaning, refer to the Vocabulary Glossary, page 852, in your student text.

	Rating Scale
1	I have never seen this word before.
2	I am not sure of the word's meaning.
3	I know this word and can teach the word's meaning to someone else.

Key Word	Check Your Understanding	Deepen Your Understanding
1 access (**ak**-ses) *noun* **Rating:** **1 2 3**	If you have **access** to a building, you have a means of _____. (**entry**) opposition	My definition: _Answers will vary._
2 bias (**bī**-us) *noun* **Rating:** **1 2 3**	A person who shows **bias** shows _____. awareness (**prejudice**)	My definition: _Answers will vary._
3 deliberate (di-**lib**-u-rut) *adjective* **Rating:** **1 2 3**	If something is **deliberate** it is _____. (**planned**) impulsive	My definition: _Answers will vary._
4 detect (di-**tekt**) *verb* **Rating:** **1 2 3**	To **detect** something is to _____ it. (**notice**) ignore	My definition: _Answers will vary._

Key Word	Check Your Understanding	Deepen Your Understanding
5 distorted (dis-**tor**-tid) *adjective* **Rating:** 1 2 3	A **distorted** picture is _____. (misleading) true	My definition: *Answers will vary.*
6 engaged (en-**gājd**) *adjective* **Rating:** 1 2 3	If you are **engaged** in an activity, you are _____. frustrated (absorbed)	My definition: *Answers will vary.*
7 objectivity (ob-jek-**tiv**-u-tē) *noun* **Rating:** 1 2 3	If you show **objectivity**, you show _____. enthusiasm (neutrality)	My definition: *Answers will vary.*
8 priority (prī-**or**-u-tē) *noun* **Rating:** 1 2 3	A **priority** is something that has high _____. insignificance (importance)	My definition: *Answers will vary.*

B. Use one of the Key Vocabulary words to describe a recent news story that affected you. How did it make you feel?

Answers will vary.

Before Reading   What Is News?

LITERARY ANALYSIS: Author's Tone

Tone is the writer's attitude about the topic or reader. A writer sometimes uses a persuasive tone to convince readers to believe his or her opinions and ideas.

A. Read the passage below. Find words and phrases that show the writer's attitude. Write the word choices in the web.

Look Into the Text

> With the pervasiveness of news today, it is important to take a look at how news affects our lives. We have come a long way from the days when the nightly news was reported at 6 p.m. on the "Big 3" broadcast networks.
>
> Today, we have access to news whenever we want—from a variety of 24-hour cable news channels, to "news when you want it" from the Internet, to instant news on one's PDA device. Instant news is just part of our lives.

Details Web

Word choice:
"pervasiveness of news"

Word choice:
"access to news whenever we want"

Opinion:
The news affects our lives.

Word choice:
"it is important to take a look"

Word choice:
"we have come a long way"

B. Look at the words and phrases the writer uses. Describe the writer's tone. Why do you think the writer chose this tone?

Possible response: The writer uses a clear and logical tone, but also a friendly one. The writer wants readers to
get involved and agree with his or her opinions.

READING STRATEGY: How to Form Generalizations

HOW TO FORM GENERALIZATIONS

1. **Record Clues** List details, word choice, and organization that show the author's tone.

2. **Combine the Information** Form a statement about the author's purpose and tone.

A. Read the passage. Use the strategies above to form generalizations as you read. Then answer the questions below.

Look Into the Text

> News has two priorities: it must be current, and it must mean something to people. A story about the environment and a story about the Super Bowl are both newsworthy, but for different reasons.
>
> On the surface at least, the (objective) of news is to inform the audience. It's the job of all the news media to tell people what's going on in their (community)—locally, nationally or globally. In this sense, the news media provide a (valuable) public (service).

1. What generalization is the author making in the passage?

   The author is defining the priorities and the purpose of the news.

2. How did recording the clues about the author's tone and purpose help you form a generalization?

   Possible response: Writing clues helped me think about the author's word choice. I combined them all into one statement.

B. Return to the passage and circle words and phrases that helped you understand the writer's tone and purpose.

Selection Review   What Is News?

EQ **How Do the Media Shape the Way People Think?**
Discover how the news media affect our understanding of events.

A. In "What Is News?" you found out how the news affects the way we think about events. Read the quotes from the text. Write notes about the author's opinions and tone.

Quote from the Text	Author's Opinion	Author's Tone
"Examining the news is important . . . so many elements, resources, and dollars go toward supporting the news."	People in our country value news, so it is important to examine the information.	straightforward, logical
"History needs to be presented in an interesting way. And there is still work to be done in order for print and electronic news to be effective."	*Possible response:* How the media present information is important since it impacts what young people know.	*Possible response:* judgmental, serious
"When taken to these extremes, 'news' can become just another type of sensational entertainment. Understanding the use of the media then becomes even more important to viewers."	*Possible response:* Some news has become entertainment, so it needs to be examined more closely by viewers.	*Possible response:* alarming, concerned

B. Use the information in the chart to answer the questions.

1. Based on your answers in the chart, how would you describe the author's attitude toward the readers and the subject?

Possible response: I can tell from the words and ideas that the writer respects the readers and how they are affected by the media.

2. What are some ways the news media show bias? Use **bias** in your answer.

Possible response: The media show bias when stories become sensationalized. Some reporters stereotype minority groups. Some stories also show age bias.

3. How might the media have more objectivity? Give two suggestions.

Possible response: Editors could choose photos that don't flatter or cast a negative light on a person. Writers could work toward not using labels to describe people, places, or events.

How to Detect Bias in the News

by Jeffrey Schank

Connect Across Texts

*"What Is News?" raises questions about **objectivity** in today's news coverage. This how-to article gives tips on how to **detect** and judge **bias** in the news that comes our way.*

Bias or Objectivity?

At one time or other we all complain about "bias in the news." Despite the journalistic goal of "objectivity," every news story is influenced by the attitudes and background of its interviewers, writers, photographers, and editors. Not all bias is deliberate. But you can watch for journalistic techniques that allow bias to "creep in" to the news.

1. Study selections and omissions.

An editor can express a bias by choosing to use or not to use specific information. These decisions give readers or viewers a different opinion about the events reported. If a few people boo during a speech, the reaction can be described as "remarks greeted by **jeers**." On the other hand, they can be ignored as "a handful of **dissidents**." Bias through omission is difficult to identify. In many cases, it can only be observed by comparing multiple news reports.

Key Vocabulary
- **objectivity** *n.*, view that is not influenced by opinions
- **detect** *v.*, to discover or notice
- **bias** *n.*, opinions that affect the way you see or present things

In Other Words
journalistic techniques that the ways that journalists
omissions the things that are left out
jeers rude comments
dissidents people who make it known they don't agree with the speaker

Interact with the Text

1. Interpret
Underline the sentence that tells the writer's purpose. What does the writer think about bias in the news?

He thinks there is always going to be some bias in the news, so it is important to learn how to identify it.

2. How-To Article
Preview the rest of the article. How is the information in this how-to article arranged? Why do you think it is organized this way?

Possible response: It is in sequential order to give the reader step-by-step instructions to examine bias.

3. Form Generalizations

Underline the main idea in Step 2. Explain how this step supports the purpose of the article.

Possible response: A

reader can detect bias

by identifying where

an article is placed or

the order in which new

stories are run. When a

story is run first or is on

the front page, readers

think it is the most

important news.

4. How-To Article

What does the writer want readers to do in Step 3? Circle the most important ideas in this step. Summarize this step in your own words.

Possible response:

Headlines are the most

important part of the

paper and the most-

read part. Headlines

can be biased, so the

writer wants readers to

examine them carefully.

When filmmaker Michael Moore gave a **controversial speech** at the 2003 Academy Awards, the news gave very different reports:

> **The London Daily:** *"He was both applauded and booed by the assembled celebrities."*
>
> **CNN:** *"The speech won him icy stares and undeniable celebrity . . . "*
>
> **ABC News:** *"Moore achieved what some may have considered impossible— getting a largely Democratic Hollywood crowd to boo."*
>
> **TV Guide:** *"That's not what I saw,"* Moore insisted. *"I saw the entire place stand up and applaud . . . "*

2. Look at item placement.

Readers of papers judge first-page stories to be more significant than those in the back. Television and radio newscasts run the most important stories first and leave the less significant for later. Where a story is placed influences what a reader or viewer thinks about its importance.

3. Consider headlines.

Many people read only the headlines of a news item. Most people **scan** nearly all the headlines in a newspaper. Headlines are the most-read part of a paper. They also can present carefully hidden bias and prejudices. They can **convey excitement where little exists**. They can express approval or **condemnation**.

In 2005, Kellenberg Memorial High School in New York canceled its prom. How do these different headlines show bias?

In Other Words

controversial speech speech that made some people upset and others happy
scan quickly look over, skim over
convey excitement where little exists make a story sound exciting even if it isn't
condemnation strong disapproval

The Boston College Observer: N.Y. Catholic School Cancels Prom

MTV News: Principal Cancels Prom, Saying "The Prom Culture Is Sick"

The Kansas City Star: Booze and Sex Sink a Prom in NY

Fox News: High School Institutes "No Prom Zone"

4. Look at names and titles.

News media often use labels and titles to describe people, places, and events. A person can be called an "ex-convict" or someone who "served time for **a minor offense**." Whether a person is described as a "terrorist" or a "freedom fighter" is another example of bias.

5. Study photos, camera angles, and captions.

Some pictures **flatter a person**. Others make the person look unpleasant. For example, a paper can choose photos to influence opinion about a candidate for election. The captions newspapers run below photos are also sources of bias.

▲ **Interpret the Photo** Photos can indicate a newswriter's attitude about a subject. Which photo might go with a positive article about actress Jennifer Lopez? Explain.

In Other Words

Institutes Establishes, Sets up
a minor offense a crime that is not too serious
flatter a person make a person look good

Interact with the Text

5. How-To Article
According to Step 4, why should a reader look at names and titles? Circle an example of a biased title.

A reader should look

at names and titles

because the news media

often use biased labels

for people like "terrorist"

instead of a "freedom

fighter."

6. Form Generalizations
Underline the sentences that tell how a photo can show bias. How does Step 5 support the purpose of the article?

Photos and captions are

another way the media

can influence a reader's

opinion.

7. Interpret

Why do companies supply news outlets with their own photos?

By supplying their own

photos, companies are

getting the reassurance

that they will not look

bad to the public.

6. Consider sources.

To detect bias, always consider where the news item "comes from." Is the information from a reporter, an eyewitness, police or fire officials, executives, or government officials? Each may have a particular bias that influences the story. Companies often supply **news outlets** with **news releases**, photos or videos. ❖

In Other Words
news outlets newspapers, magazines, and TV stations
news releases statements or stories they want the media to cover

Selection Review How to Detect Bias in the News

A. Review the six steps on how to detect bias in the news. Write a statement that summarizes what readers should do to detect bias.

Possible response: Readers can detect bias by studying selections and omissions, looking at item placement, considering headlines, looking at names and titles, studying photos and captions, and considering sources.

B. Answer the questions.

1. Form a statement about the purpose of the article and the procedure it describes.

Possible response: Readers should examine the many parts of a news story to determine if it is biased or objective.

2. The how-to article showed how to find bias in news items. Is it possible to communicate the news with complete objectivity?

Possible response: I think some bias always happens because reporters bring their own perspective no matter how hard they try to be objective. I think intentional bias can be avoided by thinking about the techniques the author outlined in the article.

WRITING: Write About Literature

A. Plan your writing. Which news medium—newspaper, TV news show, or radio broadcast—does the best job of covering the news? List the advantages and disadvantages of each medium based on what you read in each selection. *Answers will vary.*

Medium	Advantages	Disadvantages
Newspaper		
Radio		
Television		

B. Think about the advantages and the disadvantages of each news medium. Write a sentence stating your conclusion. Then explain how you arrived at that conclusion.

My conclusion: I think that _Students should support their answers with examples from the selections._

because _____

_____

_____

_____

Integrate the Language Arts

LITERARY ANALYSIS: Author's Tone

Tone is the writer's attitude toward the topic or the reader. A persuasive writer often chooses a tone that will convince the audience to believe the writer's opinions and ideas. *Answers will vary. Possible responses are shown.*

A. Read the examples below from "What Is News?" then describe the authors' tone.

Examples	Tone
"Instant news is just part of our lives."	conversational
"Media cater to their audiences. They report stories they think their consumers want to see, hear, or read about."	serious
"But a steady exposure to these images can give us a distorted view of what goes on in the world."	serious
"By knowing how the news industry works, we can find out how to reach the people who shape the news. Then we can begin to change reporting that reflects stereotyping or bias."	serious

B. Answer the questions.

1. What do the examples say about the author's attitude toward the news media? The author is cautious about the news media because the news media has great influence on our society. Also, media caters to their audiences by reporting on stories they think their consumers want to see, hear, or read about.

2. What is the author's attitude toward the reader? The author thinks that readers have a responsibility to analyze what they see on the news and become active about changing reporting that reflects stereotypes or bias.

C. Write a brief paragraph to a government leader expressing your attitude toward an issue in your community. Use words that express a serious tone to make your argument.

Answers will vary.

_____

_____

_____

_____

VOCABULARY STUDY: Denotations and Connotations

The **denotation** of a word is its dictionary meaning. The **connotations** of a word are the various feelings, images, and memories that may be associated with it. *Answers will vary. Possible responses are shown.*

A. Read the words below and write the denotation and connotation of each word.

Word	Denotation	Connotation
manipulate	to change	to alter something for a sneaky reason
mix	to mingle	to confuse
stroll	to walk	to walk carefree and relaxed
territory	an area	an area that should be protected
underfoot	at one's feet	in the way

B. Read the words below. For each, write a word that has the same denotation but a different connotation.

1. animal ___beast___

2. big ___enormous___

3. excited ___wild___

4. instruct ___direct___

5. tired ___exhausted___

C. Brainstorm five word pairs that have the same denotations but different connotations. List them below.

1. ___hungry/famished___

2. ___surprised/astonished___

3. ___mouse/rodent___

4. ___slim/scrawny___

5. ___frugal/cheap___

Key Vocabulary Review

A. Read each sentence. Circle the word that best fits into each sentence.

1. Someone who is listening closely is (**persuasive** / (**engaged**)).

2. If you buy groceries, you are a ((**consumer**)/ **minority**).

3. You can often ((**detect**)/ **manipulate**) how someone feels by watching how they behave.

4. Many restaurants offer (**distorted** / (**alternative**)) choices for people who do not eat meat.

5. Editorials are a type of opinion article that show (**racism** / (**bias**)).

6. Volunteering is one way to ((**impact**)/ **expand**) your community.

7. Commercials are an example of (**objectivity** / (**advertising**)).

8. Some companies try to increase their ((**profit**)/ **priority**) by lowering their prices and selling more products.

B. Use your own words to write what each Key Vocabulary word means. Then write a synonym for each word. *Answers will vary. Possible responses are shown.*

Key Word	My Definition	Synonym
1. access	the ability to get or use something	admittance
2. appeal	to ask for a response	request
3. convince	to influence someone to believe something	persuade
4. distorted	false or unrealistic	misleading
5. influence	to affect someone or something	control
6. objectivity	an unbiased view about a subject	neutrality
7. persuasive	able to make someone do or believe something	convincing
8. token	someone that is supposed to represent a larger group	symbolic

Unit 6 Key Vocabulary

• access	• bias	• detect	• impact	minority	profit
advertising	• consumer	• distorted	influence	• objectivity	racism
• alternative	• convince	engaged	• manipulate	persuasive	stereotype
appeal	deliberate	• expand	• media	• priority	token

• **Academic Vocabulary**

C. Complete the sentences. *Answers will vary. Possible responses are shown.*

1. The **media** I rely on most frequently are <u>TV and the Internet</u>
   _____.

2. When I hear a **stereotype** about teenagers, it makes me feel <u>angry and misunderstood</u>
   _____.

3. If I could **expand** the school building, I would add <u>a swimming pool</u>
   _____.

4. One time I was in the **minority** was when <u>I was the only female player on my baseball team</u>
   _____.

5. An example of a **deliberate** action is <u>arriving late to a party so you won't be the first one there</u>
   _____.

6. My number one **priority** this week is to <u>finish my English paper</u>
   _____.

7. One way to combat **racism** is by <u>refusing to buy products from companies that discriminate against</u>
   <u>certain groups</u> .

8. When someone tries to **manipulate** me, I react by <u>getting angry</u>
   _____.

Unit 7
Pages 588–619

Prepare to Read

▶ **A Raisin in the Sun**
▶ **My Father Is a Simple Man**
▶ **My Mother Pieced Quilts**

Key Vocabulary

A. How well do you know these words? Circle a rating for each word. Check your understanding of each word by circling *yes* or *no*. Then write a definition. If you are unsure of a word's meaning, refer to the Vocabulary Glossary, page 852, in your student text.

	Rating Scale
1	I have never seen this word before.
2	I am not sure of the word's meaning.
3	I know this word and can teach the word's meaning to someone else.

Key Word	Check Your Understanding	Deepen Your Understanding
① bond (**bond**) *noun* **Rating:** **1 2 3**	Many people often have a special **bond** with their dogs. **(Yes)** No	My definition: *Answers will vary.*
② collapse (ku-**laps**) *verb* **Rating:** **1 2 3**	People might **collapse** after they hear bad news. **(Yes)** No	My definition: *Answers will vary.*
③ integrity (in-**te**-gru-tē) *noun* **Rating:** **1 2 3**	A woman shows **integrity** when she lies to a friend. Yes **(No)**	My definition: *Answers will vary.*
④ invest (in-**vest**) *verb* **Rating:** **1 2 3**	People can **invest** in real estate by buying a house. **(Yes)** No	My definition: *Answers will vary.*

Key Word	Check Your Understanding	Deepen Your Understanding
5 **loyalty** (**loi**-ul-tē) *noun* **Rating:** 1　2　3	Your friends can show their **loyalty** by disappearing when you need them. Yes　　(No)	My definition: *Answers will vary.*
6 **pretense** (**prē**-tens) *noun* **Rating:** 1　2　3	Talking about your expensive car is showing no **pretense**. Yes　　(No)	My definition: *Answers will vary.*
7 **provider** (pru-**vī**-dur) *noun* **Rating:** 1　2　3	A good **provider** does not care when there is not enough food for the family. Yes　　(No)	My definition: *Answers will vary.*
8 **successful** (suk-**ses**-ful) *adjective* **Rating:** 1　2　3	Most **successful** people meet their goals. (Yes)　　No	My definition: *Answers will vary.*

B. Use one of the Key Vocabulary words to write about a member of your family who you think holds your family together.

Answers will vary.

Before Reading A Raisin in the Sun

LITERARY ANALYSIS: Dramatic Elements

Drama is writing that is meant to be performed for an audience. Acts and scenes, stage directions, and dialogue are **dramatic elements**.

A. Read the passage below. List the setting details, stage directions, and dialogue in the chart below.

> **Look Into the Text**
>
> **Scene 1**
>
> **SETTING**: *It's a gray Friday morning in 1950s Chicago. In a tiny, run-down apartment, a family begins to stir. The apartment has two bedrooms. The bathroom is in the hall and is shared with neighbors.*
>
> [RUTH, *a young working mother, is the first one up. She shakes her 10-year-old son, TRAVIS, who's sleeping on the sofa.*]
>
> **RUTH**. Come on now, it's seven-thirty. Wake up! Hurry to the bathroom while it's free.
>
> [*Half asleep,* TRAVIS *stumbles toward the bathroom.*]
>
> **RUTH**. Walter Lee, get up!

Setting Details	Stage Directions	Dialogue
gray Friday morning 1950s Chicago tiny, run-down apartment two bedrooms neighbors share bathroom	Ruth, young working mother, shakes son, 10-year-old Travis as Travis sleeps on the sofa	"Wake up! Hurry to the bathroom while it's free." "Walter Lee, get up!"

B. Use the dramatic elements you listed to complete the sentence.

I think this play will be about   *Possible response:* a Chicago family who has difficulties with money and
lives in a run-down apartment   .

READING STRATEGY: Form Mental Images

How to Form Mental Images

1. Pay attention to the dialogue and stage directions.

2. Look for descriptive words and phrases to help you form mental images.

3. Make a simple sketch of the characters and actions.

A. Read the passage. Use the strategies above to form mental images as you read. Then answer the questions below.

> ### Look Into the Text
>
> **RUTH.** It *is* your money. Just think—$10,000! What would *you* like to do with it?
>
> **MAMA.** Maybe we can buy a little house somewhere, with a yard for Travis.
>
> **RUTH.** Lord knows we've put enough rent into this rattrap to pay for four houses by now.
>
> [MAMA *looks around sadly.*]
>
> **MAMA.** A rattrap. Yes, that's all it is. I remember when Big Walter and I moved in here. We didn't plan to stay more than a year. I guess dreams sometimes get put on hold.
>
> [RUTH *starts ironing a big pile of clothes.* MAMA *washes the breakfast dishes. It's the beginning of another busy day.*]

1. Describe your mental image of the characters, their actions, and the setting.

   Possible response: Ruth is excited at first but then gets upset when she looks around the run-down
   apartment and begins ironing. Mama seems sad as she remembers moving there.

2. Which strategies did you use to answer question 1?

   Possible response: I used the first two strategies. I paid attention to the dialogue and stage directions and
   looked for descriptive words.

B. Return to the passage above, and underline the words or sentences that helped you answer the first question.

Selection Review A Raisin in the Sun

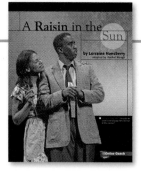

 What Holds Us Together? What Keeps Us Apart?

Consider how families hold us together.

A. In "A Raisin in the Sun," you read about how the Youngers struggle to stay together through difficult times. Complete the T Chart by comparing Walter's actions with Mama's actions.

T Chart

Walter's Actions	Mama's Actions
Walter wants to buy a liquor store with Mama's money.	Mama doesn't believe in selling liquor.
Walter wants to be successful, and he thinks having money will make him successful.	Mama says she is the head of the household.
Walter thinks no one believes in him and that they do not think he's a man.	Mama and Big Walter always dreamed of buying a home. She uses the insurance money to buy a house in a white neighborhood.
Walter gives the money for Beneatha's education to Willy. Willy steals the money.	Mama says she believes in Walter and gives him the rest of the insurance money. She tells Walter he is now the head of the household.
Walter says he is going to sell the house to Lindner.	Mama says she is ashamed of Walter when he says he is going to sell the house to Lindner.
Walter stands up to Lindner and says they will not sell the house.	Mama is proud of Walter when he stands up for the family and refuses to sell to Lindner.

B. Use the information in the chart to answer the questions.

1. Which character succeeds in holding the family together? Why?

Walter holds the family together when he stands up for the family and refuses to sell the house to Lindner. He gives Mama her dream.

2. Why does Beneatha tell Walter he doesn't have any integrity? Use **integrity** in your answer.

Possible response: Beneatha tells Walter he has no integrity because he thinks money is more important than family values.

3. What would you have done if you had to make the same decision as Walter? Explain.

Possible response: I would have told Lindner to keep his money because no one has the right to tell people where they can live.

Connect Across Texts

"A Raisin in the Sun" describes what happens when a family deals with sudden wealth. In these poems, parents share lessons about a different kind of wealth.

Family BONDS

Key Vocabulary
• **bond** *n.*, connection between people or things

Interact with the Text

1. Interpret

Look at the photo. Read the title and "Connect Across Texts." What do you predict these poems will be about?

Possible response: I predict these poems will be about the importance of family. I think the poems will describe how family connections influence people's lives.

My Father Is a
Simple Man

by Luis Omar Salinas

I walk to town with my father
to buy a newspaper. He walks slower
than I do so I must slow up.
The street is filled with children.
5   We argue about the price
of pomegranates, I convince
him it is the fruit of scholars.
He has taken me on this journey
and it's been lifelong.
10   He's sure I'll be healthy
so long as I eat more oranges,
and tells me the orange
has seeds and so is perpetual;
and we too will come back
15   like the orange trees.
I ask him what he thinks
about death and he says
he will gladly face it when
it comes but won't jump
20   out in front of a car.
I'd gladly give my life
for this man with a sixth
grade education, whose kindness
and patience are true . . .

The Oranges, 2001, Robert Ginder. Oil and gold leaf on wood, private collection.

▲ **Critical Viewing: Effect** The artist painted these oranges in a highly realistic style. Which senses do you think he wanted to appeal to?

In Other Words
Simple Plain, Ordinary
scholars smart people who have a lot
  of education
is perpetual will go on forever because
  it produces new fruits

25 The truth of it is, he's the scholar,
and when the (bitter-hard reality)
(comes at me like a punishing)
(evil stranger,) I can always
remember that here was a man
30 who was a worker and provider,
who learned the simple facts
in life and lived by them,
who held no pretense.
And when he leaves without
35 benefit of fanfare or applause
I shall have learned what little
there is about greatness.

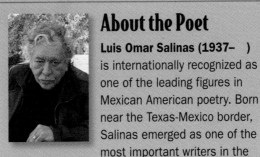

About the Poet

Luis Omar Salinas (1937–) is internationally recognized as one of the leading figures in Mexican American poetry. Born near the Texas-Mexico border, Salinas emerged as one of the most important writers in the "Fresno School" of poets in the 1970s and has since written nine books of poetry.

Key Vocabulary
provider *n.*, someone who gives necessary things to someone else
pretense *n.*, the act of pretending to do or be something

In Other Words
benefit of fanfare or applause the world celebrating the great things about his life

2. Imagery
Circle the sensory images on page 260. What do these images make you see, hear, feel, taste, or smell?

Possible response: I see the son waiting for his father. I hear children playing and the father and son arguing. I can smell and taste the oranges and pomegranates.

3. Form Mental Images
Circle the speaker's description of reality. Explain the description and what it makes you visualize.

Possible response: He describes the death of his father as an evil stranger who has come to punish him. I picture a son who feels pain and anger at the loss of his father.

4. Imagery
Underline words and phrases that describe the father. How do you "see" him?

Possible response: He is hardworking and honest. He does not pretend to be something different.

My Mother Pieced Quilts

by Teresa Palomo Acosta

they were just meant as covers
in winters
as weapons
against pounding january winds

5 but it was just that every morning I awoke
        to these
october ripened canvases
passed my hand across their cloth faces
and began to wonder how you pieced
all these together
10 these strips of gentle communion cotton
        and flannel nightgowns
wedding organdies
dime store velvets

how you shaped patterns square and oblong
        and round
positioned
15 balanced
then cemented them
with your thread
a steel needle
a thimble

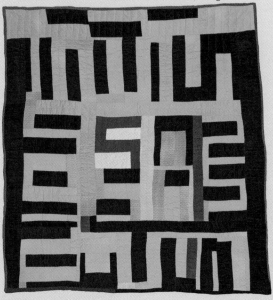

Blocks-and-Strips Quilt, 2003, Mary Lee Bendolph. Corduroy quilted fabric, collection of Tinwood Alliance, Atlanta, Georgia.

▲ **Critical Viewing: Design and Effect** What do the colors and shapes of this quilt make you think of? How do they make you feel?

In Other Words

Pieced Planned, Created
october ripened canvases quilts that we used when the weather turned cold
oblong rectangular
a thimble and other sewing tools

20 how the thread darted in and out
   galloping along the frayed edges, tucking them in
   as you did us at night
   oh how you stretched and turned and re-arranged
   your michigan spring faded curtain pieces
25 my father's santa fe work shirt
   the summer denims, the tweeds of fall

   in the evening you sat at your canvas
   —our cracked linoleum floor the drawing board
   me lounging on your arm
30 and you staking out the plan:
   whether to put the lilac purple of easter against the red plaid of winter-going-
      into-spring
   whether to mix a yellow with blue and white and paint the
   corpus christi noon when my father held your hand
   whether to shape a five-point star from the
35 somber black silk you wore to grandmother's funeral

   you were the river current
   carrying the roaring notes
   forming them into pictures of a little boy reclining
   a swallow flying
40 you were the caravan master at the reins
   driving your threaded needle artillery across the mosaic cloth bridges
   delivering yourself in separate testimonies.

   oh mother you plunged me sobbing and laughing
   into our past

In Other Words
frayed old and worn
staking out the plan planning where each
   piece would go
corpus christi noon hot day
river current flowing stream
reclining relaxing

caravan master at the reins one in control
needle artillery weapons
mosaic cloth bridges combinations of cloth
testimonies stories

5. Form Mental Images
Circle the words and phrases on page 262 that show what the quilts look like. Picture in your mind what the speaker describes. Explain how visualizing this helps you understand how the speaker feels about her mother's quilts.

Possible response:

Visualizing this helps

me understand that the

speaker sees the quilts

as works of art and as

family histories. The quilts

are all of their memories

sewn together.

6. Imagery
Underline a phrase that tells how the mother takes control of the quilts. What does this imagery help you "see"?

Possible response: This

imagery makes me see

the mother as the master

of the quilts. She drives

the needle and thread to

create her art.

7. Interpret

Highlight the words and phrases that describe how the speaker feels about the quilts. How do you think the speaker's feelings about the quilts reflect her feelings about her mother?

Possible response: The

speaker describes the

quilts with respect and

love and sees her mother

and the quilts celebrating

and living forever. The

speaker feels a bond with

her mother through the

quilts.

45 into the river crossing at five
into the spinach fields
into the plainview cotton rows
into tuberculosis wards
into braids and muslin dresses
50 sewn hard and taut to withstand the
thrashings of twenty-five years

stretched out they lay
armed/ready/shouting/celebrating

knotted with love
the quilts sing on

In Other Words
plainview wide
tuberculosis wards hospital areas
taut to withstand the thrashing strong
to survive the hard daily use

About the Poet

Teresa Palomo Acosta (1949–) grew up in the cotton country of Central Texas. She has published three books of poetry and co-authored *Las Tejanas: 300 Years of History*, about the contributions Mexican American women have made to American life.

Selection Review Family Bonds

A. Choose one of the poems. List an example of each type of imagery.

1. Sensory Image:

    Possible response: these strips of gentle communion cotton / and flannel nightgowns / wedding organdies / dime store velvets

2. Literal Image:

    Possible response: how you shaped the patterns square and oblong and round

3. Figurative Image:

    Possible response: you were the river current / carrying the roaring notes / forming them into pictures . . .

B. Answer the questions.

1. Choose one of the images you listed above. What picture does it create in your mind? Explain what you visualize.

    Possible response: The quilt is a rainbow of fabrics. The shapes and textures make the quilt warm and soft and beautiful.

Reflect and Assess

WRITING: Write About Literature

A. Plan your writing. List the characteristics of the parents in each of the three selections. *Answers will vary.*

A Raisin in the Sun	My Father Is a Simple Man	My Mother Pieced Quilts

B. Write a comparison paragraph. Describe how the parents in the three selections are similar. Use the examples from your chart to support your comparison.

Students should support their answers with examples from the selections.

_____

_____

_____

_____

_____

_____

_____

_____

_____

_____

_____

LITERARY ANALYSIS: Analyze and Compare Poetry

Poetry often uses carefully controlled language, figures of speech, and imagery to appeal to a reader's senses, emotions, and imagination. Poetic elements include the speaker, sound devices, imagery, and punctuation and line breaks.

A. Reread the poem "Rosa" below. Underline examples of imagery and sound devices that the author uses to appeal to the reader's senses, emotions, or imagination.

> **Rosa**
> How she sat there,
> the time right inside a place
> so wrong it was ready.
> That trim name with
> its dream of a bench
> to rest on. Her sensible coat.
> Doing nothing was the doing:
> the clean flame of her gaze
> carved by a camera flash.
> How she stood up
> when they bent down to retrieve
> her purse. That courtesy.

B. Consider the poetic elements from "Rosa," and write them in the chart.

Speaker	a person who admires Rosa Parks
Sound Devices (rhyme, rhythm, repetition)	time right inside; clean flame of her gaze; carved by a camera
Imagery	she sat there, sensible coat, she stood up
Punctuation and line breaks	short lines and sentences

C. Describe your favorite poem or a poem that has had a positive or negative impact on you. Describe the speaker, sound devices, and imagery.

Answers will vary.

_____

_____

VOCABULARY STUDY: Interpret Figurative Language

You can sometimes use context clues to help you understand the meaning of **figurative language**.

A. Read the lines from "A Raisin in the Sun." Write what you think the underlined words or phrases mean. Then write the context clues that helped you figure out the meaning.

Sentence	What It Means	Context Clues
WALTER. I'll do whatever it takes to put some <u>pearls around my wife's neck</u>! (p. 606)	make money	"do whatever it takes"; the knowledge that pearls are expensive
WALTER. And we decided to move into our house. Because my father, he earned it for us <u>brick by brick</u>. (p. 607)	his father worked very hard to pay for the house	earned it for us

B. Read each phrase from "My Mother Pieced Quilts." Write the meaning and identify the context clue or clues that helped you find the meaning.

1. "they were just meant as covers / in winters / as weapons / against pounding january winds" (lines 1–4)

   The words <u>winters</u> and <u>winds</u> tell me that the quilts were intended to protect against cold weather.

2. "galloping along the frayed edges, tucking them in / as you did us at night" (lines 21–22)

   This is a description of the process of sewing the quilt. I saw the word *as* and realized this is a simile that compares two things.

3. "you were the caravan master at the reins / driving your threaded needle artillery across the mosaic cloth bridges" (lines 40–41)

   This is a description of the narrator's mother sewing the quilt. I looked for related words, such as caravan master, driving, and artillery.

C. Write a sentence about a summer day using figurative language.

Answers will vary.

Prepare to Read

▶ **The Outsiders**
▶ **If There Be Pain**
▶ **Sonnet 30**

Key Vocabulary

A. How well do you know these words? Circle a rating for each word. Check your understanding of each word by circling the correct synonym. Then complete the sentences. If you are unsure of a word's meaning, refer to the Vocabulary Glossary, page 852, in your student text.

Rating Scale	
1	I have never seen this word before.
2	I am not sure of the word's meaning.
3	I know this word and can teach the word's meaning to someone else.

Key Word	Check Your Understanding	Deepen Your Understanding
❶ conquer (**kon**-kur) *verb* **Rating:** 1 2 3	To **conquer** is to _____. retreat (**defeat**)	If I wanted to help my friend conquer a bad habit, I would *Possible response:* give support and encouragement _____.
❷ devotion (di-**vō**-shun) *noun* **Rating:** 1 2 3	If you show **devotion**, you show _____. (**dedication**) faithlessness	The person I feel the most devotion toward is _____ *Possible response:* my grandmother _____.
❸ grief (**grēf**) *noun* **Rating:** 1 2 3	When people feel **grief**, they feel _____. joy (**sorrow**)	People experience grief after *Possible response:* the death of someone close to them _____.
❹ issue (**i**-shoo) *noun* **Rating:** 1 2 3	An **issue** is a _____ that matters to people. statement (**topic**)	An issue I am interested in understanding better is _____ *Possible response:* homelessness _____.

Key Word	Check Your Understanding	Deepen Your Understanding
⑤ refuge (**re**-fyūj) *noun* **Rating:** **1 2 3**	A **refuge** is a place of _____. (shelter)　　　danger	One place I could go if I needed a refuge is *Possible* *response:* my friend's house _____ _____ _____.
⑥ restore (ri-**stor**) *verb* **Rating:** **1 2 3**	To **restore** is to _____. (mend)　　　destroy	An example of something people like to restore is_____ *Possible response:* old cars _____ _____ _____.
⑦ subside (sub-**sīd**) *verb* **Rating:** **1 2 3**	To **subside** is to _____. rise　　　(lessen)	You might make someone's anger subside by _____ *Possible response:* telling a joke _____ _____ _____.
⑧ territory (**ter**-u-tor-ē) *noun* **Rating:** **1 2 3**	When a nation owns **territory**, it owns _____. buildings　　　(land)	In my community, I do not go into territory that _____ *Possible response:* has signs saying the area is private _____ _____.

B. Use one of the Key Vocabulary words to write about a time you showed loyalty to a friend.

Answers will vary. _____

_____

_____

Before Reading Pass It On

LITERARY ANALYSIS: Characterization in Drama

Playwrights create **characterization in drama** using different techniques.
Dialogue shows characters' thoughts and can give background information.
Stage directions tell how characters speak and act.

A. Read the passage below. Pay attention to dialogue and stage directions.
Complete the chart.

Look Into the Text

JUDGE. Where's Echo?

TAILLIGHT. As if you didn't know.

WHISPER. He's at the courthouse.

DOC. [*sarcastically*] "Somebody" filed an assault charge.

JUDGE. [*looking upset*] Oh, I, I, mean, Dawn just said she told the
police what happened to Gram. She didn't tell me . . . I mean, with
everything that happened, I didn't really think about . . .
  [*DOC, WHISPER, and TAILLIGHT look at each other and shake their
  heads.*]

DOC. We have to go.
  [*DOC, WHISPER, and TAILLIGHT leave.*]

JUDGE. [*speaking to himself*] I have to go, too.

Character	Dialogue	Stage Directions
Judge	"She didn't tell me . . . I mean with everything that happened,"	looking upset
Doc	"'Somebody' filed an assault charge."	sarcastically

B. What do the dialogue and stage directions tell you about the characters?

The dialogue and stage directions help me understand that Doc and Judge do not like each other. They show it

through sarcasm and getting upset.

READING STRATEGY: Identify Emotional Responses

HOW TO IDENTIFY EMOTIONAL RESPONSES

1. **Find details** that help you visualize the scene, characters, and events.

2. **Relate details** to your own life. Imagine how you would feel if you experienced those events.

3. **Record your emotional responses** in a Response Journal.

A. Read the passage. Use the strategies above to identify emotional responses as you read. Then answer the questions below.

> **Look Into the Text**
>
> **WHISPER** I'm sorry, bro'. If I hadn't brought Tiger around, this never would've happened. I just don't want you to go away again.
> **ECHO.** Nah, forget it. It was their fault. [*under his breath*] And mine.
> **TAILLIGHT.** Don't you take the blame for this.
> **ECHO.** [*not happy* that Taillight has heard his mumbled comment] I'm not taking the blame for this. I'm just saying, if I had stayed cool—
> **TAILLIGHT** [*upset*] Stayed cool? You showed force, man, you showed strength.

1. How do you visualize this scene? Describe the picture in your mind.

   Possible response: Whisper is feeling bad because his brother is now in trouble. Echo feels bad for losing his temper--but Taillight thinks Echo was right to react as he did.

2. How would you feel if you were Echo?

   Possible response: I would feel bad because I felt I let my little brother down, even though he thinks he let me down.

B. Return to the passage above and circle the details that helped you visualize the characters and their actions.

Selection Review Pass It On

Pass It On
by Franklin Just

EQ **What Holds Us Together? What Keeps Us Apart?**
Explore how friends show loyalty.

A. In "Pass It On," you found out how loyalties and rivalries affect relationships. Complete the Character Description Chart, using information you learned from dialogue and stage directions.

Character Description Chart

Character	What He Says and Does	What This Shows About Him
Doc	Wonders about Martin Luther King, Jr. "I Have a Dream" speech	Shows that he has hopes the situation can get better.
	Has an idea to speak with the Hatchets to try and work out the problem.	He has ideas, he's willing to try things.
		He sticks up for his friends.
	Calls out Judge for filing the assault charge.	He shows responsibility in being able to work with those to which he is opposed.
	Plans the game with Details.	

B. Use the information in the chart to answer the questions.

1. Why do you think Echo leaves the bus to help Gram? What do his actions tell you about his character?

   Possible response: Echo cares about people, and he knew and cared for Gram when he was younger, and she cared for him.

2. What issues keep the Hatchets and the Tigers apart? Use **issues** in your answer.

   Possible response: The issues are mostly about wealth, and the fact that the Tigers had to move out of their old neighborhood.

3. What does Judge mean when he tells Echo to "stay strong"?

   Possible response: He means that he knows it took strength and courage to act as Echo did, and he respects him for doing so.

Connect Across Texts

In "The Outsiders," Ponyboy and Johnny learn about loyalty. The following lyrics and sonnet were written centuries apart. Has the meaning of friendship and **devotion** changed?

Standing Together

On the surface, Tupac Amaru Shakur and William Shakespeare don't have much in common. After all, the two men lived centuries apart, in very different worlds. But below the surface, there may be more similarities than you think. Both Shakur and Shakespeare were writers who used poetry as a way to express their ideas about the important **issues** of their times. And both men wrote with passion about friendship, devotion, and loyalty— things that we still care about today.

Key Vocabulary
- **devotion** *n.*, love and dedication you feel toward someone or something
- **issue** *n.*, an important topic or idea that people are concerned about

Interact with the Text

1. Interpret
Underline examples of how Tupac Shakur and William Shakespeare were similar. Why is this information important?

This information shows

that writers from

different time periods

care about similar issues

and can use poetry to

express themselves.

2. Form and Style

Identify the rhyme scheme of lines 6–9.

This rhyme scheme is

called rhyming couplets.

3. Identify Emotional Responses

What do you visualize and feel when you read lines 5–9? How does your emotional response help you understand the poem?

Possible response: I see

a friend calling another

friend on the phone.

I have called people

when I have been sad

or needed help, so I can

understand what the

poet is saying. If we have

friends, we will never be

alone.

If There Be Pain...

song lyrics by Tupac Shakur
as performed by Providence
and RasDaveed El Harar

Providence:
If there be pain
All you have to do is call on me
If there be pain
All you have to do is call on me

Together (Providence and RasDaveed El Harar):
5 To be with you
And before you hang up the phone
You will no longer be alone
Together we can never fall
Because our love will conquer all

Key Vocabulary
conquer *v.*, to defeat or beat a
  person or thing

Providence:

10   If there be pain
      Reach out for a helping hand
      If there be pain
      And I shall hold you wherever I am . . .

Together:

      Wherever I am
15   Every breath I breathe will be into you
      For without you here my joy is through
      My life was lived through falling rain
      So call on me if there be pain

RasDaveed El Harar:

      (chanting)

Providence:

      Every breath I breathe will be into you
20   For without you here my joy is through
      My life was lived through falling rain
      So call on me . . .

Together:

      If there be pain

In Other Words
(chanting) (adds more lyrics of his own)

Interact with the Text

4. Interpret
Summarize lines 10–13. How does the speaker show devotion to a friend? Use **devotion** in your response.

Possible response: The speaker shows devotion to a friend when he says he will always be available to help his friend.

5. Identify Emotional Responses
Choose a line that you relate to. Based on your experience, explain your emotional response.

Answers will vary.

6. Form and Style

A sonnet is a tightly controlled form of poetry. Describe the form and style.

Possible response: The stanzas are 4 lines and have identical rhyme schemes. The last two lines form a rhyming couplet.

7. Identify Emotional Responses

Write the poet's main point in your own words. Describe your response and how it helps you understand the poem.

Possible response:

Thinking about my best friend makes sad memories go away. These lines make me grateful that I have friends. I understand how the poet feels about the importance of friendship.

Sonnet 30

by William Shakespeare

When to the sessions of sweet silent thought
I summon up remembrance of things past,
I sigh the lack of many a thing I sought,
And with old woes new wail my dear time's waste:
5 Then can I drown an eye, unused to flow,
For precious friends hid in death's dateless night,
And weep afresh love's long since cancell'd woe,
And moan the expense of many a vanish'd sight:
Then can I grieve at grievances foregone,
10 And heavily from woe to woe tell o'er
The sad account of fore-bemoaned moan,
Which I new pay as if not paid before.
But if the while I think on thee, dear friend,
All losses are restor'd and sorrows end.

Key Vocabulary
grief *n.,* sorrow and sadness
• **restore** *v.,* to return something to the way it was before

Sonnet 30

A Modern Paraphrase

When in moments of quiet thoughtfulness

I think about the past,

I regret that I did not achieve all that I wanted,

And it saddens me to think of the years that I wasted:

5   Then I cry, though I am not one who cries often,

For my good friends who have died,

And I cry again over heartbreaks that ended long ago,

And mourn the loss of many things that I have seen and loved:

Then I grieve again over past troubles,

10 And sadly I remind myself, one regret after another,

Of all the sorrows and disappointments in my life,

And they hurt me more than ever before.

But if I think of you at this time, dear friend,

I regain all that I have lost and my sadness ends.

In Other Words

achieve do, accomplish
mourn am saddened by, grieve
disappointments failures, frustrations

Interact with the Text

8. Interpret

Reread "Sonnet 30" on page 276. How did the modern paraphrase help you understand the original poem?

Possible response: It

clarified words and ideas

that I didn't understand.

It clarified the meaning.

Selection Review Standing Together

A. Describe what you visualized as you read each selection.

1. "If There Be Pain" _Possible response:_ I visualized someone reaching out to a friend. It was dark and raining, and they were talking on the phone.

2. "Sonnet 30" _Possible response:_ When I read this poem, I visualized someone walking at night, feeling unhappy and crying.

3. "Sonnet 30: A Modern Paraphrase" _Possible response:_ This poem made me picture myself thinking about the past. I saw myself looking through a calendar and remembering projects and activities I started but never finished.

Write about an experience that one of the selections made you remember. List the emotions you felt in the T Chart.

T Chart

I Remember	I Feel
Possible response: "If There Be Pain"; I remember a time when a friend really needed to talk about her life and problems.	_Possible response:_ I feel sad that people are in so much pain.

B. Answer the questions.

1. How does the rhymed couplet at the end of Shakespeare's "Sonnet 30" help you understand the sonnet's message?

Possible response: The rhymed couplet helped me understand the sonnet because the last two lines summarize Shakespeare's message: Friends can help each other.

2. What message about friendship do Shakur and Shakespeare share?

Possible response: Both Skakur and Shakespeare write about how a good friend can help you make it through difficult times.

Reflect and Assess

- Pass It On
- If There Be Pain
- Sonnet 30

WRITING: Write About Literature

A. Shakur wrote: "Together we can never Fall / because our love will conquer all." Plan your writing. List in the chart below examples from each selection that support this theme.

Pass It On	If There Be Pain	Sonnet 30

B. Use the examples you listed to write a paragraph describing how this theme applies to each of the selections. Then add your opinion about this idea of friendship.

Students should support their answers with examples from the selections.

LITERARY ANALYSIS: Literary Criticism

Literary criticism is the evaluation, analysis, description, or interpretation of literary works. A literary criticism usually follows one of these approaches:

- **Biographical:** based on how the author's life affects the work
- **Aesthetic:** focused on what makes a work appealing to the reader
- **Historical:** based on research of a specific time period and how it influenced the work

A. Read the examples in the chart. Then write which approach the critic used.

Example of Literary Criticism	Critic's Approach
Even people who do not normally read science fiction will be engaged by the lovable characters and exquisite detail.	aesthetic
My research shows that the portrayal of the old man in the novel is actually a commentary on industrialization in 1899.	historical
It is evident that the author called on memories of his troubled youth when he wrote this story.	biographical

B. Read the description of "Pass It On" from a critic. Then answer the questions.   *Answers will vary. Possible responses are shown.*

> "Pass It On" provides a true account of the urban environment in the early eighties and the deep consequences of business and political practices of the time. Impressively, the human spirit emerges from the blight of this practice, producing a significant literary achievement.

1. Which type of approach is this? How do you know?

Historical; the writer refers to the historic conditions of the eighties.

2. Do you agree with the claim? Why or why not?

Yes. It was impressive to see how Echo and Judge triumphed under the harsh social conditions.

C. Write your own brief aesthetic literary criticism of "Pass It On."

Answers will vary.

VOCABULARY STUDY: Denotation and Connotation

Denotation is the exact meaning, or definition, of a word. **Connotation** is a meaning or feeling that is commonly added or attached to the word.

A. Read the words and their denotations in the chart below. Write a negative or positive connotation for each. *Answers will vary. Possible responses are shown.*

Word	Denotation	Connotation
alone	by yourself	lonely, isolated
darkness	the absence of light	evil
private	confidential or personal	deceptive
tricky	clever or smart	dishonest, untrustworthy

B. Read the following paragraph. Rewrite the paragraph using words with negative connotations for each of the underlined words and phrases

> My dog, Skippy, is <u>wild</u>. He <u>nips</u> the neighbors <u>a lot</u>. When he <u>drinks</u> his water out of his bowl, he makes a <u>puddle</u>. He gets <u>angry</u> when we try to take his food away. He <u>does not like</u> to be brushed.

Possible response: My dog Skippy is uncontrollable. He bites the neighbors constantly. When he slurps his water out of his bowl he makes a mess. He gets furious when we try to take his food away. He hates to be brushed.

C. Study the difference between the paragraphs. Why would a writer use words or phrases with negative connotations? *Answers will vary. Possible responses are shown.*

The author may be trying to persuade or convince a reader about an opinion he or she has. The author may also be trying to emphasize dramatic elements or create humor.

Prepare to Read
▶ **Voices of America**
▶ **Human Family**

Key Vocabulary

A. How well do you know these words? Circle a rating for each word. Check your understanding by marking an *X* next to the correct definition. Then provide an example. If you are unsure of a word's meaning, refer to the Vocabulary Glossary, page 852, in your student text.

Rating Scale

1	I have never seen this word before.
2	I am not sure of the word's meaning.
3	I know this word and can teach the word's meaning to someone else.

Key Word	Check Your Understanding	Deepen Your Understanding
❶ alien (**ā**-lē-un) *noun* **Rating:** 1　2　3	☐ a native ☒ a foreigner	Example: _Possible response: an immigrant who_ moves to the United States
❷ ashamed (u-**shāmd**) *adjective* **Rating:** 1　2　3	☒ embarrassed ☐ proud	Example: _Possible response: telling a lie and then_ feeling bad about it
❸ feature (**fē**-chur) *noun* **Rating:** 1　2　3	☒ a facial part ☐ a body type	Example: _Possible response: eyes or nose_
❹ interpret (in-**ter**-prut) *verb* **Rating:** 1　2　3	☐ to change something ☒ to translate something	Example: _Possible response: asking a native_ speaker to tell you what each menu item is when you don't speak the language

Key Word	Check Your Understanding	Deepen Your Understanding
5 major (**mā**-jur) *adjective* Rating: 1 2 3	[X] serious [ ] unimportant	Example: *Possible response:* graduating from college
6 melodious (me-**lō**-dē-us) *adjective* Rating: 1 2 3	[X] pleasant-sounding [ ] harsh-sounding	Example: *Possible response:* the sound of birds singing
7 minor (**mī**-nur) *adjective* Rating: 1 2 3	[ ] large [X] small	Example: *Possible response:* disagreeing about the best brand of ice cream
8 variety (vu-**rī**-u-tē) *noun* Rating: 1 2 3	[ ] uniformity [X] diversity	Example: *Possible response:* all of the many different fruits at the supermarket

B. Use one of the Key Vocabulary words to write about what being part of a community means to you.

Answers will vary.

LITERARY ANALYSIS: Figurative Language

Poets use **figurative language** to create images and appeal to a reader's senses and emotions. They use **metaphors** to compare two different things and **personification** to give human qualities to animals, objects, or ideas.

A. Read the excerpts from the poems below. Look for examples of figurative language. Then write the poet's meaning in the chart.

> **Look Into the Text**
>
> I hear America singing, the varied
>   carols I hear,
> Those of mechanics, each one
> singing his as it should be
>   blithe and strong,
> The carpenter singing his as he
>   measures his plank or beam,
> The mason singing his as he
>   makes ready for work, or leaves
>   off work, . . .
>   —Walt Whitman
>
> I, too, sing America.
> I am the darker brother.
> They send me to eat in the kitchen
> When company comes,
> But I laugh,
> And eat well,
> And grow strong. . . .
>   —Langston Hughes

Figurative Language	Poet's Meaning
"I hear America singing, the varied carols I hear"	America is the people who live here.
"They send me to eat in the kitchen."	African Americans have not always been treated well by other Americans.
"I am the darker brother."	African Americans are Americans, too.

B. Answer the question about the poems.

How do Whitman and Hughes use metaphors and personification to describe America?

Possible response: Whitman uses personification to describe America as "singing." Hughes uses the metaphor

that African Americans are the "darker brother" who are sent away and hidden. Both use this figurative

language to describe their versions of America and its varied groups of people.

READING STRATEGY: Identify Sensory Images

Reading Strategy
Visualize

How to IDENTIFY SENSORY IMAGES

1. **Read** Look for details and descriptions that appeal to your senses.

2. **Reflect** Think about what sense the image appeals to.

3. **Respond** Describe how the image makes you feel or what it makes you think.

A. Read the excerpt from the poem. Use the strategies above to identify sensory images. Complete the chart and answer the questions below.

> **Look Into the Text**
>
> . . . American but hyphenated,
> viewed by Anglos as perhaps exotic,
> perhaps inferior, definitely different,
> viewed by Mexicans as alien,
> (their eyes say, "You may speak
> Spanish but you're not like me") . . .
> —Pat Mora

Read	Reflect	Respond
"viewed by Anglos as perhaps exotic, / perhaps inferior,"	*Possible response:* I see people looking at the speaker as if she's different and not good enough.	*Possible response:* I think some people do not treat others fairly and judge them by what they look like.
"(their eyes say, 'You may speak / Spanish but you're not like me')"	*Possible response:* I see their eyes and the suspicion in them.	*Possible response:* It's not fair that people who look different feel like they don't belong anywhere.

1. How do sensory images help you understand the speaker's feelings?

   Possible response: The speaker feels like she will never belong because she is not American and not

   Mexican but something in between.

2. Which senses do the images appeal to?

   They appeal to the sense of sight because you can see how the people look at the speaker and judge her.

Selection Review Voices of America

What Holds Us Together? What Keeps Us Apart?
Discover what it means to belong to a community.

A. In "Voices of America," you read about how some people feel connected to a community and how others feel separated. Complete the web with lines from the poems that show how people can feel like aliens in America.

Details Web

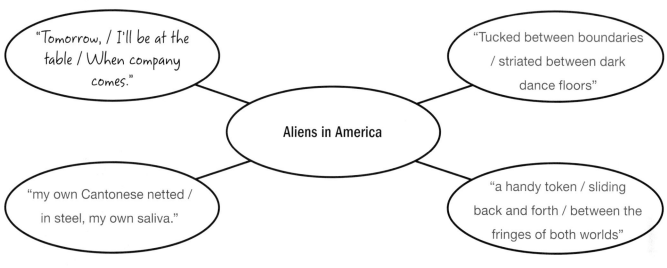

B. Use the information in the web to answer the questions.

1. What causes the speakers in the poems to feel like aliens in America? How do the images help you understand their experience?

Possible response: The speakers feel like they are not part of the American community because they also have another culture that makes up part of their identity. The images helped me see and feel how the speaker feels.

2. How does this collection of poems show the variety of cultures in America? Use **variety** in your answer.

Possible response: The poems are written by a group of poets that represent a variety of ethnicities. One poet is white, one is African American, one is Chinese, and one is Mexican American. They all see and experience America differently.

3. Which poem do you think best expresses what being part of a community should be? Explain.

Possible response: I think "I Hear America Singing" is an example of all the different people that make up a community and how they all work together to make their community strong. The poet seems to celebrate their differences, which is what a community should do.

HUMAN FAMILY

BY MAYA ANGELOU

All Human Beings are Born Free and Equal in Dignity and Rights, 1998, Ron Waddams.
Acrylic on board, private collection, The Bridgeman Art Library.

▲ Critical Viewing: Effect Study the effect of the curved arms in this painting.
How does it show the relationship among the people?

Interact with the Text

1. Interpret
Why do you think the artist
chose to paint this family in
this way?

Possible response: The
artist wanted to show
that the human family is
made up of people with
not one skin color, but
many colors.

2. Use Sensory Images
Underline the phrases that explain the variety of skin tones in the human family. How do these images help you understand the poem?

Possible response: I

picture all the people in

the world and think how

different we all look but

how we are really all the

same.

3. Rhythm and Rhyme
Circle the words that rhyme in lines 13–16. How do these words affect the rhythm of the poem?

Possible response: The

rhyming words speed up

the rhythm and bring the

stanza to a clear end.

I note the obvious differences
in the human family.
Some of us are serious,
some thrive on comedy.

5 Some declare their lives are lived
as true profundity,
and others claim they really live
the real reality.

The variety of our skin tones
10 can confuse, bemuse, delight,
brown and pink and beige and purple,
tan and blue and white.

I've sailed upon the seven seas
and stopped in every land,
15 I've seen the wonders of the world,
not yet one common man.

Key Vocabulary
  variety *n.*, mix of different things

In Other Words
declare insist, say
as true profundity in a great, meaningful way
bemuse confuse, puzzle
one common man a person who is
  totally ordinary

I know ten thousand women
called Jane and Mary Jane,
but I've not seen any two
20   who really were the same.

Mirror twins are different
although their features jibe,
and lovers think quite different thoughts
while lying side by side.

25   We love and lose in China,
we weep on England's moors,
and laugh and moan in Guinea,
and thrive on Spanish shores.

We seek success in Finland,
30   are born and die in Maine.
In minor ways we differ,
in major we're the same.

Key Vocabulary
● **minor** *adj.*, small or unimportant
● **major** *adj.*, great in size or importance

In Other Words
jibe match, go together
moors open, empty land

Interact with the Text

4. Use Sensory Images
Underline the phrases that tell about the women the speaker has met. How does the image help you understand her point?

Possible response: I know many people with the same name, but they are not the same person. Each person is unique.

5. Interpret
Circle the phrases that explain how all people are alike and different. Explain this idea in your own words, using the words **major** and **minor**.

Possible response:

Our similarities are major, like emotions and experiences. The differences are minor, like skin tone and gender. We are more the same than we are different.

6. Rhythm and Rhyme
Underline the words that change the rhythm of the poem. What is the effect of this change?

Possible response:

The phrase breaks up

the rhythm and draws

attention to itself. The

poet repeats this phrase

for emphasis.

I note the obvious differences
between each sort and type,
35 but we are more alike, my friends,
than we are unalike.

We are more alike, my friends,
than we are unalike.

We are more alike, my friends,
40 than we are unalike.

Selection Review Human Family

A. Complete the chart with words and phrases from the poem that appealed to your senses. Describe what you visualize using as many senses as you can. Answers will vary. Possible responses are shown.

You Notice	You Visualize
"I've sailed upon the seven seas / and stopped in every land"	I smell and feel the wind and the salty water. I see the sights and hear the sounds of exotic places.
"we weep on England's moors, / and laugh and moan in Guinea,"	I hear crying, see a green open field, and feel misty rain. I hear loud laughter and feel warmth.

B. Answer the questions.

1. How did recognizing rhyme and rhythm help you as you read the poem? What does the rhythm of this poem remind you of?

   The rhyme and rhythm made me enjoy the poem even more because it had a beat. It reminded me of music.

2. Why does Angelou believe that we are more alike than different?

   Maya Angelou thinks we are more alike because the things we have in common are our emotions, feelings, and dreams. These emotions are more powerful than the way we look.

WRITING: Write About Literature

A. Plan your writing. List examples from each poem that describe what it means to be an American. *Answers will vary.*

Voices of America	Human Family

B. Which poem speaks most directly to you about what it means to be an American? Write a paragraph explaining your choice. Include specific examples from the poem to support your opinion.

Students should support their answers with examples from the selections.

_____

_____

_____

_____

_____

_____

_____

_____

_____

LITERARY ANALYSIS: Allusions

An **allusion** is a reference to a well-known person, place, event, artwork, or work of literature. Understanding what a writer is alluding to can help you understand his or her meaning.

A. Read each fictional example of allusion. Then write the meaning of the allusion. *Answers will vary. Possible responses are shown.*

Allusions	Meaning
Sometimes my brother thinks it's funny to sneak up behind me and scream. I get so scared. His new nickname should be Stephen King!	The brother likes to scare people like Stephen King does.
I'll know who took the last cookie by the beating of your tell-tale heart.	The person who took the cookie will not be able to hide his or her guilt just like the man in the story by Poe.
Chris didn't like to spend money. He was no Scrooge, but he seldom purchased anything except the bare necessities.	It refers to Ebenezer Scrooge, who is a well-known character in "A Christmas Carol."

B. Answer the questions. *Answers will vary. Possible responses are shown.*

1. Why do you think the title of Hughes' poem is "I, Too?" What is it alluding to?

   The title comes from the first line of the poem, which is "I, too, sing America." The first line of the poem refers to Whitman's poem, "I Hear America Singing."

2. What is the message of "I, Too"?

   The message is that there are many different types of races and ethnicities that call America home. It's unjust that some people are discriminated against.

3. How does the allusion help you understand the message of "I, Too"?

   Having read Whitman's poem, I understood what Hughes was trying to say about equality.

C. Write a short paragraph about your dream job. Include at least one allusion in your paragraph.

   Answers will vary.

LITERARY ANALYSIS: Figurative Language

Figurative language helps readers create images in their minds. A **simile** uses *like* or *as* to make a comparison. A **metaphor** makes a comparison by saying one thing is another thing. *Answers will vary.*

A. Read the following similes. Complete the chart by describing the image that each simile creates in your mind.

Simile	Image It Creates
my car was like a rocket	
you are as slow as molasses	
the poetry is like a breath of fresh air	
the basketball player is as tall as a giraffe	

B. Read the following metaphors from the poems in this unit. Complete the chart by writing your interpretation of each metaphor.

Metaphor	My Interpretation
"Tomorrow, / I'll be at the table / When company comes."	
"my own Cantonese netted / in steel"	
"American but hyphenated"	
"a handy token / sliding back and forth / between the"	

C. Use a simile or a metaphor to describe:

the first day of summer vacation _____

your favorite sport _____

a scary movie _____

a younger sibling or relative _____

Key Vocabulary Review

A. Use these words to complete the paragraph.

bond	**invest**	**refuge**	**territory**
devotion	**major**	**successful**	**variety**

It was a _____major_____ decision when I joined a club during high school. The group met
(1)

twice a month to build a _____refuge_____ for injured animals. It was encouraging to see that we
(2)

all had great _____devotion_____ to the cause. In no time, the club felt like a second family. Our
(3)

_____bond_____ continued after the school year ended, so we decided to _____invest_____ money
(4)   (5)

in a _____territory_____ that will be the perfect site for a _____variety_____ of birds to make their
(6)   (7)

homes. I know our project will be _____successful_____ because anything is possible if you work together.
(8)

B. Use your own words to write what each Key Vocabulary word means.
Then write a synonym for each word. *Answers will vary. Possible responses are shown.*

Key Word	My Definition	Synonym
1. alien	someone who was born in a different country	foreigner
2. ashamed	feeling guilty	embarrassed
3. grief	great sadness	sorrow
4. integrity	honesty and uprightness	trustworthiness
5. loyalty	faithfulness to someone or something	devotion
6. melodious	sounding sweet and pleasant	harmonious
7. minor	small or unimportant	insignificant
8. subside	to lose strength	lessen

alien	conquer	• integrity	loyalty	pretense	subside
ashamed	• devotion	• interpret	• major	provider	successful
• bond	• feature	• invest	melodious	refuge	territory
• collapse	grief	• issue	• minor	• restore	variety

• **Academic Vocabulary**

C. Answer the questions using complete sentences. *Answers will vary. Possible responses are shown.*

1. How can you **conquer** your fears?

I can try doing what I am afraid of.

2. Describe an **issue** that affects your life.

Environmental issues, such as pollution, affect my life.

3. Which **feature** of your face is your favorite?

My blue eyes are my favorite feature.

4. How could someone **restore** a friendship?

Someone could write an email or letter to the friend.

5. Describe what a good **provider** does for his or her family.

A good provider makes sure his or her family has shelter, plenty of food, and love.

6. Why might someone **collapse**?

Someone might collapse if he or she is sick.

7. Why would it be useful to be able to **interpret** another language?

It makes it easier to read menus when you travel to foreign countries.

8. Why might someone put on a **pretense**?

Someone might put on a pretense if he or she is embarrassed.